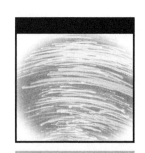

Wireless Security Essentials

Defending Mobile Systems

from Data Piracy

Russell Dean Vines

Wiley Publishing, Inc.

Publisher: Robert Ipsen
Editor: Margaret Eldridge
Assistant Editor: Adaobi Obi
Managing Editor: Micheline Frederick
New Media Editor: Brian Snapp
Text Design & Composition: Wiley Composition Services

Published by Wiley Publishing, Inc., Indianapolis, Indiana
Published simultaneously in Canada

For general information on our other products and services please contact our Customer Care Department within the United States at (800) 762-2974, outside the United States at (317) 572-3993 or fax (317) 572-4002.

Wiley also publishes its books in a variety of electronic formats. Some content that appears in print may not be available in electronic books.

Library of Congress Cataloging-in-Publication Data:

ISBN: 0-471-20936-8

Printed in the United States of America.

10 9 8 7 6 5 4 3 2 1

This book is dedicated to the heroes of 9/11/01, common people who performed uncommon deeds when the time required it.

And especially to my friend Lingard Knutson, who helped lead her Port Authority co-workers down 62 flights of stairs from Tower 1 to safety. We should all have such angels.

Contents

Preface

Each morning when I write, various birds from the neighborhood feed outside my window, searching the rain gutters for bugs. They occasionally watch me between bites, perhaps to ensure I'm not up to something they won't like; or perhaps the sight of me is odd to them. The birds vary in size and breed, but they are generally small; the large birds tend to shy away from close contact with the house. Often, I notice in particular a small, young cardinal pecking through the debris, keeping an eye on me at the same time he keeps an eye out for his breakfast.

Perhaps some will think it's a stretch to analogize bird-feeding behavior to information systems security, but the connection is clear to me: Security cannot be an all-consuming activity for the enterprise but must be as transparent, efficient, and effective as possible. (In the same way that IT systems are services to the enterprise, not an end in and of themselves.) Managing protections must not consume so much internal and external resources as to make the enterprise dysfunctional. To continue the analogy, the cardinal cannot stop feeding entirely in the effort to feel secure in its environment. It must be secure enough to *facilitate* its feeding, grooming, and breeding behaviors, by creating a protective zone around itself so that it can be assured of completing its life-preserving tasks.

If at any time while watching the bird, I stand up or make a sudden movement or gesture that startles the bird, he will fly off. At that point, all of his resources become dedicated to and focused on security; feeding is abandoned, because the cost/benefit ratio of the activity is gone; that is, protecting against a perceived threat consumes all of his available resources. Better to cut and fly and stay alive (i.e., profitable).

For information systems to remain viable, security must balance effectiveness with transparency. The Internet will never reach its full potential without the big three:

- Reliability

- Performance

- Security

Though security is a fundamental building block of IT and the enterprise, it can't consume too much of the enterprise's resources or it ceases to be useful. This is why *distributed denial-of-service* (DDoS) attacks are so damaging to an organization. They instantly create a resource drain on the organization and turn all IT personnel into security personnel for the duration of the event. A DDoS is a very effective tool for creating a diversion for other, more serious intrusions, as the DDoS attack siphons off the attention of a majority of the IT personnel into a number of other functions: detective, sys admin, reconfiguring the firewalls or routers, working with the web host or co-locating service to find/stop the source of the attacks (if the service provider will even respond on a timely basis).

A DDoS attack (using zombie, IRC bots, or some other type of unknowing accomplices to launch from multiple sources) today constitutes the greatest threat to maturity of the Internet. The major effect on computing of the recent Code Red worm and its variants' was to create a DoS, as it consumed resources and bandwidth.

So though economic espionage, disgruntled employee sabotage, and operator error, can all pose serious threats to a system's confidentiality, integrity, and availability (the C.I.A.), DDoS attacks are probably the greatest threats of all, as they confound security professionals more than any others in their attempts to stop them. Preventing a single person, or a small group of persons, from clogging the Internet, almost at will, is today incredibly difficult. In contrast, with traditional brick-and-mortar business, if customers have trouble getting to your store because of, say, increased traffic congestion, usually several other options are available: widen the street, increase parking access, move to a location with better public transportation, and so on. And overcrowding due to demand was a rare (and good) thing; and although crowd control could be an issue for a short period (recall the Cabbage Patch doll and Tickle-Me Elmo crazes, for example), such events meant good sales overall, and sold-out shelves certainly made distributors happy.

In the electronic world, however, such control issues do not help sales, as they're not reactions to market conditions or to a popular product or sale, or based on some crowd demographic. Rather, a DDoS is a malicious (and almost always successful) attempt to suspend an organization's ability to conduct business on the Web, or in the case of government or political Web sites, to limit speech freedoms.

The Internet service providers, web-hosting services, co-locating services, and so on, are largely complicit in this scenario. Security, privacy, and service guarantees are latecomers to the Internet ball, and too often are given lip service, then largely ignored. Moreover, the attitude that security is the end-user's concern continues to be prevalent. That said, as more state attorneys general become involved in sorting out this dilemma, in the future, attempts to compensate or reimburse users for service outages may become more common, and we may soon see the first class-action suits against ISPs that don't take due care or perform due diligence in providing a secure computing environment. Furthermore, the concept that computing hardware or communications lines are the primary goods supplied to the user is an old telecomm concept: organizations and users will demand secure, private Internet pathways.

And since September 11, 2001, the issue of security has come out of the shadows and into a very bright light. The simple fact is, all the good that the Internet has to offer won't come to fruition until security and privacy are guaranteed.

Introduction

Wireless is one of the newest communications technology frontiers. Offering the possibility of always-on, instant mobile communications, the potential of this technology appears to be limitless. This potential now is within our reach and is revolutionizing the computing world. Of course, as with any new technology, wireless sets some technological hurdles we must overcome. These hurdles, however, are less daunting than the vulnerabilities inherent to wireless computing; it is these vulnerabilities—to eavesdropping, session hijacking, data alteration and manipulation, in conjunction with an overall lack of privacy—that are hindering widespread adoption of the technology.

To help address, and increase understanding of, the challenges to the widespread deployment of wireless technologies, this book, *Wireless Security Essentials*, offers a snapshot of the current state of wireless security. A compilation of material from many sources, it attempts to give the reader an overview of the challenges posed by wireless technologies and the inherent security vulnerabilities.

Typically, when a new technology emerges, standards are created and a rush commences to develop the technology without a thorough security vetting. This has been the case with wireless, too. The result is that much work is now devoted to retrofitting security into the existing models and protocols, and designing new models and protocols with better security features. Fortunately, progress *is* being made, as apparent in such standards as 802.1x and newer versions of WAP. Network infrastructure design, such as implementation of VPNs and RADIUS, also can help create secure pipes for wireless sessions. Hopefully, these developments will help to fill the holes access points punch in the network.

On the contrary, still lacking in organizational implementations of wireless nets is the adoption of fundamental security methodologies, such as standard policies, internal and external testing, auditing, intrusion detection, and response.

One of the objectives of *Wireless Security Essentials* is to address all these issues.

Origin and Rationale

Initially, the idea for this book came as a result of my work with an arm of the Department of Defense, to certify and accredit a wireless technology solution, which used Xybernaut wearable computers[1], Symbol 802.11b wireless adapters and access points[2], and Blue Ridge VPN crypto servers and clients[3], the details of which I cannot divulge here. The idea was further propelled by the rapid proliferation of mobile IP devices and their impact on the basic tenets of information systems security. Finally, after the events of September 11, 2001, which clarified the vital role of cell phones, the idea was cemented.

When I began writing *Wireless Security Essentials*, I was concerned about the lack of research material to draw from. But in a short time, the problem was reversed: suddenly there was so much material available on wireless that the problem became, what to leave out? To prevent this book growing to 900 pages, I decided to make it a compilation of technology research and reviews from many sources, which are listed in Appendix E.

I need to stress an important point here: This book is a compilation of the state of wireless technology and security current *at the time of this writing*. Wireless technology is among the most dynamic and changeable of the current computing technologies, so by the time *Wireless Security Essentials* is on the shelves, no doubt much will already be different. As just one example, strides in the use of 802.1x in hardening wireless networks were reported in a January 2002 issue of *Information Security Magazine* (see the article "Wireless Insecurities"). As another example, *InfoWorld* has reported that a University of Maryland professor and his graduate assistant cracked 802.1x. In their paper, "An Initial Security Analysis of the IEEE 802.1X Standard," funded by the National Institute of Standards (NIST), Professor William Arbaugh and Arunesh Mishra reveal serious weaknesses in 802.1x they have uncovered.[4]

[1] www.xybernaut.com

[2] www.symbol.com

[3] www.blueridgenetworks.com

[4] You can read their paper in its entirety at: www.infoworld.com/articles/hn/xml/02/02/14/020214hnwifispec.xml.

It's also quite possible that by the time this book is published the world itself will be substantially different from today. It has changed since I started writing, due to the more restrictive atmosphere imposed by wartime regulations. The public may have less, not more, access to cryptographic solutions than they do today; we may go back to the old days of cryptography being classified as a "weapon."

Whatever the state of the world, as I've already said, the technology will have definitely changed by the time this book is published. Trying to get wireless to sit still long enough to enable a static review is like changing a tire on a speeding vehicle. This then raises the question: If the technology is so fluid, how can this book be useful? The book's value lies in the fact that it addresses the important issue of security where other books have not. It's rare to find any book on networking or wireless today that contains more than two or three pages on security. This is a major oversight, because effective security is the most important element missing from wireless networks. And though the technology is dynamic, the basic tenets of confidentiality, availability, and integrity are immutable. That is, though the wireless environment is exceptionally quick-paced and dynamic, the fundamental concepts of security and basic computing technology have not changed and will not, in the short term, change significantly.

Organization

The purpose of this book is threefold: one, to provide the reader with a simple background in computer technologies and standards; two, to give the reader a solid grounding in common security concepts and methodologies; and three, to identify the threats to and vulnerabilities of wireless communications.

This book is organized into two parts, "Technology Essentials" and "Security Essentials." Part I, is designed as a primer on computer, network, and wireless technologies. It comprises three chapters, which cover this material as follows:

Chapter 1, "Computing Technology." Covers the basics of computer hardware, software, and networking technologies, including:

- Essential terminology, such as the CPU, memory, operating systems, and software

- Foundation in network technologies, such as LANs, WANs, VPNs, firewalls, and protocols

Chapter 2, "Wireless Theory." Provides background on wireless and cellular technologies, then examines the fundamental concepts of wireless networking, including:

- A brief history of wireless

- Discussions on wireless cellular technologies, wireless data networking technologies, and the Wireless Application Protocol (WAP)

Chapter 3, "Wireless Reality." Begins an examination of the various ways wireless is implemented, through various wireless networking standards, devices, and applications, with sections on:

- Wireless standards and technologies
- Wireless hardware and devices
- Wireless applications

Part II, "Security Essentials," explores the various security methodologies, and opens the discussion as to how to apply them to the wireless world. Part II also contains three chapters:

Chapter 4, "Security Concepts and Methodologies." Presents an overview of various security concepts, including cryptography and certification and assurance methodologies, and examines several important ways security methodologies are used to improve the security posture of an organization.

Chapter 5, Security Technologies." Examines the ways security is implemented in wireless, including:

- Cryptographic technologies and PKI
- Wired Equivalent Privacy (WEP)
- WAP security
- Bluetooth security architecture
- Wireless tools
- Security monitoring and testing

Chapter 6, "Threats and Solutions." This, the final chapter, confronts the security issues inherent to wireless systems, and examines the solution options. The topics covered are:

- Personal electronic device threats
- Wireless network threats
- Standards and policy solutions
- Network and software solutions
- Physical hardware security

Wireless Security Essentials also includes five appendices, as follows:

- Appendix A is a glossary of wireless and networking terms.
- Appendix B gives a detailed description of how an attacker can exploit security vulnerabilities in an 802.11b WLAN, written by Mel K. Yokoyama, Jr.

- Appendix C reprints a paper titled "Using the Fluhrer, Mantin, and Shamir Attack to Break WEP," written by Adam Stubblefield, John Ioannidis, and Aviel D. Rubin, published in August 6, 2001[5].

- Appendix D reproduces a paper titled, "NASA White Paper on the Wireless Firewall Gateway," by Nichole K. Boscia and Derek G. Shaw, published by NASA's Advanced Supercomputing Division.[6]

- Appendix E lists referenced documents, articles, papers, and URLs.

What's on the website

If you're like me, one of the first things you want to know when you pick up a new book on technology is what kind of tools and workable code came with it. The *Wireless Securities Essentials* website provides both demo and live versions of several wireless security tools, a real-time security news desktop ticker, and PDFs of white papers relevant to the topic. The downloadable software includes:

- AiroPeek 1.1.1 from WildPackets

- Netstumbler 0.3.23 for Windows and Mini-Stumbler for Pocket-PC from Marius Milner

- PC-cillin for Wireless from Trend Micro for the Palm, PocketPC, and EPOC platforms

- OnlyMe from Tranzoa

- Internet Scanner 6.2 from Internet Security Systems, Inc.

- BlackICE Defender 2.9 from Internet Security Systems, Inc.

Also included on the website is a very exciting piece of software provided by Desktop News. It is a news ticker that has been adapted by DTN and the RDV Group to push real-time security news and alerts directly to your workstation. After installation and registration, the ticker can be customized to receive news and information from a variety of major news sources, in addition to virus and security vulnerability alerts from major security news clearinghouses.

---

[5]Stubblefield, A., J. Ioannidis, & A. Rubin, "Using the Fluhrer, Mantin, and Shamir Attack to Break WEP," AT&T Labs Technical Report TD-4ZCPZZ, August 6, 2001.

[6]www.nas.nasa.gov/Groups/Networks/Projects/Wireless/index.html

PART
One

Technology Essentials

"The struggle between the need to gather information versus the right to privacy will be one of the long-term repercussions of the events of Sept. 11. Only as the coming months and years unroll before us will we be able to look back and say whether or not our special kind of democracy – unlike the World Trade Center twin towers – has withstood the heat of these terrorist attacks."

WIRELESS WORLD COLUMNIST EPHRAIM SCHWARTZ

"In individuals insanity is rare, but in groups, parties, nations and epochs it is the rule."

FRIEDRICH NIETZSCHE, BEYOND GOOD AND EVIL (1886)

CHAPTER

1

Computing Technology

To understand how wireless networking works, you first need to understand the basic elements of computer hardware, software, and networking. A quick review of the basics will help lay the foundation for the concepts in the later chapters. Let's start by examining the fundamental concepts of the computing and networking environment.

NOTE Those readers who already have a firm grasp of the information in this chapter may choose to skip ahead to Chapter 2.

The chapter is divided into two sections:

- *Computer architecture.* The hardware/software elements that create a computer system.

- *Network technology.* The internetworking elements that enable computer systems to communicate with each other.

Computer Basics

The fundamental building blocks of a computer describe its architecture. These hardware and software elements combine to create the entire computing *platform*. A computer's architecture has four basic elements:

- The central processing unit (CPU) and its related processes
- Random access memory (RAM), read-only memory (ROM), and other types of memory
- Various input/output (I/O) devices
- The operating system and software

CPU

The basic functions of modern computers haven't really changed much since John von Neumann's "stored program concept" and Alan Turing's "universal machine" propositions of the 1930s. Although the technology functionality has improved exponentially, the process of binary computation (XOR, NAND, and so on) remain basically unchanged, as do the fundamental concepts of the architecture.

The CPU contains an *arithmetic logic unit* (ALU). The ALU performs arithmetic and logical operations on the binary code of the computer. The CPU also contains other processing elements and functions, including program counters, control logic, accumulators, the instruction register, and other general-purpose registers.

Bus

The computer processing elements coordinate their activities by the means of a computer bus. A *computer bus* is a collection of electronic conductors running on a common plane and connecting these different computer functions.

THE VON NEUMANN ARCHITECTURE

An excellent short paper on John von Neumann can be found at: http://ei.cs.vt.edu/~history/VonNeumann.html. His insights into the organization of computing machines came to be known as the "von Neumann architecture." Von Neumann recognized the need for computers to process in parallel but also understood that computers employing sequential processing were much more likely to be constructed.

In contrast to CPU speed, which has been steadily and dramatically increasing for years, it is only recently that bus speed, previously a major limiting factor in the computer's architecture, has been radically altered and improved. Computers may have a bus speed of 33 MHz, 66 MHz, 100 MHz, or higher. A diagram of a computer bus is shown in Figure 1.1.

Memory

The term "memory" often causes confusion because a computer's architecture uses many different types of memory for many different functions. Let's look at the main types of memory:

Random access memory (RAM).   RAM is directly addressable and alterable memory. RAM is *volatile*, meaning that data will be lost if the power is removed from the system. RAM is used for primary (sometimes called "real") memory storage. This is the high-speed memory directly addressable by the CPU and used for storage of instructions and data associated with the program being executed.

Cache memory.   Cache memory is a very small amount of high-speed RAM used to dynamically store the most recently used data and computer instructions. It improves the performance of the CPU by storing data that is most frequently accessed. Cache memory greatly improves the execution time of various processes.

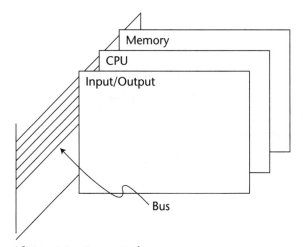

Figure 1.1   Computer bus.

INPUT/OUTPUT SYSTEMS

One of the CPU's primary functions is to interface with other devices such as input/output (I/O) adapters. I/O devices provide data buffering, and have timing and interrupt controls. Also, I/O adapters have addresses on the computer bus that are selected by computer instructions. An I/O adapter may support direct memory access (DMA), whereby data is transferred directly to and from memory without going through the CPU.

Read-only memory (ROM).   ROM provides the computer with *nonvolatile* storage, which means the data is (relatively) permanent. Nonvolatile storage retains its information even when the computer loses power. ROM is used to hold programs and data that is rarely changed, such as firmware. The contents of some ROM cannot be altered, whereas other ROM can be upgraded from the flash process, such as an EPROM.

Secondary memory.   Secondary memory is a data storage area that, like ROM, is also nonvolatile. It is a larger, slower memory storage area, and consists of the familiar hard drives, floppy-disk drives, zip drives, and tapes. These are referred to as secondary memory.

Virtual memory.   Virtual memory is a combination of primary and secondary memory that creates a large addressable memory space. This space allows the processor to access much larger amounts of memory than the RAM alone would be able to address. The Windows swap file is an example of virtual memory.

A typical memory hierarchy is depicted in Figure 1.2.

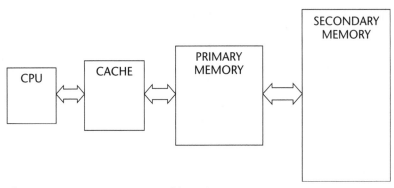

Figure 1.2   Computer memory hierarchy.

OPEN VERSUS CLOSED SYSTEMS

Open systems are vendor-independent and have published specifications that allow interoperability with other vendors' products. Closed systems use vendor-dependent proprietary hardware and/or software that is usually not compatible with other vendors' systems.

Operating Systems and Software

The primary program that controls the operations of the computer is called an operating system (OS). Windows NT, Windows 98, Windows 2000, Linux, and Unix are examples of operating systems. Operating systems manage various processes, such as memory and the file allocation tables.

The OS communicates with I/O systems through a controller, which is a device that interfaces with the peripherals and runs device drivers to communicate with the device. Examples of this type of controller are a disk controller, a network interface card (NIC), a modem, and a video controller.

Software

The CPU executes sets of instructions that tell the hardware what to do. These sets of instructions are grouped into various hierarchical levels of languages, which range from binary or mnemonic code (called assembly language) to high-level languages, like Java and BASIC.

High-level languages are converted into machine language through either interpreter or compiler programs. An interpreter operates on each high-level language source statement individually and executes the requested operation immediately, whereas a compiler first translates the entire software program into its corresponding machine language then executes them as a unit.

The high-level languages are grouped into five generations of languages (GLs), examples of which are listed in Table 1.1.

Table 1.1 Examples of Language Generations

LEVEL	DESCRIPTION
1 GL	The computer's binary machine language
2 GL	Assembly language
3 GL	BASIC, FORTRAN, C++
4 GL	FOCUS, NATURAL
5 GL	Artificial intelligence (AI) languages like LISP or Prolog

Network Technologies

In this book, the term *network technologies* refers to those hardware and software elements that allow computers to communicate with each other, whether to send email, surf the Web, or share a printer or documents. Since this book is about wireless networking, you should have some background in:

- Local area networks (LANs)
- Wide area networks (WANs)
- Virtual private networks (VPNs)
- Firewalls
- Protocols

Analog versus Digital

As shown in Figure 1.3 and Table 1.2, there are several differences between analog and digital signals. If you access the Internet via a dial-up connection at home, you probably are using a modem to create an analog circuit-switched connection. But analog technologies are more prone to interference; and they are less secure and run at slower speeds than digital technologies.

Digital has other advantages over analog as well. Long circuit-switched session setup and teardown times make analog networks unsuitable for high-speed networking, including wireless LANs. Also, digital communications can be managed by software, making it possible to build sophisticated communications switching products.

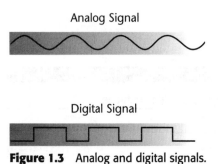

Figure 1.3   Analog and digital signals.

Table 1.2   Analog versus Digital Technologies

ANALOG	DIGITAL
Infinite wave form	Sawtooth wave form
Continuous signal	Pulses
Varied by amplification	On-off only

Local Area Networking

A data network consists of two or more computers connected for the purpose of sharing files, printers, exchanging data, email, and so on. To communicate via the network, every workstation must have a network interface card (NIC); a transmission medium such as copper, fiber, or wireless; and a network operating system (NOS). The networked computer usually connects to a network device of some sort (hub, bridge, router, or switch). Figure 1.4 shows common data networking components.

A local area network (LAN) is designed to operate in a specific limited geographic area. LANs connect workstations with file servers so they can share network resources like printers, email, and files. LAN devices are linked using a type of connection medium (copper wire, fiber optics) and use various LAN protocols and access methods to communicate through LAN devices (bridges, routers, wireless access points). LANs may be connected to a public switched network. Figure 1.5 shows three local area networks.

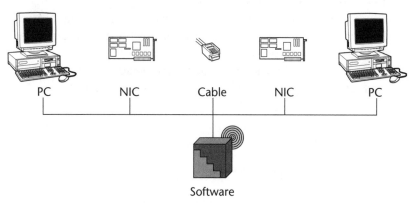

PC   NIC   Cable   NIC   PC

Software

Figure 1.4   Data networking components.

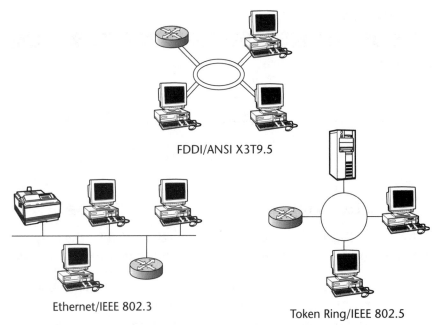

FDDI/ANSI X3T9.5

Ethernet/IEEE 802.3

Token Ring/IEEE 802.5

Figure 1.5   Local area networks.

LAN Topology

Common LAN topologies are *bus*, *ring*, and *star*. In a bus topology, all network node transmissions travel the full length of cable and are received by all other stations. Ethernet uses primarily this topology.

In a ring topology, the network nodes are connected by unidirectional transmission links to form a closed loop. Token ring and Fiber-Distributed Data Interface (FDDI) both use this topology.

In a star topology, the nodes of the network are connected directly to a central LAN device. Figure 1.6 shows a common bus Ethernet topology.

Figure 1.6   Bus topology.

The two most common LAN transmission protocol forms are carrier-sense multiple access with collision detection (CSMA/CD) used by Ethernet, and token passing, used in token ring and FDDI networks. Ethernet, ARCnet, token ring, and FDDI, the most common LAN types, use these transmission protocols.

Institute of Electrical and Electronic Engineers Standards

The Institute of Electrical and Electronic Engineers (IEEE) is a U.S. organization that participates in the development of standards for data transmission systems. IEEE has made significant progress in the establishment of standards for LANs by creating the IEEE 802 series of standards, which govern all LAN transmission methods and media access technology. Table 1.3 lists the various IEEE standards that relate to local area networking.

The LAN types are defined as follows:

Ethernet. Ethernet is a LAN media access method that uses CSMA/CD. Ethernet was originally designed to serve networks with sporadic, occasionally heavy traffic. Ethernet comes in three cabling types: thinnet coax, thicknet coax, and unshielded twisted pair (UTP). UTP is the most common of the three types, and 10BaseT/100BaseT cables and equipment are the most common. Figure 1.7 shows an Ethernet segment. Table 1.4 lists the various Ethernet 10Base standards and the types of cable used. Cable types are described later in this chapter.

Table 1.3   Common IEEE 802 Standards

STANDARD	DESCRIPTION
802.2	Specifies the logical link control (LLC).
802.3	Specifies a bus topology using CSMA/CD at 10 Mbps.
802.4	Specifies a token-passing bus access method
802.5	Specifies a token-passing ring access method.
802.10	Specifies LAN security and privacy access methods.
802.11	Specifies 1 Mbps and 2 Mbps wireless networks.
802.11a	Specifies high-speed wireless networking in the 5 GHz band up to 54 Mbps.
802.11b	Specifies high-speed wireless networking in the 2.4 GHz band up to 11 Mbps.
802.15	Specifies Bluetooth (see Chapter 2) LANs in the 2.4-2.5 GHz band.

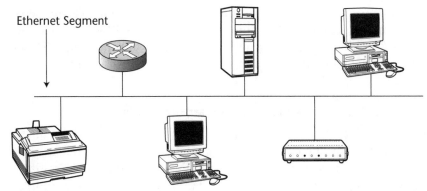

Ethernet Segment

Figure 1.7 Ethernet segment.

ARCnet.   ARCnet is one of the earliest LAN technologies. It provides predictable but slow network performance.

Token ring.   IBM originally developed token ring in the 1970s. Although it was originally the primary LAN network type, it was eventually surpassed in popularity by Ethernet. The term "token ring" can refer to either IBM's Token Ring network (in which case, it is capitalized to indicate it is a trademarked name) or any IEEE 802.5 network. In a token ring network, all end stations are attached to a device called a multistation access unit (MSAU).

Table 1.4   10Base Ethernet Standards

STANDARD	DESCRIPTION
10Base2	10 Mbps thinnet coax rated to 185 meters
10Base5	10 Mbps thicknet coax rated to 500 meters
10BaseF	10 Mbps baseband optical fiber
10BaseT	10 Mbps UTP rated to 100 meters
10Broad36	10 Mbps broadband rated to 3600 meters
100BaseT	100 Mbps UTP
1000BaseT	1000 Mbps UTP

TOKEN-PASSING BUS NETWORKS

A token-passing bus network uses a logical token-passing access method. Unlike a token-passing ring, permission to transmit is based on the node address rather than the position in the network. It uses a shared single cable with all the data broadcast across the entire LAN.

Fiber Distributed Data Interface (FDDI).   Similar to token ring, FDDI is a token-passing media access topology. It consists of dual rings operating at 100 Mbps, commonly over fiber optic cabling, although a version using category 5 copper cable exists, called Copper Distributed Data Interface (CDDI). FDDI employs a token-passing media access with dual counter-rotating rings, with only one ring active at any given time. If a break or outage occurs, the ring will wrap back in the other direction, keeping the ring intact.

LAN Cabling

LAN cabling comes in three common varieties: coaxial (called coax), unshielded twisted pair (called UTP), and fiber optic. Let's briefly look at each type.

Unshielded twisted pair (UTP).   UTP wiring consists of four wire pairs (eight connectors) individually insulated and twisted together. UTP comes in several categories based on how tightly the insulated copper strands are twisted together. The tighter the twist, the higher the rating and its resistance against interference and attenuation. Table 1.5 shows the various categories of UTP cabling.

Table 1.5 UTP Cable Categories

CATEGORY	DESCRIPTION
Category 1	Used for early analog telephone communications; not suitable for data.
Category 2	Used in early token ring networks; rated for 4 Mbps.
Category 3	Common in 10BaseT networks; rated for 10 Mbps.
Category 4	Common in later token ring networks; rated for 16 Mbps.
Category 5	Current standard; rated for 100 Mbps.
Category 6	Rated for 155 Mbps.
Category 7	Rated for 1 Gbps.

Figure 1.8 LAN cable types.

Coaxial cable.   Coaxial cable (commonly called coax) consists of a hollow outer cylindrical conductor that surrounds a single inner wire conductor. Coax comes in two common types: thinnet (RG58), and thicknet (RG8 or RG11). Because the shielding reduces the amount of electrical noise interference, coax can extend to much greater lengths than twisted pair wiring.

Fiber optic.   Fiber optic cable is a physical medium capable of conducting modulated light transmission, thereby creating higher transmission speeds and greater distances. It is the most resistant to electromagnetic interference. Fiber optic cable is a very reliable cable type but is very expensive to install and terminate.

Figure 1.8 shows the three different LAN cable types.

LAN Network Devices

LANs are connected by communication devices, such as hubs, bridges, routers, switches, or gateways. Let's take a look at these.

Hubs.   Hubs amplify the data signals to extend the length of the network segment and help compensate for signal deterioration due to attenuation. They don't add any intelligence to the process; that is, they don't filter packets, examine addressing, or alter anything in the data packet. Hubs are used to connect LAN devices into a concentrator. Figure 1.9 shows a hub or repeater.

Bridges and switches.   Bridges are like hubs, but they add some intelligence. A bridge forwards the data to all other network segments if the media access control (MAC) or hardware address of the destination computer isn't on the local network segment. If the destination computer is on the local network segment, it doesn't forward the data. Figure 1.10 shows a bridged network. A switch is similar to a bridge or a hub, except that a switch will send the data packet only to the specific port where the destination MAC address is located, rather than to all ports attached to the hub or bridge. This improves performance.

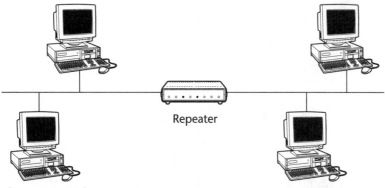

Figure 1.9 Hub or repeater.

Routers.   Routers add even more intelligence to the process of forwarding data packets. A router opens up the data packet and reads either the hardware or network address (IP address) before forwarding it, then forwards the packet only to the network to which the packet was destined. This prevents unnecessary network traffic from being sent over the network by blocking broadcast information and blocking traffic to unknown addresses. Figure 1.11 is an example of a routed network.

Gateways.   Gateways are primarily software products that can be run on computers or other network devices. They can be multiprotocol (link different protocols) and can examine the entire packet.

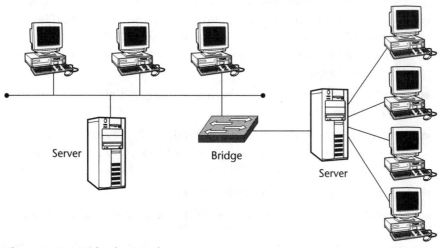

Figure 1.10 Bridged network.

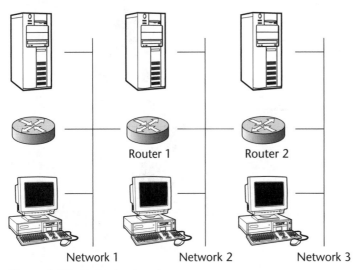

Figure 1.11   Routed network.

Wireless Access Protocol (WAP) gateway.   A gateway device, called a WAP gateway, is used to serve HTML-style content to WAP-enabled devices, such as Internet-enabled cell phones. WAP gateways are discussed in more detail in Chapter 3.

Wireless access points (APs).   An AP functions like a bridge or router, but is made for wireless, 802.11 communications. The most common APs on the market today are 802.11b Ethernet-compatible, but a new Ethernet format with a faster transmission speed, 802.11a, is becoming available for the home and office market. However, 802.11b will continue to dominate the market for some time. A more complete description of wireless access points is given in Chapter 2. Figure 1.12 shows a common home networking 802.11b AP by GigaFast Ethernet[1]. Some APs made for use in the home or small office/home office (SOHO) often have several additional functions, for example:

- Broadband routing, to allow sharing of a single high-speed cable modem or DSL Internet line.
- Dynamic Host Configuration Protocol (DHCP) service, which provides the workstation with a usable IP address, and provides network address translation (NAT); see the NAT sidebar.
- Printer sharing through a printer server.
- Redundant dial-up access, in case of failure of the broadband line.

[1] www.gigafast.com

Figure 1.12   GigaFast 802.11b wireless access point.
(Courtesy of GigaFast Ethernet USA)

Figure 1.13 shows the GigaFast USB 802.11b network interface adapter. It is designed to operate with the Gigafast access point shown earlier, but like most 802.11b USB adapters, can operate with any WLAN-compliant network.

Figure 1.13   GigaFast 802.11b USB adapter.
(Courtesy of GigaFast Ethernet USA)

DOMAIN NAME SERVICE (DNS)

The Domain Name Service matches Internet URL (Uniform Resource Locator) requests with the actual address or location of the server providing that URL. DNS is a distributed database system used to map host names to IP addresses. The Domain Name Service is not to be confused with the Domain Name System (also abbreviated as DNS), which is a global network of servers that provide these domain name services.

Figure 1.14 shows an 802.11b AP manufactured by SMC Networks[2] with these additional routing features. Features of this kind were unheard of in the home or SOHO environment just a couple of years ago. SMC's most recent product introduction, the Barricade Plus Cable/DSL Broadband Router, offers integrated stateful packet inspection (SPI) and a VPN tunneling feature, which supports up to five VPN tunnels.

Another recent vendor with an entry into the 802.11b home or SOHO market is Belkin Components[3], more well known as a maker of cables and PC accessories. Like Gigafast and SMC, they offer several WLAN products, including a wireless Cable/DSL gateway router (shown in Figure 1.15), and a wireless USB network adapter (shown in Figure 1.16.)

Figure 1.14   SMC Barricade wireless broadband router.
(Courtesy of SMC Networks)

[2] www.smc.com
[3] www.belkin.com

Figure 1.15   Belkin Wireless Cable/DSL gateway router.
(Courtesy of Belkin Components)

Wide Area Networking

A wide area network (WAN) is a network of subnetworks that physically or logically interconnects LANs over a large geographic area. Basically, the WAN is everything outside of the LAN. It may be privately operated for a specific user community, it may support multiple communication protocols, or it may provide network connectivity and services via an interconnected public packet data network, like the Internet.

Circuit-Switched versus Packet-Switched Networks

Circuit-switching technology uses a dedicated physical circuit path between the sender and receiver for the duration of the connection, and consists of a physical, permanent data connection. Though this technology predates packet-switching, it is the preferred choice for communications that need to be continuously on and that have a limited distribution scope (one transmission path only). Modems and analog voice phone calls are circuit-switched.

NETWORK ADDRESS TRANSLATION

Network address translation (NAT) is the process of preventing a "real" IP address from being seen from outside the network. The Internet Assigned Numbers Authority (IANA) reserved three blocks of IP addresses for private networks: 10.0.0.0(10.255.255.255; 172.16.0.0(172.31.255.255; and 192.168.0.0(192.168.255.255. NAT masks the host's true IP address by translating it into a private, internal address.

Figure 1.16   Belkin USB network adapter.
(Courtesy of Belkin Components)

In contrast, packet-switching is a network communications technology that lets nodes share bandwidth with each other by sending packets. A packet-switched network (PSN) or packet-switched data network (PSDN) uses packet-switching technology for data transfer. Unlike circuit-switched networks, the data in packet-switched networks is broken up into relatively small units of data, called *packets*, and is then sent to the next destination based on the destination address contained within each packet. At that destination the packets are reassembled based on the originally assigned sequence numbers. Though the data is manhandled a lot in this process, it results in a network that is very resilient to error.

It's important to note that this type of communication between sender and receiver is known as connectionless communication, as opposed to connection-oriented dedicated communications. Dividing communications into packets allows the same data path to be shared. Packet-switched networks are more cost-effective than dedicated circuits because they generate virtual circuits that are created and discarded dynamically, in contrast to a static continuous dedicated circuit.

A couple of analogies might help to clarify the difference between dedicated and connectionless networks. Calling someone on the phone creates a dedicated circuit, because you've established a direct connection with the party at the other end. That party may or may not be the person you want to speak to, nevertheless, you know you made contact. A connectionless network can be likened to sending a letter: You write your message, address it, and mail it. If, however, you divide the message into several parts, address each of them separately to the same person, then mail them, you have no way of confirming they will get there in the same order—or at all.

Packet-Switched Technologies

Examples of packet-switching networks are X.25, link access procedure balanced (LAPB), frame relay, Switched Multimegabit Data Services (SMDS), Asynchronous Transfer Mode (ATM), and voice over IP (VoIP). Most traffic over the Internet uses packet switching, and the Internet is basically a connectionless network.

X.25. A terminal interface standard for a packet-switching network. X.25 was developed by the Comité Consultatif International Télégraphique et Téléphonique (CCITT; in English, the International Telegraph and Telephone Consultative Committee) as the first public packet switching technology during the 1970s and is still available. It offers connection-oriented virtual circuits at 64 Kbps. It was designed to operate effectively regardless of the type of systems connected to the network. It has become an international standard and is now much more prevalent overseas than in the United States.

Link access procedure balanced (LAPB). Created for use with X.25, LAPB defines frame types and is capable of retransmitting, exchanging, and acknowledging frames, as well as detecting out-of-sequence or missing frames.

Frame relay. Frame Relay is an upgrade from X.25 and LAPB. It's a packet-switching interface that operates at data rates of 56 Kbps to 2 Mbps and utilizes no error correction. Carriers offer frame relay as permanent connection-oriented virtual circuit service.

Asynchronous Transfer Mode (ATM). ATM is a very high-bandwidth, low-delay technology that uses both switching and multiplexing. It uses 53-byte fixed-size cells instead of frames, like Ethernet. It can allocate bandwidth on demand, making it a good solution for bursty applications, that is, applications that require intensive bandwidth for short periods of time, rather than steady, constant bandwidth. It requires a high-speed, high-bandwidth medium such as fiber optics.

Switched Multimegabit Data Services (SMDS). SMDS is a high-speed technology used over public-switched networks. It helps companies exchange large amounts of data with other companies over WANs on a bursty, or noncontinuous, basis by providing connectionless bandwidth on demand.

Private Circuit Technologies

Private circuits evolved before packet-switching networks. A private circuit network is composed of a dedicated analog or digital point-to-point connection that joins geographically diverse networks. The following defines the types of private circuit technologies:

Dedicated and leased lines.   A dedicated line is defined as a communications line that is indefinitely and continuously reserved for communication. A leased line is a type of dedicated line reserved by a communications carrier for the private use of a customer.

Serial Line Internet Protocol (SLIP).   SLIP supports TCP/IP over low-speed serial interfaces. Windows NT computers can use TCP/IP and SLIP to communicate with remote hosts using Window's Remote Access Server (RAS) service. This is an older technology but still in use.

Point-to-Point Protocol (PPP).   PPP is a specification used by data communications equipment for communicating over dial-up and dedicated links. It was built to replace the Serial Line Internet Protocol (SLIP), which only supported IP. PPP has built-in security mechanisms such as Challenge Handshake Authentication Protocol (CHAP) and Password Authentication Protocol (PAP).

Integrated Services Digital Network (ISDN).   ISDN is combination of digital telephony and data-transport services offered by telecommunications carriers. It supports voice and other digital services (data, music, video) over existing telephone wires. It has recently been replaced by Digital Subscriber Line (DSL), described next.

Digital Subscriber Line (DSL).   DSL is a broadband technology that uses existing twisted pair telephone lines to move high bandwidth data to remote subscribers, with download speeds commonly faster than upload speeds. The installation must be within 15,000 feet of a provider's central office (CO). Some types of DSL are: Asymmetric Digital Subscriber Line (ADSL), Single-Line Digital Subscriber Line (SDSL), High-Rate Digital Subscriber Line (HDSL), and Very-High-Data-Rate Digital Subscriber Line (VDSL).

Virtual Private Networking (VPNs)

A virtual private network (VPN) is created by building (often dynamically) a secure communications link between two nodes, using a secret encapsulation method. This link is commonly called a secure encrypted tunnel, although it's more accurately defined as an encapsulated tunnel, as encryption may or may not be used.

CABLE MODEMS

A cable modem is a broadband technology that is used like DSL, but with some differences. A cable modem is a shared connection, whereas DSL is a direct, unshared connection; therefore, speed can degrade during peak usage times. Also, a cable modem commonly has a larger starting bandwidth than DSL, which may offset the shared usage degradation.

VPN Communications Standards

The three most common VPN communications protocol standards are:

Point-to-Point Tunneling Protocol (PPTP).   PPTP works at the data link layer of the Open Systems Interconnect (OSI) model, which is described shortly. It is designed for individual client-to-server connections as it allows only a single point-to-point connection per session. PPTP is commonly used by Windows clients for asynchronous communications. PPTP uses the native PPP authentication and encryption services.

Layer 2 Tunneling Protocol (L2TP).   L2TP is a combination of PPTP and the earlier Layer 2 Forwarding Protocol (L2F); it, too, works at the data link layer. L2TP is an accepted tunneling standard for VPNs, as dial-up VPNs use this standard frequently. Like PPTP, it was designed for single point-to-point client-to-server connections. Multiple protocols can be encapsulated within the L2TP tunnel.

Internet Protocol Security (IPSec).   IPSec operates at the network layer and allows multiple simultaneous tunnels. IPSec contains the functionality to encrypt and authenticate IP data. While PPTP and L2TP are aimed more at dial-up VPNs, IPSec also encompasses network-to-network connectivity.

Firewalls

Let's look at three different types of firewall architectures. This will help when we discuss WAP gateways and security methodologies later. A firewall is a set of programs residing on a device on the perimeter of the network that protects the resources of a private network from users from other networks. An organization commonly installs a firewall to prevent outsiders from accessing its own private data resources and for controlling to what outside resources its own users have access.

Packet-Filtering Firewall

The simplest form of firewall is the packet-filtering firewall, also called a *screening router*. This type of firewall examines both the source and destination address of the incoming data packet and either blocks the packet or passes the packet to its intended destination network, usually the local network segment upon which it resides. The firewall can deny access to specific applications and/or services based on access control lists (ACLs), port numbers, or service numbers.

The packet-filtering firewall uses the information of the source and destination addresses of the incoming packet, the session's communications protocol, and the source and destination application port for the desired service. A packet-filtering router sits between the private trusted network and the untrusted network. Figure 1.17 illustrates a simple packet filtering firewall.

Application-Level Firewalls

An application-level firewall, or application layer gateway, is commonly implemented as a proxy server. The firewall transfers a copy of each authorized data packet from one network to another, thereby masking the origin of the data. This controls which services are allowed to be used by the workstation and aids in protecting the network from outsiders who may be trying to get information about the design of the network.

Stateful Inspection Firewall

In a stateful inspection firewall, data packets are captured by an inspection engine operating at the faster network layer; they are then queued and analyzed at higher OSI layers. This type of firewall is commonly faster than an application-level firewall while providing a thorough inspection of the data. The stateful inspection firewall examines the state and context of the incoming data packets and helps track connectionless protocols, like UDP.

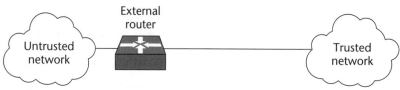

Figure 1.17   Packet-filtering firewall.

Protocols

A protocol describes the format that a message must be in when computers communicate; that is, protocols enable different types of computers to communicate despite their differences. They do this by describing a standard format and method for communications by adhering to a layered architecture model. A layered architecture divides communications processes into logical groups called *layers*.

Open Systems Interconnect (OSI) Model

The Open Systems Interconnection (OSI) model was created in the early 1980s by the International Standards Organization (ISO) to help vendors develop interoperable network devices. The OSI model describes how data and network information is communicated from one computer to another computer through the network media. This model breaks this information into seven distinct layers, each with a unique set of properties. Each layer directly interacts with its adjacent layers. The seven OSI layers are shown in Figure 1.18.

> **Application layer (layer 7).**   The application layer is the highest level of the OSI model and is the direct interface to the user. It supports the processes that deal with the communication aspects of an application. The application layer is responsible for identifying and establishing the availability of the intended communication partner. This layer is also responsible for determining whether sufficient resources for the intended communication exists.

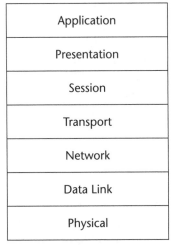

Figure 1.18   The OSI seven-layer reference model.

Presentation layer (layer 6). The presentation layer presents data to the application layer. It's essentially a translator. Tasks like data compression, decompression, encryption, and decryption are associated with this layer. The presentation layer defines how applications can enter the network.

Session layer (layer 5). The session layer makes the initial contact with other computers and sets up lines of communication. It formats the data for transfer between end nodes, provides session restart and recovery, and performs general maintenance of the session from end to end. It also splits up a communication session into three different phases: connection establishment, data transfer, and connection release.

Transport layer (layer 4). The transport layer is responsible for maintaining the end-to-end integrity and control of the session. It defines how to address the physical locations and/or devices on the network, makes connections between nodes, and handles the internetworking of messages. Services located in the transport layer both segment and reassemble the data from upper-layer applications and unite it onto the same data stream, provide end-to-end data transport services, and establish a logical connection between the sending host and destination host on a network.

Network layer (layer 3). The network layer defines how the small packets of data are routed and relayed between end systems on the same network or on interconnected networks. At this layer, message routing, error detection, and control of node data traffic are managed. Sending packets from the source network to the destination network is the network layer's primary function. The IP protocol operates at this layer.

Data link layer (layer 2). The data link layer defines the protocol that computers must follow to access the network for transmitting and receiving messages. Token ring and Ethernet operate within this layer, which establishes the communications link between individual devices over a physical link or channel. The data link layer ensures that messages are delivered to the proper device, and translates messages from above into bits for the physical layer (layer 1) to transmit. The data link layer formats the message into data frames and adds a customized header that contains the hardware destination and source address. It also contains the logical link control and the media access control (MAC) sublayers.

Physical layer (layer 1). The physical layer has only two responsibilities: to send and receive bits. The physical layer defines the physical connection between the computer and the network and converts the bits into voltages or light impulses for transmission. It defines the electrical and mechanical aspects of the interface of the device to a physical transmission medium, such as twisted pair, coax, or fiber.

Transmission Control Protocol/Internet Protocol (TCP/IP) Model

Transmission Control Protocol/Internet Protocol (TCP/IP) is the common name for the suite of protocols developed by the Department of Defense in the 1970s to support the construction of worldwide networks. The Internet is based on TCP/IP, which are the two best-known protocols in the suite.

As shown in Figure 1.19, TCP/IP adheres roughly to the bottom four layers of the OSI model. This figure reflects the original Department of Defense (DoD) concept of the TCP/IP model.

Application layer.   This layer isn't really in TCP/IP, it's made up of whatever application is trying to communicate using TCP/IP. TCP/IP views everything above the three bottom layers as the responsibility of the application, so that the Application, Presentation, and Session layers of the OSI model are considered folded into this top layer. Therefore, the TCP/IP suite primarily operates in the Transport and Network layers of the OSI model.

Host-to-host layer.   The host-to-host layer is comparable to the OSI transport layer. It defines protocols for setting up the level of transmission service. It provides for reliable end-to-end communications, ensures the error-free delivery of the data, handles packet sequencing of the data, and maintains the integrity of the data.

Internet layer.   The Internet layer corresponds to the OSI network layer. It designates the protocols relating to the logical transmission of packets over the network. It gives network nodes an IP address and handles the routing of packets among multiple networks. It also controls the communication flow between hosts.

Network access layer.   At the bottom of the TCP/IP model, the network access layer monitors the data exchange between the host and the network. The equivalent of the data-link and physical layers of the OSI model, it oversees hardware addressing and defines protocols for the physical transmission of data.

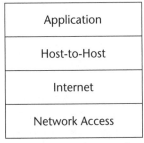

Figure 1.19   The DoD layered model for TCP/IP.

Table 1.6   TCP/IP Protocols

LAYER	PROTOCOL
Host-to-host	Transmission Control Protocol (TCP)
Host-to-host	User Datagram Protocol (UDP)
Internet	Internet Protocol (IP)
Internet	Address Resolution Protocol (ARP) l
Internet	Reverse Address Resolution Protocol (RARP)
Internet	Internet Control Message Protocol (ICMP)

TCP/IP Protocols

Let's look at the various protocols that populate the TCP/IP model. Table 1.6 lists some important TCP/IP protocols, and their related layers.

Transmission Control Protocol (TCP).   TCP provides a full-duplex, connection-oriented, reliable connection. Incoming TCP packets are sequenced to match the original transmission sequence numbers. Any lost or damaged packets are retransmitted.

User Datagram Protocol (UDP).   UDP is similar to TCP but gives only a "best effort" delivery, which means it offers no error correction, does not sequence the packet segments, and does not care in which order the packet segments arrive at their destination. Consequently, it's referred to as an *unreliable protocol*. It's also considered a connectionless protocol. Table 1.7 points out the differences between the TCP and the UDP protocols.

Internet Protocol (IP).   IP provides an *unreliable datagram service*, meaning that it does not guarantee that the packet will be delivered at all, that it will be delivered only once, or that it will be delivered in the order in which it was sent.

On the Internet, and in networks using the IP protocol, each data packet is assigned the IP address of the sender and the IP address of the recipient. Each device then receives the packet and makes routing decisions based upon the packet's destination IP address.

Address Resolution Protocol (ARP).   IP needs to know the hardware address of the destination of the packet so it can send it. ARP is used to match an IP address to an Ethernet address. An Ethernet address is a 48-bit address that is hard-wired into the NIC of the network node. ARP is used to match up the 32-bit IP address with this hardware address, technically referred to as the media access control (MAC) address or physical address.

Table 1.7 TCP versus UDP Protocol

TCP	UDP
Sequenced	Unsequenced
Connection-oriented	Connectionless
Reliable	Unreliable
High overhead	Low overhead
Slower	Faster

Reverse Address Resolution Protocol (RARP).   In some cases, the reverse of the preceding is required: the MAC address is known but the IP address needs to be discovered. This is sometimes the case when diskless machines are booted onto the network. The RARP protocol sends out a packet that includes its MAC address along with a request to be informed of which IP address should be assigned to that MAC address. A RARP server responds with the answer.

Internet Control Message Protocol (ICMP).   ICMP's primary function is to send messages between network devices regarding the health of the network. It can inform hosts of a better route to a destination if there is trouble with an existing route, and help identify the problem with a route. The Packet INternet Groper utility (PING) uses ICMP messages to check the physical connectivity of machines on a network.

Figure 1.20 shows how TCP/IP protocols correspond to the OSI model layers.

The Wireless Application Protocol

Chapter 2 addresses the Wireless Application Protocol (WAP) in more detail, but it's described briefly here to enable a comparison with the previous two protocol models, OSI and TCP/IP.

The WAP architecture is loosely based on the OSI model, and was created from the following layers (top to bottom):

Application layer.   The WAP application layer is the direct interface to the user, and contains the wireless application environment (WAE), This top layer consists of several elements, including a microbrowser specification for Internet access, the Wireless Markup Language (WML), WMLScript, and wireless telephony applications (WTA).

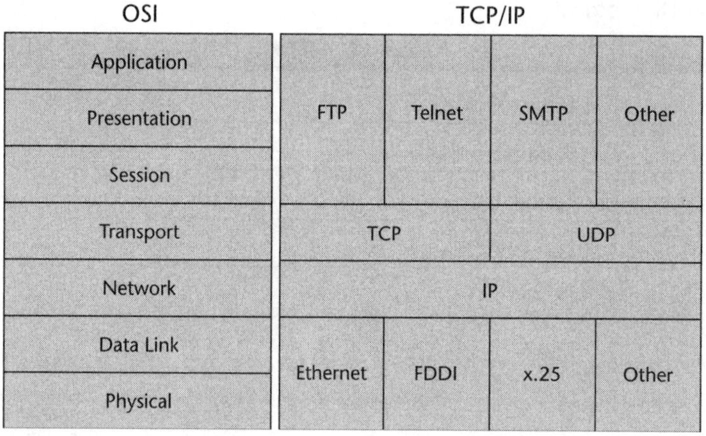

OSI   TCP/IP

Application				
Presentation	FTP	Telnet	SMTP	Other
Session				
Transport	TCP		UDP	
Network	IP			
Data Link	Ethernet	FDDI	x.25	Other
Physical				

Figure 1.20   OSI model layers mapped to TCP/IP protocols.

Session layer.   The WAP session layer contains the Wireless Session Protocol (WSP), which is similar to the Hypertext Transfer Protocol (HTTP), as it is designed for low-bandwidth, high-latency wireless networks. As explained in Chapter 3, WSP facilitates the transfer of content between WAP clients and WAP gateways in a binary format. Additional functionalities include content push and suspension/resumption of connections.

Transaction layer.   The WAP transaction layer provides the Wireless Transactional Protocol (WTP), which provides the functionality similar to TCP/IP in the Internet model. WTP is a lightweight transactional protocol that allows for reliable request and response transactions and supports unguaranteed and guaranteed push.

Security layer.   The security layer contains Wireless Transport Layer Security (WTLS). WTLS is based on Transport Layer Security (TLS, similar to the Secure Sockets Layer, or SSL). It provides data integrity, privacy, authentication, and denial-of-service (DoS) protection mechanisms.

Transport layer.   The bottom WAP layer, the transport layer, supports the Wireless Datagram Protocol (WDP), which provides an interface to the bearers of transportation. It supports the CDPD, GSM, Integrated Digital Enhanced Network (iDEN), CDMA, TDMA, SMS, and FLEX protocols.

Figure 1.21 diagrams the layers of the Wireless Application Protocol.

Since you've immersed yourself in this chapter, you now have a good understanding of computing and network fundamentals. Now you're ready to take this knowledge into the next chapter, "Wireless Theory." Here you will begin to see the building blocks of wireless protocols and concepts.

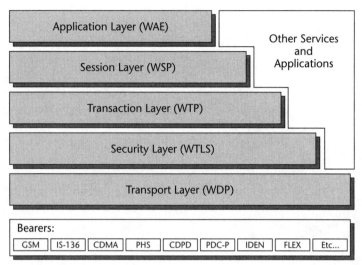

Figure 1.21 The Wireless Application Protocol.

CHAPTER

2

Wireless Theory

This chapter tracks the evolution of wireless technologies and gives an overview of the kinds of wireless protocols, standards, and technologies that are currently available. The descriptions presented here are intended solely as a necessary foundation to understanding the wireless security technologies described later; therefore, they are neither highly technical nor detailed.

A Painless History of Wireless Technology

Radio waves are measured in different cycles per second, based on the number of times a wave occurs in a second. A single cycle or wave is called a Hertz, named for Heinrich Rudolph Hertz (1857–1894), the German physicist who discovered it. Sound waves normally range from about 20 Hertz (Hz) to 20 Kilohertz (thousands of Hertz, kHz).

The number of times a wave occurs per second is also called its *frequency*. Low-pitched sound waves have lower frequencies than high-pitched sound waves. The full range of frequencies is called the *electromagnetic spectrum*, which is divided into distinct regions from the lowest to the highest. The lowest range of frequencies contains audible sound, what we can hear. The next group of frequencies consist of the radio spectrum, ranging from about 100 kHz to 100 Gigahertz (one billion Hertz, GHz). Above the radio spectrum is what we can see, that is, visible light, followed by ultraviolet, and X ray, and, finally, gamma rays at the highest layer.

Wireless data uses a subset of the radio frequency spectrum, currently from 800 kHz to 5 GHz. Although wireless data is often identified as operating at some fixed frequency, it really uses a small range of frequencies within the radio frequency. An excellent chart showing the allocation of the United States radio frequency spectrum can be found in PDF format at the National Telecommunications and Information Administration Web site: www.ntia.doc.gov/osmhome/allochrt.html. The NTIA also offers a wall-size poster for sale, which is really cool (to some of us). Because radio waves don't travel great distances, various governmental organizations representing many countries and/or groups of countries decide who can use which parts of the spectrum and how. The Federal Communications Commission (FCC) does this for the United States. In spite of (or because of) this governmental control, the same wireless communication system can exist in two countries on different frequencies; and, often, the allocated wireless frequencies don't match the frequencies allocated in other countries. In the United States alone, many different wireless communications carriers battle for market share of a finite spectrum.

The Cellular Phone Network

The first radio mobile phone service was provided for police, emergency, and private vehicles. Only a couple of channels handled by operators were available, so the demand for mobile communications soon exceeded the resources. It wasn't possible to simply provide more channels, because of the intense competition for these limited frequencies.

Two developments improved radio telephone service: advanced techniques in ultra-high frequency (UHF) radio and advancements in computers. UHF provides much larger bandwidth, and larger bandwidth means more channels for mobile service. The transmitter/receivers of the radio signals are located in *cells* that divide a serving area. As the cell phone user moves about, the signal is handed off to the receiver that is getting the strongest signal. This can only be done with a network system centrally controlled by a computer.

PERSONAL COMMUNICATIONS SYSTEM

The FCC "auctioned off" the 1900 MHz radio spectrum in the 1990s to a digital wireless communications system called the Personal Communications System (PCS). Various large and small companies used this spectrum to deploy new PCS systems, such as the Sprint PCS wireless network.

Worldwide Cellular via LEO Satellites

Modern low Earth orbit (LEO) satellite networks are being constructed now that will begin to reach their service potential in the next few years. Modern LEOs have greatly changed since the first communications satellite, Telstar, which was launched in the early 1960s. Telstar was basically a silver balloon that reflected microwave signals back to Earth, but was significant at the time because it did so from a low, rather than geosynchronous (that is, completing one revolution in the same time that the Earth completes one rotation), orbit.

Besides extending basic voice service to new customers, LEOs can offer advanced services, such as Internet access and video. LEO systems use the same interface technologies as today's digital wireless networks. Some use code division multiple access (CDMA) technology, while others employ a variation on time division multiple access (TDMA) technology. CDMA and TDMA are discussed in more detail later in this chapter.

Medium Earth orbit satellite systems, which begin at an altitude of about 12,000 kilometers, also can be used for communication, but to date, these systems have mostly been devoted to use by weather satellites.

Cellular Network Elements

Let's take a quick look at the components of a wireless cellular network's architecture.

Cell tower.   A cell tower is the site of a cellular telephone transmission facility. Wireless coverage is divided into hexagonal-shaped coverage boundaries, with one cell tower covering each region. This hexagonal shape varies depending on the network's geographic coverage.

Base station controller (BSC).   Also commonly called a *base station*, a BSC controls a cluster of cell towers. It is responsible for setting up a voice or data call with the mobile terminal and managing handoff when the phone moves from one cell tower boundary to another, without disruption of service.

Mobile switching center (MSC).   An MSC connects all the base stations to pass communications signals and messages to and from subscribers operating on the network. An MSC is connected to a visitor location register (VLR), a home location register (HLR), an authentication center (AuC), and an equipment identity register (EIR).

Home location register (HLR).   An HLR keeps track of information about the subscriber, including a record of the last time the mobile cell phone was registered on the network. Mobile devices register with a wireless network every few seconds to identify their location. This helps to speed call setup when BSCs have to find the mobile device.

Visitor location register (VLR). A VLR records information about mobile devices that have roamed into its network from other networks, that is, out of their home calling area. For example, if your mobile device is registered to operate with a network in New York but you're initiating a call from Boston, the VLR registers details about the mobile and its plan in Boston.

Mobile identity number (MIN) and electronic serial number (ESN). All mobile devices used in a wireless network carry these identification numbers, which are used for verification, authentication, and billing purposes.

Equipment identity register (EIR). An EIR stores and checks the status of MINs and ESNs.

Authentication center (AuC). An AuC is responsible for authentication and validation of services for each mobile device attempting to use the network.

Operations and maintenance center (OMC). An OMC is connected to the network to provide functions such as billing, network management, customer care, and service provisioning.

The Call Process

The cellular calling process works as follows:

1. To initiate the call setup, a mobile device's radio frequency (RF) transceiver sends a message request to the nearest base station.

2. The base station recognizes the call signal and routes it to the MSC.

3. The MSC queries the HLR or VLR (if the original registration of the mobile device is local, HLR will be queried; otherwise, VLR will be queried.), EIR and AuC for location, service qualification and features, and authentication.

4. Depending on the destination of the call, it's routed to another base station, the same base station (if the destination of the communication in the same area), to a landline via the public-switched telephone network (PSTN), or to an Internet device via the Internet if it's a data transmission.

Wireless Cellular Technologies

Over the past few years, wireless technologies have improved significantly. This section reviews some of the predominant wireless cellular technologies. The next section examines wireless data technologies.

Wireless Transmission Systems

Several different transmission systems are used around the world for cellular telephone service, none of which is compatible with any of the others. Europe uses Global System for Mobile Communications (GSM) for digital communications; parts of Asia, mainly Japan, use Personal Digital Cellular (PDC for digital communication, which will not work in any other system. Because of these incompatible systems, a person using a WAP phone or even a cellular phone will find it difficult to use anywhere other than the continent on which it was purchased. Even in the United States, if you change carriers, you will have to purchase another WAP phone that was manufactured specifically for your new carrier.

Worldwide efforts are underway to create a global standard for mobile telephone/mobile WAP telephone use. The front-runner standard is known as the Universal Mobile Telecommunications System (UMTS), also known as wideband CDMA or WCDMA, and it is expected to be in place by 2004. This system meets the requirements put forth by the International Telecommunications Union (ITU), an agency of the United Nations responsible for making recommendations and standardization regarding telephone and data communications systems for public and private telecommunications organizations. This effort is also known as IMT-2000 (International Mobile Telephone 2000), an international standardization effort.

Wireless cellular networks that can provide data connections in the 50 Kbps (thousand bits per second) range are currently in development. Speeds should eventually reach 2 Mbps (million bits per second). Several high-speed wireless data technologies, such as GPRS, CDMA2000, and EDGE, are being tested in limited trials in various parts of the world. Cell phones, BlackBerrys, and two-way pagers will get faster, cheaper, and easier to use.

Following are a few of the primary modes used for cellular communications, listed somewhat by generation.

Advanced Mobile Phone System

Advanced Mobile Phone System (AMPS) is the U.S. standard for analog cellular service, a first-generation (1G) wireless technology. AMPS is the analog cellular transport used throughout North America and in other parts of the world, notably Central and South America, and New Zealand and Australia. It has the best coverage of all North American systems.

AMPS operates at 800 MHz and is a voice-only analog transport, although it can be used with a cellular modem for circuit-switched data communications. AMPS is slowly being replaced by various competing digital networks.

Time Division Multiple Access

Time Division Multiple Access (TDMA) was the first U.S. digital standard to be developed by the Telecommunications Industry Association (TIA) in 1992; it also has been in use for quite some time in Europe as the basis for the GSM, and has been implemented in North America in some PCS systems. TDMA is a digital transport scheme, wherein multiple subscribers are granted access to the same radio frequency source by limiting subscribers' transmit and receive signals to time slots. TDMA is also referred to as the first digital cellular frequency modulation (FM) system standardized in North America; it is considered a second-generation (2G) wireless technology.

TDMA divides the frequency range allotted to it into a series of channels. Each channel is then divided into time slots. Each conversation within a channel gets a time slot, which explains the word "division" in its name.

It's possible to overlay TDMA on an AMPS transport, thus converting an analog network to a hybrid analog/digital network. Some AMPS carriers in North America have been doing this to add security, capacity, and data capabilities to their older voice systems. This type of network goes by several names, including Digital AMPS (D-AMPS) and North American TDMA (NA-TDMA).

Code Division Multiple Access

Code Division Multiple Access (CDMA) is an airlink interface coding scheme, wherein multiple subscribers are granted access to the same radio frequency source by assigning subscriber's transmit and receive signals a spectrum-spreading code. CDMA is considered a second-generation technology.

Developed originally by QUALCOMM, CDMA is characterized by its high capacity and small cell radius, and the fact that it employs spread-spectrum technology and a special scheme. It was adopted by the Telecommunications Industry Association (TIA) in 1993. Though CDMA has been used as a digital transport by the U.S. military since the 1940s, as a commercial wireless transport, it is considered the new kid on the block compared to TDMA and AMPS.

A CDMA transmitter assigns a unique code to each wireless connection and then broadcasts its data out on the channel simultaneously with all other connections. The receiver is able to decode each conversation by deciphering the unique code assigned to each connection.

CDMA supports more simultaneous users than either AMPS or TDMA: approximately 10 to 20 times that of AMPS, and three times that of TDMA. It uses less power, thereby providing longer phone battery life. It is also more secure, because it hops from one frequency to another during a conversation, making it less prone to eavesdropping and phone fraud.

Global System for Mobile Communications

Global System for Mobile Communications (GSM) is similar to TDMA except that it uses 200-KHz-wide channels with eight users per channel and has a vocoder rate of 13 Kbps. It is the first digital cellular system to be used commercially, and has been adopted in Europe and many Pacific Rim countries. It is a second-generation technology.

GSM is the first, and the de facto, standard in Europe; more than 80 GSM networks are now operational, making it the most widely deployed digital network in the world to date, used by millions of people in more than 200 countries.

Although GSM started out operating in the 900 MHz frequency, additional networks are being deployed in the 1800 MHz frequency range. An alternate name for GSM is PCN (Personal Communication Network), the European equivalent of PCS, Personal Communication Services.

Cellular Digital Packet Data

Cellular Digital Packet Data (CDPD) is a TCP/IP-based mobile data-only service that runs on AMPS networks. It is deployed as an enhancement to the existing analog cellular network. CDPD runs on analog networks; therefore, it requires a modem to convert the TCP/IP-based data into analog signals when sending and receiving. CDPD networks offer analog voice, circuit-switched data, and packet data services at a raw throughput of 19,200 bits per second (bps). However, effective data throughput is about 9,600 bps because of protocol overhead.

CDPD, though a uniquely North American protocol, is not widely deployed in the United States. And though CDPD is designed for relatively quick setup and teardown, it's not as efficient as digital-only networks for bursty data communications, consequently CDPD will likely be replaced by various all-digital networks in the future.

Nordic Mobile Telephone

Nordic Mobile Telephone (NMT) is the original 1981 Nordic Countries standard for analog cellular service. It is a first-generation wireless technology.

Total Access Communication System

Total Access Communication System (TACS) is an analog FM communication system used in some parts of Europe and Asia (e.g. United Kingdom and Malaysia). It is another first-generation wireless technology.

Personal Digital Cellular

Personal Digital Cellular (PDC) is a TDMA-based Japanese standard OS, operating in the 800- and 1500-MHz bands. It is a Japanese standard for digital cellular service, and is considered a second-generation technology.

Short Message Service

The Short Message Service (SMS) is not specifically a wireless transmission mode, but nevertheless should be listed here, as it provides instantaneous two-way message-handling service over two-way pagers or data-enabled cellular phones. SMS lets users send and receive relatively small data messages, even when making a telephone call.

SMS became popular with second-generation digital systems, especially GSM. It uses a packet-based architecture that sends data over the control channel. SMS messages are limited to 160 characters in GSM, 256 bytes in TDMA, and 255 characters in CDMA. SMS-based services are very popular in Europe, where the use of simple applications such as weather, email, and instant messaging has skyrocketed in the past few years.

Nextel uses TDMA technology in the Specialized Mobile Radio (SMR) spectrum block, which is adjacent to the 800 MHz AMPS spectrum in the United States to implement a hybrid analog/digital network called iDEN (Integrated Dispatch Enhanced Network). iDEN provides voice service, plus circuit-switch data connections, and 140-character short message services.

The Generation Gap

As you've no doubt noticed in the preceding discussion, wireless technologies and cellular transmission modes are often referred to within the context of technology generations. This is a handy way to distinguish levels of advances. First generation (1G) technology refers to the earliest wireless networks (and a lot of them are still in service), followed by 2G, 2.5G, 3G, and so on.

First-generation wireless technologies, such as AMPS in North America, TACS in Europe, and NMT in Japan, were based on analog transmissions. And even though, today, digital networks are becoming widely deployed, analog networks still service more than 40 percent of cellular phones in the United States.

Second-generation technologies, such as TDMA and CDMA in the United States, PDC in Japan, and GSM in Europe, are digital in nature and provide improved system performance and security. Most new deployments are digital, with a few notable exceptions, such as those in South America and the United States. Third-generation (3G) technologies include UMTS and CDMA2000 technologies.

It is estimated that any given wireless technology has an average of a 15-year maturity life cycle. Data rates available for the first generation of wireless technologies were 9.6 Kbps or lower. Second-generation technology data rates vary from 9.6 to 14.4 Kbps. Third-generation wireless technologies promise data rates ranging from 14.4 Kbps to 2 Mbps, which would enable acceptable performance from wireless Internet applications and services.

Apart from the three main generational groupings of technologies, there is a mid-generational group, referred as 2.5G wireless technologies, so called because they enhance the existing 2G technologies and make a transition to the 3G technologies.

Fourth-generation technologies are expected to focus on Wireless Asynchronous Transfer Mode (WATM) with the potential to provide data rates of 10 Mbps to 150 Mbps, low bit error rate, and high quality of service—in short, truly high-speed wireless data networking.

Each of these generations is described more fully in the following subsections.

2.5G Technologies

The technologies known as 2.5G promise much improved bandwidths and the capability to push more complex content to mobile devices, meaning increased revenues for their networks. These technologies include High-Speed Circuit-Switched Data (HSCSD), General Packet Radio Service (GPRS), and Enhanced Data Rates for Global Evolution (EDGE). HSCSD, GPRS, and EDGE. These technologies give carriers the option of deploying enhancements to their networks before they invest in expensive new 3G infrastructure. (More aggressive network operators, however, such as NTT DoCoMo of Japan, are going directly into deployment of 3G technologies, bypassing the 2.5 generation.)

Here are brief descriptions of these 2.5G technologies.

High-Speed Circuit-Switched Data (HSCSD). HSCSD is a circuit-switched protocol based on GSM. Available rates for HSCSD are up to 38.4 Kbps, and it can use four control channels simultaneously and provide up to four times the speed available in GSM (14.4 Kbps). Though some of the European carriers have already started to offer HSCSD services, the technology still lacks widespread support. It's considered an interim technology to GPRS (see next), which offers instant connectivity at higher speeds.

General Packet Radio Service (GPRS). GPRS-based systems are already being deployed in some wireless networks; available data rates are up to 144 Kbps. GPRS is a IP-based packet-switched wireless protocol that allows for burst transmission speeds up to 1.15 Mbps. The GPRS device is always connected to the network, meaning that it and terminal get instant IP connectivity. The network capacity is used only when data is actually transmitted. Due to high available speeds, GPRS, along with EDGE (see next), provides a smooth transition for operators who are not keen on investing in 3G infrastructure up front.

Enhanced Data Rates for Global Evolution (EDGE).   EDGE is a higher-bandwidth version of GPRS, with transmission speeds up to 384 Kbps and theoretical data rates hovering around 384 Kbps. Such high speeds will allow for wireless multimedia applications.

3G Technologies

The most recent generation of cellular radio systems for mobile telephony are referred to as third-generation (3G) technologies, and generally refer to those that promise to provide very high (for wireless) transmission speeds and performance. The technical framework for 3G has been defined by the International Telecommunication Union (ITU) as part of its International Mobile Telecommunications 2000 (IMT-2000) program, which is described in detail next.

The third generation will be the first cellular radio technology designed from the outset to support wideband data communications at the same level of its voice communications. The Bluetooth specification (described later in the chapter) will support 3G systems in the delivery of a wide range of services by extending their reach to localized devices, such a handheld computers and PDAs, wherever they are and wherever they are going.

IMT-2000

The International Mobile Telephone Standard 2000 (IMT-2000) project facilitates cooperation between 3G developers. IMT-2000 is the term used by the International Telecommunications Union (ITU) for a set of standards for third generation (3G) mobile telecom services and equipment

One of the most important attributes of IMT-2000 is to enable the capability for global roaming with a single low-cost terminal, which many hope will be the basis for a wireless information society where access to information and services such as electronic commerce are available at all times to everyone.

The key goals of IMT-2000 are to:

- Increase efficiency and capacity.

- Enable new services, such as WANs for PCs and multimedia.

- Offer bandwidth on demand; that is, the capability to dynamically allocate the required spectrum, depending on the application-sensitive data rate requirement.

- Increase flexibility-multiple standards, frequency bands, environments, and backward compatibility.

- Enable seamless roaming across dissimilar networks.

- Integrate satellite services and fixed wireless access services with the cellular network.

- Enable higher data-rate services (384 Kbps mobile; 2 Mbps fixed in the early phase, increasing to 20 Mbps in the later stages).

Move information about the IMT-2000 project can be found at www .imt-2000.org.

Universal Mobile Telecommunications System

Universal Mobile Telecommunications System (UMTS) is a project of the Special Mobile Group (SMG), a committee of the European Telecommunication Standards Institute (ETSI). UMTS is the first European implementation of the 1MT-2000 standard.

UMTS is the next generation of global cellular, which should be in place by 2004. UMTS has a proposed data rate of 2 Mbps using a combination of TDMA and WCDMA operations at 2 GHz.

CDMA2000 and WCDMA

Two 3G modes of CDMA are Wideband CDMA (WCDMA) and CDMA2000. WCDMA is a third-generation technology that increases data transmission rates in GSM systems by using CDMA instead of TDMA. WCDMA is being backed by Ericsson, Nokia, and Japanese handset manufacturers. A slighter different version, CDMA2000, is supported by QUALCOMM and Lucent.

The NTIA, the FCC, the DOD, and other executive branch agencies have developed a new plan for spectrum assessment for advanced 3G wireless services. Part of this plan will include auctioning some of the spectrum. After the federal government has completed the assessment, the executive branch, through NTIA, will coordinate with the FCC to reach solutions for allocating spectrum for advanced commercial wireless services, including 3G, formulate service rules, and conduct auctions as necessary. Although the current auction deadline for the 1710-1755 and 2110-2150 MHz bands is September 30, 2002, the administration has proposed legislation to postpone this deadline until September 30, 2004.

911 POSITION LOCATORS

In 1997, the FCC mandated that mobile carriers must have the capability to identify the latitude and longitude of mobile units making 911 calls within a radius of 100 meters 67 percent of the time, and 300 meters 95 percent of the time for network-based technologies. For handset-based technologies, the accuracy requirement is within 50 meters 67 percent of the time and 100 meters 95 percent of the time.

Wireless Data Networking Technologies

This section attempts to give some order to the various standards and components of wireless networking—pure data, no voice. Demand for wireless access to LANs is fueled by the growth of mobile computing devices, such as laptops and personal digital assistants, and by users' desire for continual network connections to the Internet without having to physically plug into wired systems. It is estimated that there will be more than a billion mobile devices in use by 2003.

Spread Spectrum Technology

The de facto communication standard for wireless LANs is *spread spectrum*, a wideband radio frequency technique originally developed by the military for use in secure, mission-critical communications systems. Spread spectrum uses a radio transmission mode, which broadcasts signals over a range of frequencies. The receiving mobile device must know the correct frequency of the spread-spectrum signal being broadcast.

Most wireless LANs use spread spectrum technology, as it helps mobile devices circumvent the absence of interference immunity often associated with narrowband systems. Spread spectrum uses a transmission mode that consumes more bandwidth than narrowband transmission, but produces a signal that is stronger and easier to detect by other devices. Thus, spread spectrum trades off some bandwidth efficiency for gains in security, integrity of transmission, and reliability of transmission.

Two very different, but equally popular, spread spectrum RF technologies for 2.4 GHz wireless LANs currently exist: direct-sequence spread spectrum (DSSS) and frequency-hopping spread spectrum (FHSS).

Direct Sequence Spread Spectrum (DSSS)

Direct-sequence spread-spectrum (DSSS) is a wideband spread spectrum transmission technology that generates a redundant bit pattern for each bit to be transmitted. This bit pattern is called a *chip*, or the *chipping code*. The longer the chip, the greater the probability that the original data can be recovered. But using this chipping code requires more bandwidth for a transmission than narrowband transmission methods.

The ratio of chips per bit is called the *spreading ratio*. A high spreading ratio increases the resistance of the signal to interference, whereas a low spreading ratio increases the net bandwidth available to a mobile device. Embedded statistical algorithms can recover the original data if bits are damaged in the transmission without requiring retransmission.

DSSS spreads the signal over a wide frequency band in which each bit of data is mapped by the source transmitter into a pattern of chips. At the receiving mobile device, the original data is recreated by mapping the chips back into a data bit. The DSSS transmitter and receiver must be synchronized to operate properly. A DSSS signal appears as low-power wideband noise to a non-DSSS receiver, and therefore is ignored by most narrowband receivers.

Because DSSS spreads across the spectrum, the number of independent, nonoverlapping channels in the 2.4 GHz band is small (typically only three); therefore, only a very limited number of co-located networks can operate without interference. Some DSSS products allow users to deploy more than one channel in the same area, by separating the 2.4 GHz band into multiple subbands, each of which contains an independent DSSS network.

Frequency-Hopping Spread Spectrum (FHSS)

Frequency-hopping spread spectrum (FHSS) uses a narrowband carrier that continually changes frequency in a known pattern. The FHSS algorithm spreads the signal by operating on one frequency for a short duration and then *hopping* to another frequency.

The source mobile device's transmission and the destination mobile device's transmission must be synchronized so that they are on the same frequency at the same time. When the transmitter and receiver are properly synchronized, it maintains a single logical communications channel. Similar to DSSS, FHSS appears to be noise of a short-duration to a non-FHSS receiver, hence is ignored.

Proponents of FHSS say that it has greater immunity to outside interference than DSSS because of this frequency-hopping technique, as noise on any given frequency will typically disappear after hopping to another frequency. Also, it has been suggested that a FHSS transmission cannot be blocked by a single narrowband interferer, as opposed to the preselected frequency of a DSSS transmission. If interference or corruption occurs on one frequency, the data is simply retransmitted on a subsequent hop. This is intended as a solution to narrowband interference from 2.4 GHz sources, such as microwave ovens.

The minimum number of frequencies engaged in the hopping pattern and the maximum frequency dwell time (how long it stays on each frequency before it changes) are restricted by the FCC, which requires that 75 or more frequencies be used with a maximum dwell time of 400 ms.

FHSS make it possible to deploy many nonoverlapping channels. Because there are a large number of possible sequences in the 2.4 GHz band, FHSS products allow users to deploy more than one channel in the same area, by implementing separate channels with different hopping sequences.

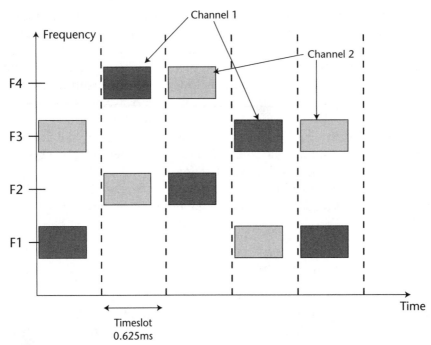

Figure 2.1   Frequency hopping.

(Courtesy of "*GPRS and 3G Wireless Applications*", by Christoffer Anderson, John Wiley & Sons, Inc., 2001)

Another FHSS feature is that multiple access points in the same FHSS geographic network area can be added if more bandwidth is needed or if there is an increase in the number of users who need to access the wireless network. Mobile devices roaming into the area will be randomly assigned to one of the two access points, effectively doubling the available bandwidth in that area. This currently is not possible with DSSS.

Finally, it appears that the power amplifiers for FHSS transmitters are more efficient than DSSS transmitters, resulting in significantly lower power consumption in the FHSS products. By requiring lighter batteries and fewer recharges, the mobile device user can stay mobile longer. Figure 2.1 shows frequency hopping in action.

Orthogonal Frequency Division Multiplexing

Another wireless transmission mode, different from spread spectrum, is called Orthogonal Frequency Division Multiplexing (OFDM), with a variation called Coded Orthogonal Frequency Division Multiplexing (COFDM).

OFDM is a form of multicarrier modulation, using a frequency-division multiplexing (FDM) modulation technique for transmitting large amounts of digital data over a single radio wave. OFDM splits the radio signal into multiple smaller subsignals that are then transmitted simultaneously at different frequencies to the receiving mobile device. In this way, OFDM reduces the amount of cross-talk in signal transmissions.

OFDM is very useful when transmitting broadband and high-data-rate information. One of the benefits of OFDM is the robustness of the transmission system and its resistance to interference. OFDM has been standardized for discrete multitone (DMT), which is the world standard for Asymmetric Digital Subscriber Lines (ADSL).OFDM is also incorporated into the Digital Audio Broadcasting (DAB) scheme, which is used primarily in Europe as defined by the European Telecommunication Standard ETS 300 401. IEEE 802.11a WLAN technology (see the next section) uses OFDM.

IEEE 802.11 Specifications for Wireless LANS

IEEE 802.11 refers to a family of specifications for wireless local area networks (WLANs) developed by a working group of the Institute of Electrical and Electronics Engineers (IEEE). (Note: 802.11 also generically refers to the IEEE Committee responsible for setting the various wireless LAN standards.) This standards effort began in 1989, with the focus on deployment in large enterprise networking environments, effectively a wireless equivalent to Ethernet. The IEEE accepted the specification in 1997.

The 802.11 specification identifies an over-the-air interface between a mobile device wireless client and a base station or between two mobile device wireless clients. To date, there are four completed specifications in the family: 802.11, 802.11a, 802.11b, and 802.11g, with a fifth, 802.11e, in development as a draft standard. All four existing standards use the Ethernet protocol and carrier sense multiple access with collision avoidance (CSMA/CA) for path sharing.

There are several specifications in the 802.11 family:

802.11. The original IEEE wireless LAN standard that provides 1 or 2 Mbps transmission speed in the 2.4 GHz band, using either FHSS or DSSS. The modulation used in 802.11 is commonly phase-shift keying (PSK).

802.11a. An extension to the original IEEE 802.11 wireless LAN standard that provides up to 54 Mbps in the 5 GHz band. 802.11a uses an orthogonal frequency division multiplexing encoding scheme rather than FHSS or DSSS.

NOTE Though listed here in alphabetical order, in fact 802.11b was an earlier extension than 802.11a; see the following subsections for more on this.

802.11b. An extension to the 802.11 wireless LAN standard; it provides 11 Mbps transmission speed, but that automatically slows down to 5.5 Mbps, 2 Mbps, or 1 Mbps speeds in the 2.4 GHz band, based upon the strength of the signal. 802.11b uses only DSSS. 802.11b, a 1999 ratification to the original 802.11 standard, allows wireless functionality comparable to Ethernet; it is also referred to as 802.11 High Rate or Wi-Fi.[1]

802.11g.   A new IEEE wireless standard that applies to wireless LANs, 802.11g provides 20 Mbps to 54 Mbps in the 2.4 GHz band. As of this writing, this standard has not yet been approved, so is not available in the marketplace, unlike 802.11b or 802.11a.

802.11e.   The latest IEEE draft extension to provide quality-of-service (QoS) features and multimedia support for home and business wireless environments.

Each of these specs is defined more fully in the following subsections.

Original IEEE 802.11 LAN Standard

The IEEE 802.11 wireless LAN standard provides for 1 Mbps or 2 Mbps wireless communications in the 2.4 GHz industrial, scientific, medical (ISM) band using either FHSS or DSSS. The modulation used in 802.11 is commonly phase-shift keying (PSK).

In a typical WLAN installation, wireless stations (STAs) are associated with a fixed access point (AP), which provides a bridging function to the wired network. The combination of the AP and its associated STA is referred to as a *Basic Service Set* (BSS). BSS is described later in the chapter.

The 802.11 standard is aimed at medium-range, higher-data-rate applications. This technology can be used in shop-floor areas in factory environments or in other enterprises in which the wireless interaction is confined to a limited range and can tolerate 1 Mbps to 2 Mbps wireless connectivity.

IEEE 802.11b

In 1999, the Institute of Electrical and Electronics Engineers ratified an extension to the IEEE 802.11 standard and called it IEEE 802.11b. The IEEE 802.11b standard addresses transmission for WLANs in the 2.4 GHz range. It offers 1 Mbps, 2 Mbps, and 5.5 Mbps, and a peak data rate of 11 Mbps transmission speeds. Most implementations of 802.11b allow for slow-down of the transmission speeds when the client is farther away from the access point, thereby allowing the communications to continue uninterrupted, albeit at a slower speed.

IEEE 802.11b is the most commonly implemented wireless networking communications standard, with the largest number of vendor implementations available to the business, home, or small office home office (SOHO) consumer. IEEE 802.11b, like HomeRF and Bluetooth, uses the 2.4 GHz band, and uses a linear modulation known as complementary code keying (CCK) with a coding variation of DSSS.

---

[1] The term "Wi-Fi" is used by the Wireless Ethernet Compatibility Alliance (www.weca.net) to specify products that conform to the 802.11b standard.

The 802.11b standard, also called Wi-Fi, is backward-compatible with 802.11. The modulation used in 802.11 has historically been phase-shift keying (PSK), but the modulation method selected for 802.11b, as just noted previously is CCK, which allows higher data speeds and is less susceptible to multipath-propagation interference.

The 11 Mbps data rate makes wireless LAN technology viable in enterprises and other large organizations, making it the current de facto standard for wireless business LANs. The home market has also seen an explosion in the use of 802.11b LANs, with many traditional wired LANs component vendors hopping on the 802.11b bandwagon.

Interoperability of wireless LAN products from different vendors is overseen by an independent organization called the Wireless Ethernet Compatibility Alliance (WECA; www.wi-fi.com), which brands compliant products as "Wi-Fi."

IEEE 802.11a

As noted, 802.11a came after 802.11b. The IEEE 802.11a standard was passed in an attempt to remedy some of the major problems that arose in early 802.11 and 802.11b implementations. It operates at radio frequencies between 5 GHz and 6 GHz range. It uses a modulation scheme known as orthogonal frequency-division multiplexing (OFDM) that makes data speeds as high as 54 Mbps possible (though most current implementations transmit at 6 Mbps, 12 Mbps, or 24 Mbps).

Figure 2.2 shows the next generation of SOHO wireless networking device, the SMC 802.11a Wireless Access Point. SMC's 802.11a-compliant wireless access point offers transmission speeds of up to 54 Mbps in standard mode and 72 Mbps in so-called turbo mode. Operating in the 5 GHz frequency range, it offers compatibility with Bluetooth, microwave, and cordless phones, and is backward-compatible with current 802.11b installations. It also supports up to 64 simultaneous wireless clients and includes enhanced security features such as 64-bit, 128-bit, and 152-bit WEP encryption and MAC address filtering.

One advantage of 802.11a is that it largely quiets many of the current interference concerns about 802.11b and mitigates somewhat the network density limitations of 802.11b by operating in the 5 GHz range and using OFDM, rather than the spread spectrum technology.

Although several vendors are currently developing products to expand their 802.11b product line with 802.11a-compliant products, the technology is still new and inevitable problems have emerged; for one, some initial implementations of the standard do not function up to the range and performance specs promised. The primary obstacle to business adoption of 802.11a products is the significantly reduced range at its peak data rate. As of this writing, many businesses feel that the 802.11a systems aren't as reliable as the older 802.11b systems, hence they are continuing to implement and expand the older systems. Another issue is that 802.11a is not backward-compatible to existing 802.11b-based networks.

Figure 2.2   SMC2755W 802.11a Wireless Access Point.
(Courtesy of SMCNetworks Inc.)

These issues will most likely be resolved in the near future, however, and 802.11a products will soon be as ubiquitous as those using the 802.11b standard.

IEEE 802.11g

The newly proposed standard, IEEE 802.11g, offers wireless transmission over relatively short distances at speeds from 20 Mbps up to 54 Mbps, compared with the 11 Mbps of the 802.11b standard. Like 802.11b, 802.11g operates in the 2.4 GHz range and is thus backward-compatible with existing 802.11b-based networks, a major advantage for the standard over 802.11a.

However, the IEEE working group has been divided for some time over which coding technology is preferable for the new standard. At last report the IEEE's new standard was slated to borrow from Intersil's OFDM modulation technology, touted as one of the key components of 802.11g, as well as Texas Instruments' rival technology, PBCC.

IEEE 902.11g is expected to see vendor implementations by late 2002, using OFDM, and CCK modulation, which is complementary code keying from 802.11b.

IEEE 802.11e

The latest IEEE draft specification for wireless networks, 802.11e, will focus on interoperability between business, home, and public environments, such as airports and hotels. Unlike other wireless initiatives, this is the first wireless standard that intentionally spans home and business environments.

It also adds QoS features and multimedia support to the existing 802.11b and 802.11a wireless standards, while maintaining full backward compatibility with these standards. QoS and multimedia support are an essential ingredient to offering residential customers video-on-demand, audio-on-demand, voice over IP (VoIP), and high-speed Internet access.

802.11 Wireless Network Operational Modes

The IEEE 802.11 wireless networks operate in one of two operational modes: *ad hoc* or *infrastructure* mode. The IEEE standard defines the ad hoc mode as Independent Basic Service Set (IBSS), and the infrastructure mode as Basic Service Set (BSS). Ad hoc mode is a peer-to-peer type of networking, whereas infrastructure mode uses access points to communicate between the mobile devices and the wired network.

Ad Hoc Mode

In ad hoc mode, each mobile device client communicates directly with the other mobile device clients within the network. That is, no access points are used to connect the ad hoc network directly with any wired local area network. As shown in Figure 2.3, ad hoc mode is designed such that only the clients within transmission range (within the same cell) of each other can communicate. If a client in an ad hoc network wants to communicate outside of the cell, a member of the cell must operate as a gateway and a perform routing service.

802.16

Another wireless 802 standard, called IEEE 802 Broadband Wireless Access (802.WBA, or 802.16), is under development. IEEE 802.16 standardizes the air interface and related functions associated with the wireless local loop (WLL) for wireless broadband subscriber access. Three working groups have been chartered to produce standards:

    IEEE 802.16.1: Air interface for 10 to 66 GHz
    IEEE 802.16.2: Coexistence of broadband wireless access systems
    IEEE 802.16.3: Air interface for licensed frequencies, 2 to 11 GHz

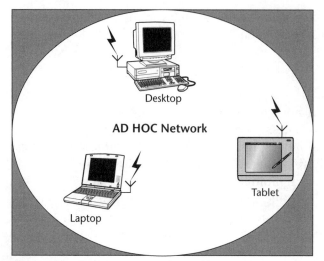

Figure 2.3   An 802.11 network in ad hoc mode.

Infrastructure Mode

As shown in Figure 2.4, each mobile device client in infrastructure mode sends all of its communications to a network device called an access point (AP). The access point acts as an Ethernet bridge and forwards the communications to the appropriate network, either the wired local area network or another wireless network.

Association Frames

Before they can communicate data, mobile wireless clients and access points must establish a relationship, or an *association*. Only after an association has been established can the two wireless stations exchange data. In infrastructure mode, the clients associate with an access point.

Forming an association is an eight-step process that moves through these three states:

- Unauthenticated and unassociated
- Authenticated and unassociated
- Authenticated and associated

To transition between the states, the communicating parties exchange messages, called *management frames*. Here's how this is done:

1. All access points transmit a beacon management frame at a fixed interval.
2. To associate with an access point and join a BSS, a mobile device client listens for beacon messages to identify the access points within range.

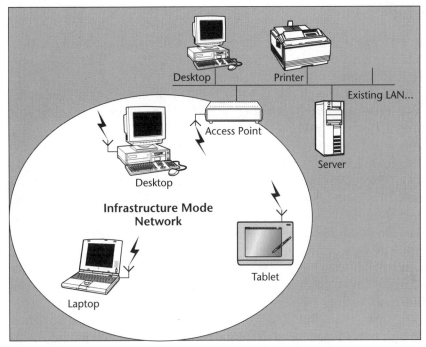

Figure 2.4 An 802.11 network in infrastructure mode.

3. The mobile device client selects the BSS to join in a vendor-independent manner.

4. The client may also send a probe request management frame to find an access point affiliated with a desired service set identifier (SSID). An SSID is an identification value programmed into a wireless access point.

5. After identifying an access point, the client and the access point perform a mutual authentication by exchanging several management frames as part of the process.

6. After successful authentication, the client moves into the second state, authenticated and unassociated.

7. Moving from the second state to the third and final state, authenticated and associated, involves the client sending an association request frame, and the access point responding with an association response frame.

8. The mobile device client becomes a peer on the wireless network, and can transmit data frames on the network.

Chapter 5 discusses 802.11 authentication in greater detail.

Bluetooth

Bluetooth is a simple peer-to-peer protocol created to connect multiple consumer mobile information devices (cellular phones, laptops, handheld computers, digital cameras, and printers) transparently. It uses the IEEE 802.15 specification in the 2.4 to 2.5 GHz band with FHSS technology. Bluetooth-enabled mobile devices avoid interference from other signals by hopping to a new frequency after transmitting or receiving a packet.

Bluetooth is a low-power-consuming technology with transmission distances of up to 30 feet and a throughput of about 1 Mbps. The range will be extended to 300 feet by increasing the transmit power to 100 mW (milliwatts). Though each Bluetooth network can accommodate only eight devices, thanks to frequency hopping, many Bluetooth networks can operate in the same vicinity. The Bluetooth MAC layer is TDMA-based. Bluetooth can carry either voice or low-rate data connections.

Bluetooth's FHSS technology uses a much higher hop rate than HomeRF (described in the next section) and other radios, transmitting at 1,600 hops per second. Bluetooth defines 10 different ranges of hopping sequences, five in the 79 MHz range and five in the 23 MHz range. Therefore, Bluetooth is designed to operate in a noisy frequency environment, using a fast acknowledgment and the quick frequency-hopping scheme.

Figure 2.5 shows the internal structure of the Bluetooth protocol stack.

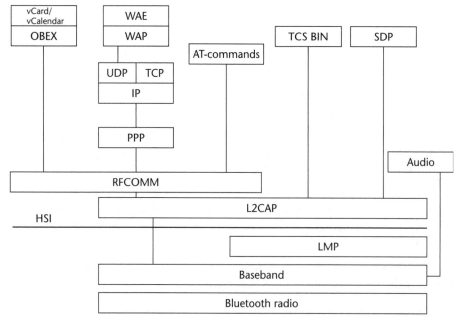

Figure 2.5 The Bluetooth protocol stack.

(Figure source: Bluetooth specification 1.0)

Bluetooth Advantages and Disadvantages

The advantage of faster hopping is a lower likelihood of interference, because less time is spent on a channel. The disadvantage is twofold: faster hop rates result in a very inefficient use of bandwidth, due to the time wasted hopping; and the length of the data packet the system is able to transmit is necessarily shorter.

But whether the hop rate matters depends on individual needs; for example:

- For a mobile device sending delay-sensitive traffic with a concern for latency, faster hopping is preferred because its moves the device off a given channel sooner.

- For mobile devices that must send relatively long Ethernet packets, slower hop rates are better, because of reduced probability that a given target packet will collide with the interference source.

The 2.4 GHz band is becoming very crowded, and the coexistence of various spread spectrum technologies sometimes causes unexpected results. This has led to research into 2.4 GHz band interference and contention between 802.11, HomeRF, Bluetooth devices, digital phones, and microwave ovens. Bluetooth is often considered a noisy neighbor, because it creates a bubble of radio waves within what's called the piconet area. A piconet is a collection of devices connected in an ad hoc fashion using Bluetooth technology, which communicate with each other using this bubble of radiation.[2] To that end, the Bluetooth Special Interest Group (SIG), led by a nine-member Bluetooth SIG Promoter group, has been formed. The Promoter group, which includes 3Com, Ericsson, Intel, IBM Corporation, Lucent Technologies, Microsoft, Motorola Inc., Nokia, and Toshiba Corporation, is working to create, enhance, and promote the Bluetooth technology, and provide a vehicle for interoperability testing. As of this writing, more than 1,000 companies worldwide support and/or are working on standardizing the technology.

HomeRF

Another wireless networking standard, called HomeRF, was designed specifically for broadband Internet home use, hence is not commonly found in the business networking environment, which is the realm of IEEE 802.11. HomeRF networks are designed to support home entertainment and integrated home automation applications, and is priced to appeal to the general home market.

HomeRF products operate in the 2.4 GHz ISM band using FHSS at 50 to 100 hops per second; that is, it changes the channel 50 to 100 times per second (more often than I do). First-generation HomeRF (1.0) products have peak data rates of 1.6 Mbps, typically with a 150-foot indoor range. Second-generation HomeRF

---

[2] A very good white paper on Bluetooth interference can be found at www.intersil.com called "Effects of Microwave Interference on IEEE 802.11 WLAN Reliability."

A TYPICAL BLUETOOTH SESSION

Here's the sequence a Bluetooth session follows:

A Bluetooth-based mobile device listens to determine whether there are any other Bluetooth radios in its vicinity. If it doesn't find any, it configures itself as the master device, then it configures its radio transmission to a randomly selected frequency.

When another Bluetooth-enabled mobile device (say, a printer) is turned on, it searches for any other Bluetooth radio frequency transmissions in its vicinity.

When the printer finds the master device's broadcast, it matches its transmitter to the same frequency pattern as the master device, and identifies itself to the master device.

After the two devices exchange privilege and capability information, the printer becomes the slave of the master device's piconet.

If a user walks into the room carrying a Bluetooth-equipped PDA and hears the master broadcast, the PDA automatically tunes its transmitter to the frequency pattern and identifies itself to the master device and becomes another slave to the master's piconet.

The three devices exchange information on each other's access privileges and capabilities, thereby allowing the PDA to access both the desktop and the printer.

(2.0) products operate at up to 10 Mbps peak data rates. Both versions provide low-power consumption (less than 10 mW standby with full TCP/IP connectivity) and are small in size (world's only Compact Flash WLAN).

Another feature of HomeRF is that it supports near wire-line voice quality by incorporating the Digital Enhanced Cordless Telephony (DECT) standard.

Third-generation HomeRF devices are planned to be in the 20 Mbps data rate range, with shipments expected to begin in late 2002.

HomeRF Technology Overview

A typical HomeRF network for what is called the "Broadband Internet Home" consists of multiple device types, as shown in Figure 2.6.

The HomeRF specification, like most networking interface standards, describes fundamentally the lowest two layers of the seven-layer OSI network stack model, as shown in Figure 2.7. The lowest layer, the physical (PHY) layer, sets most of the cost, data rate, and range characteristics. The second layer, the data link control (DLC)—or, as used here, the media access control (MAC) layer—defines the types of data services, such as voice or prioritized streaming, as well as other attributes like security, roaming, and mapping to standard upper layers.

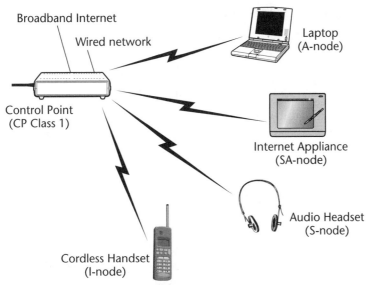

Broadband Internet

Wired network

Control Point
(CP Class 1)

Laptop
(A-node)

Internet Appliance
(SA-node)

Audio Headset
(S-node)

Cordless Handset
(I-node)

Figure 2.6   HomeRF network device types.

(Courtesy the HomeRF Working Group)

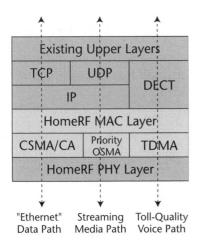

Figure 2.7   HomeRF network stack model.

(Courtesy the HomeRF Working Group)

The HomeRF MAC layer provides three distinct service flow categories:

- An asynchronous, connectionless wireless Ethernet packet data service for TCP/IP traffic.
- A prioritized and repetitive connection-oriented data service typically used for streaming media sessions using UDP/IP flows.
- An isochronous, full-duplex, symmetric, two-way voice service typically used to map multiple toll-quality voice connections, as defined by the DECT protocol.

HomeRF and Shared Wireless Application Protocol

The Home Radio Frequency Working Group has produced a specification called Shared Wireless Application Protocol (SWAP) that allows a variety of devices, such as PCs, wireless phones, and other consumer devices to share voice and data in and around the home environment.

SWAP features include:

- Available data rates that currently range from 1 Mbps to 2 Mbps.
- Up to 150 feet broadcast range.
- Capability to network up to 10 PCs.
- Capability to work with DSL, modems, and cable modems.
- Capability to secure data using a unique network ID.
- Support for near-line-quality voice and telephony service with minimized radio interference.

Examples of what HomeRF believes users will be able to do with products that adhere to the SWAP specification include:

- Set up a wireless home network to share voice and data between PCs, peripherals, and PC-enhanced cordless phones.
- Access the Internet from anywhere in and around the home from portable display devices.
- Share an ISP connection between PCs and other new devices.
- Share files, modems, and printers in multi-PC homes.
- Forward incoming telephone calls to multiple cordless handsets, fax machines, and voice mailboxes.
- Review incoming voice, fax, and email messages from a small, PC-enhanced cordless telephone handset.
- Activate other home electronic systems simply by speaking a command into a PC-enhanced cordless handset; or engage in multiplayer games based on PC or Internet resources.

High-Performance Radio LANs

High-Performance Radio Local Area Networks (HiperLAN) is a set of wireless local area network communication standards primarily used in European countries. There are two specifications: HiperLAN/1 and HiperLAN/2. Both have been adopted by the European Telecommunications Standards Institute (ETSI).

The HiperLAN standards provide features and capabilities similar to those of the IEEE 802.11 wireless local area network standards, used in the United States and other adoptive countries. HiperLAN/1 provides communications at up to 20 Mbps in the 5 GHz range of the RF spectrum.

The newer HiperLAN/2 standard operates at up to 54 Mbps in the same 5 GHz range. HiperLAN/2 is compatible with 3G WLAN systems for sending and receiving data, images, and voice communications. It has the potential, and is intended, for worldwide implementation in conjunction with similar systems in the 5-GHz RF band. HiperLAN/2 uses coded orthogonal frequency division multiplexing (COFDM).

HiperLAN/1

ETSI work on private and business radio networks, known under the generic name of HiperLAN, was initiated at the end of 1991, and resulted in the Hiper-LAN Type 1 Functional Specification EN 300 652. HiperLAN Type 1 is a radio LAN standard designed to provide high-speed communications of up to 20 Mbps between portable devices in the 5 GHz range. It is intended to enable the creation of flexible wireless data networks, without the need for an existing wired infrastructure. In addition, it can be used as an extension to a wired LAN. The support of multimedia applications is also possible.

HiperLAN/2

The newer, faster HiperLAN/2 standard is being developed by ETSI in hopes that it will become a worldwide standard. A HiperLAN/2 network typically has a topology as depicted in Figure 2.8. As shown, the mobile terminals (MT) communicate with the access points (AP) over an air interface, as defined by the HiperLAN/2 standard. (Note: There is also a direct mode of communication between two MTs, which is still in its early phase of development and is not further described in this version of the document.) The user of the MT may move around freely in the HiperLAN/2 network, which will ensure that the user and the MT get the best possible transmission performance. An MT, after association has been performed (can be viewed as a login), only communicates with one AP in each point in time.

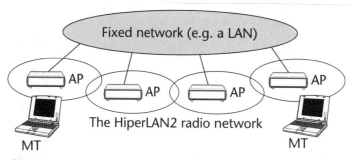

Figure 2.8   A HiperLAN/2 network.
(Courtesy of the HiperLAN/2 Global Forum)

This short-range variant is intended for complementary access mechanism for UMTS systems as well as for private use as a wireless LAN. It will offer high-speed access up to 54 Mbps to a variety of networks including the UMTS core networks, ATM networks and IP-based networks. Spectrum has been allocated for HiperLAN/2 in the 5 GHz range.

HiperLAN/2 Protocol Architecture

The HiperLAN/2 protocol stack is divided into a control plane part and a user plane part, similar to the semantics of ISDN functional partitioning. The user plane includes functions for transmission of traffic over established connections, and the control plane includes functions for the control of connection establishment, release, and supervision. The HiperLAN/2 protocol has three basic layers as depicted in Figure 2.9: Physical layer (PHY), Data Link Control layer (DLC), and the Convergence layer (CL). At the moment, there is only control plane functionality defined within DLC.

Following the work done on the HiperLAN/1 standard, ETSI is currently developing standards for Broadband Radio Access Networks (BRAN), which include the HIPERACCESS and HIPERLINK systems.

HIPERACCESS

This long-range variant is intended for point-to-multipoint, high-speed 25 Mbps access by residential and SOHO customers to a wide variety of networks, including UMTS core networks, ATM networks, and IP-based networks. In this scheme, HiperLAN/2 might be used for distribution within premises. Spectrum allocation in the 40.5 GHz to 43.5 GHz band are being discussed in the relevant Committee on European Postal Regulations/European Radiocommunications Committee (CEPT/ERC) working groups. The first group of HIPERACCESS specifications are being readied for publication.

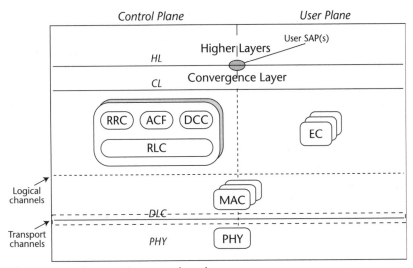

Figure 2.9   HiperLAN/2 protocol stack.

(Figure courtesy of the HiperLAN/2 Global Forum)

HIPERLINK

This variant will provide short-range very high-speed interconnection of HiperLAN networks and HIPERACCESS up to 155 Mbps over distances up to 150 meters. The available spectrum for HIPERLINK is in the 17 GHz range. The work on HIPERLINK standardization has not started as of this writing.

Wireless Application Protocol

While the Hypertext Markup Language (HTML) and related technologies such as JavaScript, Java, and Flash work well for desktop computers and laptops with large displays, they're less effective for devices with small screens and limited resolution. Enabling color graphics, animation, and sound poses a challenge to developers under the best of conditions. Additionally, these types of devices lack the processing power and memory to handle multimedia.

To meet that challenge, in 1997, Ericsson, Motorola, Nokia, and Unwired Planet announced the creation of a new technology for delivering Internet content to all types of mobile and wireless devices, and, along with it, the formation of the WAP Forum. WAP was developed as a set of technologies related to HTML, but tailored to the small screens and limited resources of handheld, wireless devices. The most notable of these technologies is the Handheld

Device Markup Language (HDML). On paper, HDML looks similar to HTML, but, again, has a feature set and programming paradigm tailored to wireless devices with small screens. HDML and other elements of this architecture eventually became the Wireless Markup Language (WML) and the architecture of WAP.

Since its initial release, WAP has evolved twice. Releases 1.1 and 1.2 of the specification have the same functionality as 1.0, but with added features to align with what the rest of the industry is doing. Version 1.3 is used most often in WAP products as of this writing.

In August 2001, the WAP Forum approved and released the specifications for WAP 2.0 for public review, and Ericsson, Nokia, and Motorola all announced support for WAP 2.0. The WAP 2.0 specification contains new functionality that allows users to send sound and moving pictures over their telephones, among other things. WAP 2.0 will also provide a toolkit for easy development and deployment of new services, including XHTML.

WAP 2.0 includes Multimedia Messaging Services (MMS), a service that allows users to combine sounds with images and text when sending messages, much like the text-only SMS. It also contains an improved WAP Push, used for services such as online auctions, where users can receive information on-demand rather than having to search.

Products incorporating WAP 2.0 are expected to arrive on the market by the end of 2002. More information on WAP 2.0 can be found at the WAP Forum, at www.wapforum.org.

WAP Layers

As others already covered, the WAP architecture is drawn from the OSI model. To review, OSI is intended to connect open systems and, therefore, observes the following principles:

- A layer should be created where a different level of abstraction is needed.
- Each layer should perform a well-defined function.
- The function of each layer should be chosen with an eye toward defining internationally standardized protocols.
- The layer boundaries should be chosen to minimize the information flow across the interfaces.
- The number of layers should be large enough so that distinct functions do not have to be thrown together in the same layer out of necessity, and small enough so that the architecture does not become unwieldy.

Unlike the seven layers of OSI or the four layers of the TCP/IP model, WAP has five layers: application, session, transaction, security, and transport. Let's look at each one.

Application Layer

The WAP application layer contains the Wireless Application Environment (WAE). It encompasses devices, content-development languages (WML and WMLScript), wireless telephony APIs (WTA) for accessing telephony functionality from within WAE programs, and some well-defined content formats for phone book records, calendar information, and graphics.

The WAE has four key components:

Microbrowser.   Defines how WML and WMLScript are interpreted by a WAP-enabled device for presentation to the end user.

Wireless Markup Language (WML).   Similar to HTML, WML defines how data should be formatted and presented to the user. It is based on the eXtended Markup Language (XML) and provides support for text and images and Wireless Bitmap Format (WBMP), user input, user navigation, multiple languages, and state and context management features.

WMLScript.   Similar to JavaScript, WMLScript provides some programming logic for performing calculations within an application. The scripting language extends WML's functionality.

Wireless Telephony Applications (WTA).   Provides functionality so that developers can integrate microbrowser functions with the telephone. It provides the framework for accessing telephony commands using WML and WMLScript.

Session Layer

The WAP session layer contains the Wireless Session Protocol (WSP). WSP is similar to HTTP, as it is designed for low-bandwidth, high-latency wireless networks. It facilitates the transfer of content between WAP clients and WAP gateways in a binary format. Additional functionalities include content push and suspension/resumption of connections.

The WSP layer provides a consistent interface to WAE for two types of session services: a connection mode and a connectionless service. This layer provides:

- Connection creation and release between the client and server.

- Data exchange between the client and server using a coding scheme that is much more compact than traditional HTML text.

- Session suspend and release between the client and server.

Transaction Layer

The WAP transaction layer provides the Wireless Transactional Protocol (WTP). WTP provides the functionality similar to TCP/IP in the Internet model. WTP is a lightweight transactional protocol that allows for reliable request and response transactions and supports unguaranteed and guaranteed push.

WTP provides transaction services to WAP. It handles acknowledgments so that users can determine whether a transaction has succeeded. It also provides retransmission of transactions in case they are not successfully received, and removes duplicate transactions.

WTP manages different classes of transactions for WAP devices: unreliable one-way requests, reliable one-way requests, and reliable two-way requests. An unreliable request from a WAP device means that no precautions are taken to guarantee that the request for information makes it to the server.

Security Layer

The Wireless Transport Layer Security (WTLS) layer is based on Transport Layer Security (TLS, formerly known as Secure Sockets Layer, or SSL), and can be invoked similar to HTTPS in the Internet world. It provides data integrity, privacy, authentication, and denial-of-service protection mechanisms. Data integrity guarantees that the data that is sent is the same data that is received. WAP privacy services guarantee that all transactions between the WAP device and gateway are encrypted. Authentication guarantees the authenticity of the client and application server. Finally, denial-of-service protection detects and rejects data that comes in the form of unverified requests.

Transport Layer

The bottom WAP layer, the transport layer supports the Wireless Datagram Protocol (WDP). WDP provides an interface to the bearers of transportation. It supports the CDPD, GSM, Integrated Digital Enhanced Network (iDEN), CDMA, TDMA, SMS, and FLEX protocols.

The Wireless Datagram Protocol provides a consistent interface to the higher layers of the WAP architecture, meaning it does not matter which type of wireless network the application is running on. Among other capabilities, WDP provides data error correction.

The bearers, or wireless communications networks, are at WAP's lowest level. WAP is designed to run on a variety of networks, including short message services (SMS), circuit-switched connections, and packet-switched networks. Each type of network has pros and cons in terms of performance, delay, and errors.

In this chapter you have explored wireless theory and protocols. This will be a good help in understanding the next chapter "Wireless Reality." In it you will see how these theories apply to current wireless devices and systems.

Wireless Reality

This chapter builds on the information covered in Chapters 1 and 2, presenting a more detailed description of the various wireless devices and topologies currently available. We'll investigate in greater detail the standards introduced in Chapter 2, look at some specific wireless network topologies, and examine a sampling of wireless mobile devices and operating systems.

For a company's workforce, wireless technologies provide exciting new features, one of which is to enable mobile employees to quickly move to new locations to set up and resume previously interrupted networked communications. Wireless technologies also enable a mobile workforce to form workgroups at a client's site. The rapid deployment of networked communications at an off-site location helps to give an organization more network connectivity options.

Wireless Standards and Technologies

The most common and promising of the new wireless standards and technologies are IEEE 802.11, HomeRF, Bluetooth, and IrDA (described later). These standards compete with each other in some arenas, while complementing each other in others. Moreover, many of these standards and technologies overlap, meaning we may see more than one of these competing technologies survive. Let's look at these technologies a little closer.

802.11

As described in Chapter 2, the most common WLAN standard is the wireless Ethernet-like connectivity identified with the IEEE 802.11 standard suite, which supports extensions of existing wire-based local area networks, (LANs). Today's wireless LANs operate at high speeds, speeds that were considered state-of-the-art for wired networks in the mid-90s. Recall that the functional range for 802.11 devices may reach up to 100 meters, at data rates up to 11 Mbps in the 2.4-GHz range for 802.11b, and 54 Mbps in the 5-GHz range for 802.11a.

Wired local area networks were the technology story of the 1980s; the Internet was the story of the 1990s; and so far in this decade, wireless LANs (WLANs) have begun to emerge as a flexible alternative to the world of wired LANs. Until recently the speed of the WLAN was limited to 2 Mbps, but newer standards have increased that speed to 11 Mpbs, and 54 Mbps is on the horizon.

Wireless LANs are built using two basic topologies, which are called by a variety of names, including managed and unmanaged, hosted and peer-to-peer, and infrastructure and ad hoc. The two WLAN topologies, ad hoc and infrastructure mode were described in Chapter 2. A WLAN is similar to a wired LAN in that the intent of WLANs is to enable user access to corporate network resources, such as shared data and applications or peripherals. Wireless LANs frequently augment, rather than replace, wired LAN networks; providing the final few meters of connectivity between a backbone network and the mobile user. But the emphasis of a WLAN is on a semipermanent wireless connection that doesn't inhibit a user's mobility, and defines a distinct region of coverage using wireless access points. High-speed wireless LANs can provide the benefits of network connectivity without being restricted to a location or tethered by wires.

Benefits of WLAN

The primary benefits of the WLAN technology are threefold:

- *Installation flexibility*. Networks can extend to areas that wires can't reach, with significantly lower cabling costs.
- *Scalability*. WLAN configurations can be easily changed, increased, and updated.
- *Installation speed*. A WLAN can be installed quickly enough to support mobile workgroups and assist in disaster recovery implementation.

802.11b Encryption

This subsection only touches on the WEP and 802.11 security process, for the purpose of this discussion; we'll delve into it more in Chapter 5. The WEP protocol uses a 40-bit shared secret key, a Rivest Code 4 (RC4) pseudorandom number generator (PRNG) encryption algorithm, and a 24-bit initialization vector (IV). The basic process works as follows:

1. A checksum of the message is computed and appended to the message.

2. A shared secret key and the initialization vector (IV) are fed to the RC4 algorithm to produce a key stream.

3. An exclusive OR (XOR) operation of the key stream with the message and checksum grouping produces ciphertext.

4. The initialization vector is appended to the cipher text to form the encrypted message, which is sent to the intended recipient.

5. The recipient, who has a copy of the same shared key, uses it to generate an identical key stream.

6. XOR'ing the key stream with the ciphertext yields the original plaintext message.

NOTE The 802.11 standard has security issues, which are addressed in Chapter 6 and in Appendix B. IEEE is attempting to address these issues with a new addendum to the 802.11 standard, 802.1x, which is discussed below.

Other Notable IEEE 802 Wireless Standards and Drafts

Chapter 2 described a number of the IEEE 802.11 variations; here we'll look at some of the latest developments in standards and drafts being pursued by the IEEE.

802.1x Port-Based Network Access Control

The 802.1x standard was drafted in 2001 by the IEEE to provide enhanced security for users of 802.11b wireless LANs. It provides port-level authentication for any wired or wireless Ethernet client system.

Originally designed as a standard for wired Ethernet, 802.1x is applicable to WLANs. It leverages many of the security features used with dial-up networking; it uses encryption keys that are unique for each user and each network session, and supports 128-bit key lengths. It has a key management protocol built into its specification, which provides keys automatically. Keys can also be changed rapidly at set intervals. It will also support the use of Remote Authentication Dial-in User Service (RADIUS) and Kerberos.[1]

The 802.1x standard can be used with Windows XP to provide link-layer authentication, making employee authentication by active directories and

---

[1] A good source for 802.1x information is at http://www.drizzle.com/~aboba/IEEE/.

databases easier (see the sidebar titled "802.1x and Airport Wireless"). The standard defines a client/server-based access control and authentication protocol that restricts unauthorized devices from connecting to a LAN through publicly accessible ports. The authentication server verifies each client connected to a switch port before making available any services offered by the switch or the LAN. Until the client has been authenticated, 802.1x access control allows only Extensible Authentication Protocol over LAN (EAPOL) traffic through the port to which the client is connected. Once the client has been authenticated, normal traffic can pass through the port.

Most of the major wireless vendors have announced plans to support the new standard; products due late 2002. Cisco Systems, Inc. has already introduced the Lightweight Extensible Authentication Protocol (LEAP) for its Aironet devices. Using LEAP, client devices dynamically generate a new WEP key, instead of using a static key as part of the log-in process.

802.15 Wireless Personal Area Networks

The project scope of 802.15 (official name: IEEE P802.15.1/D0.9.2, Draft Standard for Part 15.1: Wireless Media Access Control (MAC) and Physical Layer (PHY) specifications for Wireless Personal Area Networks (WPAN) is to define PHY and MAC specifications for wireless connectivity with fixed, portable, and mobile devices within or entering a personal operating space (POS).

The project's purpose is to provide a standard for low-complexity, low-power consumption wireless connectivity to support interoperability among devices within or entering the POS. This includes devices that are carried, worn, or located near the user's body. The proposed project will address quality of service to support a variety of traffic classes.

802.1X AND AIRPORT WIRELESS

Wayport Inc., a provider of wireless and wired Internet connections at a variety of airports and hotels, recently completed a pilot implementation of the Microsoft Windows XP operating system, used in conjunction with IEEE 802.1x. Wayport and Microsoft began testing the combination at the Seattle-Tacoma airport in 2001, where Wayport had WLAN service already installed.[2] As of this writing, Wayport has wireless at 4 major airports (all terminals and gates at Dallas/Fort Worth, Seattle-Tacoma, San Jose and Austin-Bergstrom) and now 13 Laptop Lane locations at 7 airports. Wayport hopes to implement the 802.1x/WinXP zero configuration service at many more major U.S. airports and hotels.[3]

---

[2] http://www.80211-planet.com/columns/article/0,,1781_875651,00.html
[3] http://www.internetnews.com/wireless/article/0,,10692_973961,00.html

802.16 Broadband Wireless Access

The 802.16 standard includes the following:

- Approved Draft 802.16-2001, IEEE Local and Metropolitan Area Networks, Part 16: Standard Air Interface for Fixed Broadband Wireless Access Systems

- Broadband Wireless LANs (802.16) IEEE Standard 802.16.2-2001 IEEE Recommended Practice for Local and Metropolitan Area Networks: Coexistence of Fixed Broadband Wireless Access Systems 802.16.2-2001 IEEE Recommended Practice for Local and Metropolitan Area Networks: Coexistence of Fixed Broadband Wireless Access System 2001

This IEEE recommended practice provides guidelines for minimizing interference in fixed broadband wireless access (BWA) systems operating in the frequency range 10 to 66 GHz, with particular focus on the range 23.5 to 43.5 GHz. It analyzes coexistence scenarios and provides guidance for system design, deployment, coordination, and frequency usage.

802.11g

IEEE 802.11g is a draft standard that, when complete, will extend the family of IEEE 802.11 wireless standards, with data rates of up to 54 Mbps in the 2.4 GHz band. The first draft standard of IEEE 802.11g is based on complementary code keying (CCK), orthogonal frequency division multiplexing (OFDM) and packet binary convolutional coding (PBCC) technologies. The 802.11g working group is expected to publish the standard sometime in the second half of 2002.

Nonwireless IEEE Standards

Many IEEE working groups have cross-pollinated, for the obvious reason: They can't work in isolation from the LAN bridging working group. Therefore, each group tries to work in conjunction with the other IEEE working groups to define draft standards that are properly interoperable. The following subsections list some nonwireless standards and draft that apply to WLANs. For more on the most recent IEEE wireless standards, visit: www.ieee802.org/11/.

802.1v VLAN Classification by Protocol and Port

Classifying multiple protocols into a single VLAN often imposes VLAN boundaries that are inappropriate for some of the protocols, thus requiring the presence of a nonstandard entity to relay between VLANs the frames bearing the protocols for which the VLAN boundaries are inappropriate.

The nonstandard relay makes the boundaries of the VLANs transparent to the relayed protocols, depriving those protocols of the benefits of VLANs. The proposed supplement (IEEE 802.1v-2001, IEEE Standards Amendment to IEEE 802.1Q: IEEE Standards for Local and Metropolitan Area Networks: Virtual Bridged Local Area Networks—Amendment 2: VLAN Classification by Protocol and Port) will benefit users of multiprotocol LANs by permitting them to specify VLAN structures suitable for each protocol present in a LAN, and removing the need for a nonstandard relay function between VLANs.

802.17 Resilient Packet Ring Access Protocol

In metropolitan and wide area networks, fiber optic rings are widely deployed. These rings are currently using protocols that are neither optimized nor scalable to the demands of packet networks, including speed of deployment, bandwidth allocation and throughput, resiliency to faults, and reduced equipment and operational costs.

The IEEE 802.17 Resilient Packet Ring Working Group (RPRWG) is defining a Resilient Packet Ring Access Protocol for use in local, metropolitan, and wide area networks for transfer of data packets at rates scalable to many gigabits per second. The new standard will use existing physical layer specifications and will develop new "PHYs" where appropriate.

Other Standards Working Groups

Other working groups currently developing standards, primarily for use in local, metropolitan, and wide area networks, include:

- IEEE 802.1t-2001 (Amendment to IEEE Std 802.1D, 1998 Edition) IEEE Standard for Information technology—Telecommunications and Information Exchange between Systems—Local and Metropolitan Area Networks—Common Specifications, Part 3: Media Access Control (MAC) Bridges: Technical and Editorial Corrections.

- IEEE 802.1u-2001 (Amendment to IEEE Std 802.1Q, 1998 Edition) IEEE Standard for Local and Metropolitan Area Networks—Virtual Bridged Local Area Networks—Amendment 1: Technical and Editorial Corrections.

- IEEE 802.1w-2001, IEEE Standard for Information Technology—Telecommunications and Information Exchange between Systems—Local and Metropolitan Area Networks—Common Specifications, Part 3: Media Access Control (MAC) Bridges—Amendment 2: Rapid Reconfiguration [Amendment to IEEE Std 802.1D, 1998 Edition (ISO/IEC 15802-3:1998) and IEEE Standard 802.1t-2001].

- IEEE P802.3ae/D4.0 Draft IEEE Supplement to ISO/IEC 8802-3 (IEEE 802.3)—Media Access Control (MAC) Parameters, Physical Layer, and Management Parameters for 10Gb/s Operation.

- IEEE P802.3af/D3.0 Draft IEEE Supplement to IEEE 802-3-2000 (ISO/IEC 8802-3)— Data Terminal Equipment (DTE) Power via Media Dependent Interface (MDI).

- IEEE 1802.3-2001, IEEE Conformance Test Methodology for IEEE Standards for Local and Metropolitan Area Networks—Specific Requirements, Part 3: Carrier Sense Multiple Access with Collision Detection (CSMA/CD) Access Method and Physical Layer Specifications.

- IEEE Std 802.5w-2000 (Corrigendum to ISO/IEC 8802-5:1998 including ISO/IEC 8802-5:1998/Amd.1: 1998) Information technology—Telecommunications and Information Exchange between Systems—Local and Metropolitan Area Networks, Part 5: Token Ring Access Method and Physical Layer Specifications, Corrigendum 1.

- IEEE Std 802.5v-2001, IEEE Standard for Information Technology—Telecommunications and Information Exchange between Systems—Local and Metropolitan Area Networks—Specific Requirements, Part 5: Token Ring Access Method and Physical Layer Specifications, Amendment 5: Gigabit Token Ring Operation Print.

HomeRF

Though HomeRF was covered in some depth in Chapter 2, we'll revisit it briefly here; and we'll discuss security issues involving HomeRF in Chapter 6.

HomeRF is a subset of the International Telecommunications Union (ITU), dedicated primarily to the development of a standard for inexpensive RF voice and data communication. The HomeRF Working Group recently ratified the HomeRF 2.0 specification, which operates at data rates up to 10 Mbps, and is intended to meet the wireless networking requirements of home users. It reportedly supports toll-quality voice, and attempts to integrate voice, data, and streaming media capabilities across a wide range of devices, including phones, PDAs, PCs, and audio and video devices.

A summary of its technical capabilities breaks out like this:

- 10 Mbps peak data rate, with fallback modes of 5 Mbps, 1.6 Mbps and 0.8 Mbps.

- Backward compatibility, with installed base of HomeRF devices operating at 1.6 Mbps and 0.8 Mbps.

- Simultaneous host/client and peer/peer technology.

- Up to eight simultaneous prioritized streaming media sessions for audio and video.

- Up to eight simultaneous toll-quality two-way cordless voice connections.

- Implemented security measures against eavesdropping and denial of service (DoS).

Other important HomeRF features are that it:

- Operates in the 2.45 GHz range of the unlicensed ISM band.

- Has up to 150-foot radiation range.

- Employs frequency hopping at 50 hops per second.

- Supports both a TDMA service to provide delivery of interactive voice and CSMA/CA service for delivery of high-speed data packets.

- Has a network capable of supporting up to 127 nodes.

- Offers 100-mW transmission power.

- Offers 1-Mbps data rate, using 2 FSK modulation and 2 Mbps data rate using 4 FSK modulation.

- Supports up to six full duplex voice conversations.

- Uses the Blowfish encryption algorithm for security and the LZRW3-A algorithm for data compression.

Recall from Chapter 2 that the HomeRF Working Group developed the Shared Wireless Access Protocol (SWAP). SWAP is similar to the CSMA/CA protocol of IEEE 802.11, but with an extension to voice traffic. The SWAP system can operate either as an ad hoc network or as an infrastructure network under the control of a connection point.

In an ad hoc network, all stations are peers; control is distributed between the stations; and it supports only data. In an infrastructure network, a connection point is required to coordinate the system; it provides the gateway to the public switched telephone network (PSTN). Walls and floors don't cause any problem for its functionality, and some security is also provided through the use of unique network IDs. It is robust, reliable, and minimizes the impact of radio interference.

Proxim Inc. is currently the major vendor of HomeRF products in the United States. The company also distributes 802.11b and HomeRF solutions for the Macintosh.

Comparing 802.11b to HomeRF

HomeRF and 802.11 are not interoperable with each other or with other wireless LAN solutions. HomeRF was designed primarily for the home environment, whereas 802.11b was designed for and is being deployed in homes, small and medium-sized businesses, as well as large enterprises and in a growing number of public wireless networking hot spots. Several major laptop vendors are shipping or plan to ship their product with internal 802.11b NICs. And though 802.11 currently has a substantial lead in the market over HomeRF, HomeRF's price structure is very appealing to the home user.

HomeRF Security

The HomeRF standard defines 128-bit key encryption, uses a 32-bit initialization vector (IV), and sets the time for repeated IVs to half a year. HomeRF specifies an IV management procedure that is designed to minimize the possibility of IV value repetition. The HomeRF working group believes that a brute-force attack on HomeRF encryption is inconceivable for organizations without the resources of a government security agency, and therefore contends that HomeRF offers a number of significant security advantages over WLAN, which we will examine in Chapter 6.

Bluetooth

Like HomeRF, Bluetooth was introduced in Chapter 2, but we'll delve a little deeper into it here. Bluetooth, named for Denmark's first Christian king, Harald Bluetooth, is a technology specification for small form-factor, low-cost, short-range radio links between electronic devices. Bluetooth was designed to enable simple, low-bandwidth wireless connections, using a high-speed, low-power microwave wireless link technology.

Table 3.1   Bluetooth SIG Promoter Group

FOUNDING COMPANIES	NEW MEMBERS
Ericsson	3Com Corporation
IBM Corporation	Lucent Technologies
Intel Corporation	Microsoft Corporation
Nokia	Motorola Inc.
Toshiba Corporation	Agere

Bluetooth was designed to connect phones, laptops, PDAs, and other portable equipment with little effort required of the user. The technology, notable for its small size and low cost, uses modifications of existing wireless LAN technologies. Whenever any Bluetooth-enabled devices come within range of each other, they instantly transfer address information and establish small networks between each other, without user involvement.

Because Bluetooth technology has no line-of-sight requirements (unlike infrared), it can operate through walls or from within a briefcase. Portable PCs can connect wirelessly to printers, transfer data to desktop PCs or PDAs, or interface with cellular phones for wireless WAN access to corporate networks or the Internet.

The Bluetooth standard defines layers 1 and 2 of the OSI model. The application framework of Bluetooth is aimed to achieve interoperability with IrDA and WAP. In addition, a host of other applications will be able to use the Bluetooth technology and protocols.

Bluetooth is an open specification that is governed by the Bluetooth Special Interest Group (SIG), which is led by its five founding companies and four member companies added in late 1999 (these companies are listed in Table 3.1).

System Architecture Features

Bluetooth technology provides the user with a 10-meter diameter radio sphere that supports simultaneous transmission of both voice and data for multiple devices. Up to eight data devices can be connected in a piconet (described next), and up to 10 piconets can exist within the 10-meter bubble. Each piconet supports up to three simultaneous full-duplex voice devices.

Other important Bluetooth features are that it:

- Operates in the globally available 2.56 GHz ISM band, which has no FCC license requirement.
- Uses frequency hop spread spectrum (FHSS).
- Can support up to eight devices in a piconet.
- Is capable of omnidirectional, nonline-of-sight transmission through walls.
- Has a 10- to 100-meter range.
- Cost only around $20.
- Consumes less power—1mW.
- Has an extended range with external power amplifier (100 meters).

The Piconet

The simplest way Bluetooth devices interact with one or more other Bluetooth devices is via an ad hoc network called a piconet. Recall from Chapter 2 that this scheme is used when at least two devices are involved, one acting as the master and the other as a slave for the duration of the connection. Thus, a piconet can begin with as few as two point-to-point connected devices but can grow to eight connected devices.

Although all Bluetooth devices are peer units and have identical implementations, each piconet is identified by a different frequency hopping sequence to keep them separate from other Bluetooth piconets. All users participating on the same piconet are synchronized to this hopping sequence.

By definition, a piconet is any Bluetooth network with one master and one or more slaves. When multiple slaves are involved, the communication topology is referred to as *point-to-multipoint*. In this case, the channel (and bandwidth) is shared among all the devices in the piconet. There can be up to seven active slaves in a piconet. Each of the active slaves has an assigned 3-bit active member address (AM_ADDR).

That said, there can be additional *inactive* slaves that remain synchronized to the master but that do not have an active member address. The inactive slaves are referred to as *parked*, and are assigned 8-bit parked member addresses (PM_ADDR), thus limiting the number of parked members to 256. For both active and parked units, all channel access is regulated by the master. And because parked devices remain synchronized to the master clock, they can very quickly become active and begin communicating in the piconet. Figure 3.1 shows an example of a Bluetooth piconet.

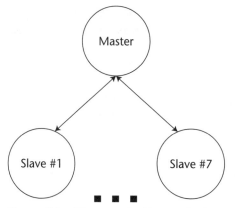

Figure 3.1 Diagram of a Bluetooth piconet.
(Courtesy of the Bluetooth SIG)

The Scatternet

Slaves in one piconet can participate in another piconet as either a master or slave through time division multiplexing. When two piconets have overlapping coverage areas, it is referred to as a *scatternet*. A scatternet is a collection of piconets joined by a Bluetooth device that is a master in one piconet and a slave in another piconet.

To prevent slaves from participating in a piconet that is unintentionally close to another piconet, the two piconets are neither time nor frequency-synchronized. Each of the piconets operates in its own frequency-hopping channel, whereas any devices in multiple piconets participate at the appropriate time via time division multiplexing.

Bluetooth Hardware Elements

Bluetooth hardware can be divided into two primary parts: the *Radio Module* and the *Link Module*. These parts are quite inexpensive: a complete Bluetooth hardware module, including both radio and link subsystems, is expected to approach $25 within the next couple of years.

The Radio Module

As mentioned in Chapter 2, Bluetooth devices operate in the 2.4 GHz Industrial Scientific Medicine (ISM) band. This is an unlicensed band and, in most countries, includes the frequency range from 2400 to 2483.5 MHz, with the exception of France (2446.5 to 2483.5 MHz) and Spain (2445 to 2475 MHz). Bluetooth products for these two markets are currently not interoperable.

The Radio Module , shown in Figure 3.2, uses RF channels from 2402 to 2480 MHz with a channel spacing of 1 MHz. Because it uses FHSS, the channel hops 1600 times every second to another frequency within the 2402 to 2480 MHz range. Each piconet has a unique hopping sequence that is determined by an algorithm using the Bluetooth device address of the master device. All devices in the piconet are then synchronized to this hopping sequence.

For modulation, Bluetooth Radio Modules use Gaussian Frequency Shift Keying (GFSK). A binary system is used, in which a 1 is signified by a positive frequency deviation and a 0 is signified by a negative frequency deviation. The data is transmitted at a symbol rate of 1 Mbps.

NOTE For detailed information on the Bluetooth Radio Module, refer to Part A of the of the Bluetooth System Specification, published by the Bluetooth SIG, available from www.bluetooth.com.

Figure 3.2   Bluetooth Radio Module.
(Courtesy of the Bluetooth SIG)

The Link Module

Bluetooth's Link Module, and the closely associated Link Manager software, are responsible for the baseband protocols and some other low-level link functions. This includes sending and receiving data, setting up connections, error detection and correction, data whitening (defined later), power management, and authentication.

The Link Module, shown in Figure 3.3, is responsible for deriving the hop sequence. This is accomplished using the Bluetooth device address of the master device. All Bluetooth devices are assigned a 48-bit IEEE 802 address. This 48-bit master device address is used by each of the devices in the piconet to derive the hop sequence.

The Link Module is also responsible for performing the three defined Bluetooth error-correction schemes:

- One-third rate forward error correction scheme (FEC)
- Two-thirds rate FEC
- Automatic retransmission request (ARQ) scheme for the data

Figure 3.3   Bluetooth Link Module.
(Courtesy of the Bluetooth SIG)

The purpose of the two FEC schemes is to reduce the number of retransmissions; the ARQ scheme causes the data to be retransmitted until either an acknowledgment is received indicating a successful transmission, or a predetermined time-out period has elapsed. A cyclic redundancy check (CRC) code is added to each packet and is used by the receiver to determine whether the packet has arrived error-free.

In order to reduce highly redundant data and minimize DC bias, a data-whitening scheme is used to randomize the data. The data is scrambled by a data element, called a data-whitening word, and subsequently unscrambled using the same word at the receiver. This descrambling is done after the error-detection/correction process.

Battery Conservation

Bluetooth radio devices are classified according to three different power classes, as shown in Table 3.2.

Most Bluetooth radio devices are in power class 1 or 2, due to cost issues and battery life requirements. A more costly and power-hungry class 1 device provides up to 100 meters of range, which should be sufficient for home networking and other applications that require a greater range.

Bluetooth also provides provisions for three low-power modes to conserve battery life. These states, in decreasing order of power requirements are *sniff*, *hold*, and *park*, defined as follows:

Sniff mode. The device listens to the piconet at a reduced rate. The sniff interval is programmable, providing flexibility for different applications.

Hold mode. Similar to park mode, except that the active member address is retained.

Park mode. The device's clock continues to run and remains synchronized to the master, but the device does not participate at all in the piconet, and does not have an active member address.

Table 3.2 Bluetooth Radio Power Classes

POWER CLASS	MAXIMUM OUTPUT	POWER
1	100 mW	20 dBm
2	2.5 mW	4 dBm
3	1 mW	0 dBm

Bluetooth Versions

Version 1.0A of the Bluetooth specification was completed and released July 28, 1999. Following the publication of errata to the original specs, version 1.0B was published in December 1999; and in November 2000, the Bluetooth SIG released version 1.1 of the specification.

Essentially, there are no profile and usage model variations from versions 1.0, 1.0A, 1.0B, and 1.1. The 1.1 specification contains approximately 200 errata corrections to the RF protocol, baseband host controller interface (HCI) command set, and tolerances; these represent technical differences, which the end user will not recognize.

Various hardware products and solutions are hitting the market, and Bluetooth is becoming integrated into a number of notebook computers, peripherals, and other mobile devices. The technology is intended to deliver wireless solutions that are ubiquitous across a broad range of devices.

One Bluetooth-enabled product to come on the market recently is the HP Deskjet 9995c color inkjet printer. This inkjet printer can print from Bluetooth-enabled devices, Infrared Data Association (IrDA)-enabled devices, or from a USB connection. The printer comes with all connection software required, including 3Com Bluetooth connectivity software, PrintConnect Suite for laptop IrDA connectivity, and IrPrint for Palm OS IrDA connectivity. Figure 3.4 shows the HP 995c printer.

Figure 3.4 HP Deskjet 995c Color Inkjet Printer.
(Courtesy, Porter Novelli Convergence Group for HP)

Bluetooth 2.0

In contrast to the 1.0 specification, which focused primarily on cable replacement scenarios, the Bluetooth 2.0 specification is an attempt to deliver more advanced usage models. The Bluetooth SIG has created several working groups to investigate a variety of usage models that will return new profiles for the 2.0 specification. These working groups include:

Radio 2.0 Group. Investigates increased data rates and improved coexistence with other 2.4-GHz systems.

Personal Area Networking (PAN) Group. Concentrates on general IP networking (including security) in an ad hoc connection environment.

Human Interface Device (HID) Group. Develops profiles for the use of computer peripherals such as keyboards, mice, and joysticks transmitting over Bluetooth.

Audio/Video Group. Investigates high-end multimedia capabilities over Bluetooth.

Printer Profile Group. Investigates direct-to-printer scenarios using peer-to-peer Bluetooth connections.

Local Positioning Group. Implements Bluetooth as a system to determine local (as opposed to global) geographic proximity.

Still Image Group. Investigates Bluetooth-enabled device wireless photo imaging systems.

The slowing economy, however, has delayed rapid adoption of the new Bluetooth, as the expected numbers of Bluetooth-enabled devices is lower than previously estimated. Original estimates of 13-36 million units shipped for 2002 will actually be closer to 4 million.[4] Also, the delay until summer 2002 of inclusion of Bluetooth support by Microsoft in its new XP operating systems also slowed unit deliveries.

Common Bluetooth Applications

Many types of new and advanced applications are being developed for the Bluetooth spec. Those following are in production, in development, or still fairly conceptual.

Cable replacement. Bluetooth radio technology built in to both the cellular telephone and the laptop replaces the cable used today to connect a laptop to a cellular telephone.

Wireless Internet. Enables Internet surfing via a laptop connection to a mobile phone or a wire-bound connection (PSTN, ISDN, LAN, xDSL).

Automatic synchronizer. Enables automatic background synchronization between a desktop, portable PC, notebook, and mobile phone.

[4] http://www.business2.com/articles/web/0,,36430,FF.html.

Interactive file transfer. Connects all participants for instant data exchange in meetings and conferences.

Instant postcard. Via a connection from a digital camera to a portable PC, enables wireless transmission of photos and video clips.

Cordless computer. Enables connection from a portable PC to peripherals or to a LAN.

Transparent email. Sends an alert to a mobile device when a portable PC receives email, and allows browsing of the email on the mobile device. Also makes it possible to compose emails offline on a portable PC, for later transmission when the mobile phone is turned on.

Bluetooth Security

With up to 128-bit public/private key authentication, and streaming cipher up to 64 bits, based on A5 security,[5] Bluetooth wireless technology is designed to be as secure as a wired LAN. Though encryption can be very robust, which is good for establishing a secure link, there may be export problems when shipping from the United States. Different hardware with smaller encryption key lengths may be required to meet U.S. export controls.

Bluetooth's main built-in security features are:

Challenge-response routine. For authentication: prevents spoofing and unwanted access to critical data and functions.

Stream cipher. For encryption: prevents eavesdropping and maintains link privacy.

Session key generation. Enables session key change at any time during a connection.

Three components are used in the security algorithms:

- The Bluetooth device address (BD_ADDR/48 bits), a public entity unique for each device. The address can be obtained through the inquiry procedure.

- A private user key (128 bits), a secret entity. The private key is derived during initialization and is never disclosed.

- A random number (128 bits), different for each new transaction. The random number is derived from a pseudo-random process in the Bluetooth unit.

---

[5] A5 is a symmetric cryptosystem used in GSM mobile phones. A5 comes in two flavors, A5/1 and A5/2. A5/1 is the stronger version of the encryption algorithm used by about 130 million GSM customers in Europe to protect the over-the-air privacy of their cellular voice and data communication. Since encryption algorithm security could not be exported, A5 had to be weakened to A5/2.

In addition to these link-level functions, frequency hopping and the limited transmission range also help to prevent eavesdropping. Bluetooth security features and issues are described in greater detail in Chapter 6.

Wireless Personal Area Network

The term *wireless personal area network* (WPAN) describes a wireless technology that is, one, intended to enable instant connectivity between devices that manage personal data or, two, facilitate data sharing between small groups of individuals, within a very small physical area.

NOTE A PAN is literally a personal area network working with electric body-field sensing capability. Electrostatically coupled PAN devices use the human body as a "wet wire," and can operate on several milliwatts of power. Personal area networks use a near-field electric field to send data across various devices using the body as a medium. However, the term PAN now commonly refers to the Bluetooth network technology that uses far-field radio technology to enable communication between devices in the ISM band, and that is the sense in which it is used here.

One example of a WPAN implementation would be instantaneous document sharing or data synchronization between mobile devices. WPAN data-sharing scenarios are often ad hoc and spontaneous, thus reducing complexity. The short-range RF transmitters of Bluetooth are being used to support a wide variety of PANs, such as in cars or on a human body for example, wireless headphones.

NOTE The IEEE standard for PANs (IEEE 802.15 with subparts 1-3) is still in draft, hence is subject to change.

Infrared Data Association (IrDA)

The initials IrDA stand for the Infrared Data Association. IrDA is a non-profit trade association with a membership of over 160 companies representing computer and telecommunications hardware, software, components, and adapters. The term IrDA is also commonly used to refer to infrared communications that comply with IrDA standards. The Infrared Data Association (IrDA) international organization creates and promotes interoperable, low-cost infrared data interconnection standards. IrDA has a set of protocols covering all layers of data transfer, including some limited network management and interoperability.[6]

[6] More information on infrared can be found at www.irda.org.

IrDA provides wireless connectivity technologies for devices that would normally use cables. It is a point-to-point, narrow angle (30° radiation cone), ad hoc data transmission standard that uses infrared and is designed to operate over a distance of 0 to 1 meter at speeds of 9600 bps to 16 Mbps. Infrared devices can be seen in cordless keyboards, television remote controls, printers, watches, and serial PC adapters.

IrDA protocols have IrDA DATA as the vehicle for data delivery and IrDA CONTROL for sending control information. Adapters now include traditional upgrades to serial and parallel ports.

IrDA features include the following:

- Transmission range up to 1 meter, plus extensions of up to 2 meters. A low-power version relaxes the range objective for operation from contact to at least 20 centimeters between low-power devices and 30 centimeters between low-power and standard-power devices. This implementation affords 10 times lower power consumption.

- Bidirectional communication.

- Primary data transmission speed of 9600 bps, with the capability to step up to 115 Kbps and even 4 Mbps in some implementations.

- Protected data packets, using a CRC-16 for speeds up to 1.152 Mbps and CRC-32 for speeds up to 4 Mbps.

Object Exchange Protocol (OBEX)

The Object Exchange Protocol (OBEX) is a session level protocol often described as a binary HTTP protocol. OBEX is optimized for ad-hoc wireless links and can be used to exchange all kind of objects like files, pictures, calendar entries (vCal), and business cards (vCard).

OBEX was specified by the Infrared Data Association, and although the protocol is very good for Infrared connections, it is not limited to it. In fact OBEX does not specify the top or bottom applications programming interface (API) making it very flexible and able to run over most transports like TCP/IP and Bluetooth. Therefore OBEX is also called IrDA Object Exchange Protocol (IrOBEX) to differentiate the infrared version from other transport versions.

Today, OBEX is implemented in several types of devices, including PDAs and mobile phones. Vendor implementations of OBEX can be found in some Palm Wireless Handhelds, the Ericsson R320, Siemens S25, Nokia NM207, and Nokia 9110 Communicator. The HP CapShare 920 can also talk OBEX in addition to JetSend. Microsoft Windows2000 has also built-in OBEX support.[7]

---

[7] A good source of information about the Open-OBEX initiative can be found at www.ravioli. pasta.cs.uit.no/open-obex/. Information about IrOBEX can be found at www.irda.org/ standards/pubs/IrOBEX12.pdf.

Comparing Bluetooth to IrDA

Bluetooth and IrDA both occupy important niches in the marketplace, and appear to complement, rather than compete with, one another. But because each technology has unique advantages and disadvantages, the choice of which to use is user-dependent.

Directionality

Bluetooth's capability to penetrate solid objects, along with its maximum mobility within the piconet, allows for data-exchange applications that are very difficult or impossible to use with IrDA. With Bluetooth, users can, for example, synchronize their phones with their PCs without taking the phone out of their purses or briefcases; this is not possible with IrDA. The omnidirectional radiation zone of Bluetooth transmission allows synchronization to start when the phone is brought into range of the PC.

But in applications involving a one-to-one data exchange, IrDA has the advantage. Because of the monodirectional nature of IrDA, electronic business cards can be exchanged between two people sitting across a table in a meeting by pointing the infrared devices at each other. This scenario could pose a problem for Bluetooth, since the Bluetooth device will detect all similar devices in the room, so some kind of filtering would have to be employed.

Other Comparisons

Other notable comparisons between the Bluetooth and IrDA technologies include:

Bluetooth provides security mechanisms that are not present in IrDA; however, IrDA's narrow infrared beam provides an ad hoc low security level.

IrDA is cheaper than Bluetooth. A manufacturer can implement an IrDA solution for about $1; a Bluetooth radio unit is more expensive, in the $25 range, although prices are expected to drop.

Windows has enhanced IrDA support for file transfer and synchronization, meaning that IrDA will probably continue—at least in the short term—to enjoy an edge over Bluetooth in terms of installed base. IrDA will likely continue to be integrated into PCs, laptops, and handheld devices. But as the installed base for Bluetooth grows, the need for IrDA will likely decrease, though this is not expected to happen for several years. For the near to medium term, IrDA and Bluetooth will coexist.

Although IrDA attempts to compete in the WPAN space, Bluetooth is emerging as the preferred wireless technology in this arena. IrDA has functional shortcomings that make it more difficult to use in a WPAN than Bluetooth.

Wireless Hardware and Devices

Wireless communication between various devices makes it possible to provide unique and innovative services. As explained in this and the previous chapter, in the past few years, many wireless connectivity standards and technologies have emerged. These technologies enable users to connect a wide range of computing and telecommunications devices easily and simply, without cables. These technologies also deliver on the promise of quick establishment of ad hoc connections and automatic connectivity between devices. In short, by eliminating the need for cabling to connect individual devices, wireless devices will make it possible to use mobile data in a variety of applications, a number of which are described in this section.

Personal Electronic Devices

The product category known as *personal electronic devices* (PEDs) includes many types of products, though here the focus is on those that offer some kind of wireless or Internet mobile communications technology. These wireless devices usually subscribe to a commercial Internet or message service provider that is not under the full control of the company providing the device to the employee.

Examples of mobile communications devices and systems meeting this criterion are:

- *Personal digital assistants (PDAs).* Windows handhelds, Palm OS handhelds, and other operating systems commonly using wireless modems for Internet connectivity.

- *Web-enabled cellular phones.* Internet-enabled cell phones using WAP, and Symbian OS, or other systems.

- *Digital text devices.* BlackBerry and two-way pagers.

PDAs

PDA use has increased significantly in the last three years. Not only do PDAs comprise one of the fastest-growing areas of consumer electronics, many companies and government agencies are issuing them to their employees to increase productivity. But while PDAs can enhance productivity, they can also introduce security vulnerabilities that must be addressed by company PDA policies.

There are essentially two classes of PDAs:

- Those using the Palm operating system (Palm OS), such as PalmPilots (shown in Figure 3.5) and the Handspring Visor.

- Windows OS handhelds, such as Compaq, HP Jornada, and Casio, which run Windows CE or Microsoft Pocket PC 2002.

These two operating systems, Palm OS and Windows OS, represent the largest segment of the current PDA market. There are others, but they constitute a very small share of the PDA market.

PDAs can have a wide variety of accessories, including modems, synchronization cables, wireless connections, and flash memory storage. Let's look at some features of each.

The Palm OS

The Palm OS is a proprietary system available on PalmPilot devices and a few other PEDs. The Palm OS is optimized for a specific hardware platform. There is very little functional difference between the two main Palm OS platform vendors, 3Com, and Handspring.

As just stated, Palm OS performance has been optimized for vendor-specific hardware, but it is quite limited as to the number of functions it can execute. Its ROM can support very few tasks because there are only enough task slots for the ROM's needs. In order to support more tasks, the ROM would have to be rebuilt.

The OS is written very compactly, but it does not address major areas of security, such as auditing or object reuse. It supports an optional use of passwords, but does not have a fully developed data-protection security scheme. Palm OS vulnerabilities and countermeasures are examined in more detail in Chapter 6.

Figure 3.5 shows a Palm VIIx Handheld Wireless Device.

Figure 3.5   PalmVIIx Handheld Wireless Device.

(Courtesy, Palm Inc.)

Windows Handhelds

Windows OS handhelds currently run either a version of Windows CE or the newer Microsoft Pocket PC 2002 OS.

Windows CE

Microsoft Windows CE originated as a stripped-down version of Windows95 and was targeted at the PED market, primarily PDAs. Unlike Palm, however, Windows CE was designed to support a much wider range of hardware. In comparison to the single-version Palm OS, Windows CE is a general-purpose OS, designed to support a number of hardware platforms, as opposed to being optimized for a specific hardware platform, as was the Palm OS.

There are many different versions of the Windows CE kernel built for various CPUs, such as NEC MIPS, Intel or AMD x86, and Sega Dreamcast. Also, CE isn't just for PDAs; it was adapted to operate on Windows terminals, light notebook PCs, and even on car computers.

Windows CE is modular in design and is very expandable; actually, it is more similar to personal computer operating systems than to the Palm OS.

Unlike the Palm OS, CE was designed to run multiple programs and tasks simultaneously, that is, multitask. Multitasking is important to wireless field-data collection applications (such as record-keeping and medical diagnostics type programs); for example, a handheld device can upload stored information to a remote database while the user is keying in information. This is beneficial during synchronization (Windows CE devices synchronize continually when plugged into their docking cradles). CE is also a good fit for wireless applications, where email and Web pages might be downloaded over the airwaves in the background while the user is doing something else, such as reading email or searching through a contacts database.

Microsoft Pocket PC 2002 OS

In October 2001, Microsoft introduced the Pocket PC 2002, the company's third major PDA OS release. PPC 2002, as its called, features many significant improvements over the CE platform; its design tries to capture the look and feel of Microsoft Windows XP OS on a PDA screen.

Refinements include improved access to PIM data, communication alerts, one-tap volume control, and customizable desktop skins. Also, different icons pop up on the screen to alert the user to email or instant message delivery.

A field-upgradeable ROM chip lets companies flash user PDAs with Microsoft and third-party applications, making deploying and upgrading a fleet of PDAs easier.

PPC 2002 also enables users to make direct contact with the Internet when the device is plugged into the docking cradle: all they have to do is tap on Internet Explorer; no network connection setting is required. Palm-to-PPC infrared beaming is also integrated into the OS, so users can trade contact information wirelessly with a Palm user.

PPC 2002 includes a terminal services client and integrated VPN support for remote operation and access to corporate systems. Password support with encryption, Windows 2000 password rules, and a user-configurable active period (after which authentication stops) helps improve security over that of the CE platform.

Other PDA Devices

Other PDA devices include the Psion Series 7, devices using PsiWin 2.3, and various EPOC devices using EPOC release 5.

A recent addition to the wireless handheld device category is the Hiptop, from Danger, Inc. (shown in Figure 3.6). While it could not be considered a full-featured PDA like the Palm or PocketPC, the Hiptop is a device that connects to wireless networks and allows users to browse the Internet, exchange instant messages, and send and receive email with attachments. Additional Hiptop features include a full-featured phone, personal information management (PIM), entertainment applications, and a camera accessory. The Hiptop is an attempt to appeal to a younger demographic with features like Musical Instrument Digital Interface (MIDI) 8 voice synthesizer and instant messaging (IM).[8]

The Hiptop weighs 5 ounces and is 4.5" x 2.6" x 1.1".

Other Hiptop specifications include:

- GSM / GPRS radio with vibration, 24-bit color illuminated LED push wheel, MIDI ringtones email notification options
- Screen resolution of 240 x 160 with backlit keyboard and screen
- 16MB RAM
- IrDA, USB, headset/accessory ports:
- Optional camera accessory attaches via Accessory Port

Internet-Enabled Cell Phones

Various Internet-enabled cell phones use WAP, include the Symbian OS or other operating systems, and employ various digital transmission schemes, such as TDMA, CDMA, and GSM (which were discussed in Chapter 2).

---

[8] www.danger.com

Figure 3.6 Hiptop Wireless Device.
(Courtesy Danger Inc.)

WAP-Enabled Phones

A wide variety of WAP-enabled phones are on the market today, but for use only in the United States. For example, AT&T subscribers can only use their WAP phone in the United States and only through AT&T. Ericsson, Mitsubishi, and Nokia all manufacture phones for AT&T using TDMA. Similarly, Sprint subscribers can access only Sprint for their service; they cannot use Sprint phones through AT&T, because Sprint uses CDMA for its digital mode for communication. Motorola, Samsung, and Sanyo manufacture for Sprint WAP-enabled phones.

Most of these manufacturers also manufacture GSM-only WAP phones for use in Europe. New global standards are not expected to be in place until 2004, at the earliest, and the adoption curve will add a few years before all cellular phones and WAP phones are standardized for global use.

Symbian OS

An operating system designed primarily for 2.5G and 3G phones is the Symbian OS. Designed for optimal flexibility, Symbian OS gives mobile phone manufacturers broad scope for differentiation and innovation in user interfaces, hardware designs, and connectivity. Symbian is an efficiently written operating system that is gaining popularity as can be seen in several major consumer communications products, such as the Nokia 7650, Ericsson R380, and the Nokia 9290 Communicator. The current OS release is version 6.x.

The Symbian OS is owned by several of the major suppliers in the mobile telecommunications world: Ericsson, Nokia, Motorola, and Psion. Symbian has several characteristics that make it user-friendly and power-efficient. It has been designed from scratch to be a fast, real-time operating system.

The Symbian OS supports a range of different devices, defined within three broad categories of the mobile phone market:

Keyboard-based information-centric mobile phones. Crystal is the code name for a Symbian reference design for keyboard-based mobile phones with the capability to enter and manage information and support email as well as content creation, word processing, and other enterprise vertical applications, particularly with Symbian OS support for Personal Java.

Pen-based information-centric mobile phones. Quartz is the code name for a Symbian reference design for tablet devices, which fit in the palm of the user's hand. Targeted to the consumer and corporate markets, users can browse the Internet with these pen-operated devices and still be able to make voice calls.

Advanced mobile phones with information capability. Though primarily focused on voice, these mobile phones can include handwriting recognition, email, WAP and i-mode,[9] short messaging (SMS), contacts, and agenda applications.

Nokia

Nokia, a major player in the wireless communications area, has created a solid niche for its products through several initiatives, notably the Nokia Developer Network. Also, the Nokia Knowledge-Sharing Network helps support open discussion on topics including WAP, xHTML, and SMS. Two of its products are described here.

Nokia 8390 Phone

The Nokia 8390, shown in Figure 3.7, is a good example of a WAP Internet-enabled phone with many features. Noncommunications-related features include voice dialing for up to 10 numbers, voice commands for 5 menu items, and the capability to record up to 3 minutes of memos and phone conversations.

Wireless communications features include:

- Email, text, and picture-messaging services
- IrDA device-to-device communications

---

[9] First introduced in Japan in February 1999 by NTT DoCoMo, i-mode is one of the world's most successful services offering wireless Web browsing and email from mobile phones. Whereas until recently, mobile phones were used mostly for making and receiving voice calls, i-mode phones allow users also to use their handsets to access various information services and communicate via email. In Japan, i-mode is most popular among young users, 24 to 35 years of age. The heaviest users of i-mode are women in their late 20s. As of November 2000, i-mode had an estimated 14.9 million users. When using i-mode services, you do not pay for the time you are connected to a Web site or service, but are charged only according to the volume of data transmitted.

Figure 3.7   The Nokia 8390 WAP phone.
(Courtesy, Nokia Corporation)

- High-speed data transmission via GPRS
- Wireless Internet using a WAP 1.2.1 microbrowser transmitting via GPRS and circuit-switched data (CSD)
- Wireless modem
- Multiuser games via infrared

Nokia 9290 Communicator

The Nokia 9290 Communicator (shown in Figure 3.8) is kind of an odd device. A little different device from a cell phone, it's an example of the next generation of cellular systems-based wireless information devices; that is, it is a combination cell phone/wireless PDA/mini-office productivity center.

The 9290's noncommunications features include a 4096 color screen, a full QWERTY keyboard for a PC-like environment, and the capability to synchronize the calendar, to-do list, and contacts with Microsoft Outlook and Lotus Notes, and Office productivity software. The 9290 can multitask: Users can use the telephone at the same time they are using other applications.

Figure 3.8 The Nokia 9290 Communicator.
(Courtesy, Nokia Corporation)

The 9290's wireless communications features include:

- IrDA functionality
- SMS services
- Wireless fax modem
- Email wireless with the capability to send and receive attachments; support for the IMAP4, POP3, MIME1 & 2, MHTML, and SMTP mail protocols
- Full-color Internet access with built-in 3.2 HTML browser; support for frames, SSL security, bookmark functionality, and full-color images
- Integrated cellular phone with hands-free speakerphone and conference calling capability

Ericsson R380e

The latest entry in Ericsson's R380 mobile phone series is the R380e (shown in Figure 3.9). It continues in the market trend by integrating PDA functions and enhancing wireless data communications: It is a combination mobile phone, personal organizer, and address book.

Figure 3.9 The Ericsson R380e mobile phone.
(Courtesy, Telefonaktiebolaget LM Ericsson)

The Ericsson R380e is a full-featured mobile phone, offering:

- Email, SMS, and fax messaging over SMS
- PC calendar synchronization
- Internet access through a touch-sensitive screen and a WAP 1.2.1 micro-browser that employs enhanced WTLS security, classes 1 and 2
- Notepad, voice memo, games, calculator, and other functions.

The R380e uses WAP profiles, network settings that users enter into the phone only once. Thereafter, users can simply switch between the different profiles; they do not have to reenter the settings every time they want to change a network connection. For example, one WAP profile can be connected to the user's network operator, another to a bank, and a third one to a company's intranet.

The R380 uses the Symbian OS, supports WAP 1.2.1, and can use either Baltimore, Entrust, or VeriSign digital certificates.

Motorola i90c iDEN

Motorola's i90c digital cellular phone (shown in Figure 3.10) uses the company's new iDEN technology, which is described in a moment.

The i90c features include:

- Digital two-way radio with group call feature
- Digital cellular phone with voice-activated dialing
- Java2 Micro Edition capability

Figure 3.10 Motorola's i90c iDEN phone.
(Courtesy, Motorola Inc.)

- Capability to send and receive files, faxes, email, and text messages
- Built-in microbrowser

The i90c is equipped with a Smart Button, meaning that users can perform multiple tasks with a one-keypress command. For example, they can access recent calls, send incoming calls directly to voicemail, end conference calls, and clear alerts.

The i90c is Internet-ready, capable of sending and receiving emails. The Motorola i90c can function as an external wireless modem if a landline is unavailable.

iDEN Technology

The iDEN digital technology developed by Motorola integrates four network communications services into one device. This effort marks Motorola's attempt to bring together in one product the features of dispatch radio, full-duplex telephone interconnect, short message service, and data transmission. iDEN phones incorporate a number of messaging services, such as voice messaging, text messaging, numeric paging, and alphanumeric messaging. Other iDEN features are:

- Automatic callback
- Radio group call

■ Wireless Internet

■ Wireless fax

■ Wired LAN connection

■ Wireless modem

Currently available Motorola iDEN products with Internet capabilities include: i55sr, i50sx, i80s, i85s, i90c, i500plus, i550plus, i700plus, i1000plus, i2000plus, and the r750plus.

iDEN utilizes time division multiple access (TDMA), which you'll recall from Chapter 2, divides a channel into different slots. Each slot can carry one voice or data transmission. TDMA utilizes GPS satellites to reference a synchronized time, then divides the channel into time slots. By concerting one channel to multiple voice or data transmission pipelines, channel capacity can be increased by as much as six times their current analog networks, according to estimates.

iDEN also employs Vector Sum Excited Linear Prediction (VSELP), which digitally codes and compresses voice signals, thereby increasing radio channel capacity by reducing the amount of information that needs to be transmitted. VSELP provides iDEN systems with the capability to fit voice transmission into the smaller transmissions pipeline that results from TDMA.

iDEN appears to provides more robust security than 802.11b wireless LANs. *Information Security Magazine* recently reported that Aeronautical Radio Inc. (Arinc), a communications services provider owned by a consortium of airlines, plans to abandon the 802.11b-based bag-matching system it operates as a shared resource system for all carriers with international flights at San Francisco International Airport in favor of a private wireless system operating in the 800-MHz band. That system will be based on iDEN voice and data terminals. Figure 3.11 shows the current iDEN network worldwide access map.

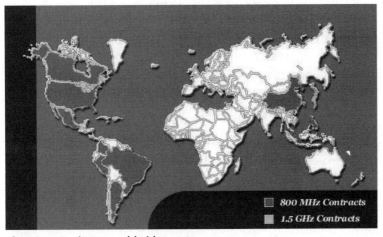

Figure 3.11   iDEN worldwide access map.

(Courtesy, Motorola Inc.)

BlackBerry

One of the faster-growing consumer communications products is the Black-Berry device from Research In Motion Limited (RIM), a designer, manufacturer, and marketer of wireless solutions for the mobile communications market. RIM's products include the RIM Wireless Handheld line, the Black-Berry wireless email solution, embedded radio modems, and software development tools.

BlackBerry is an integrated package device that provides mobile access to email, contacts, calendars, and task lists. It is offered in two basic flavors: BlackBerry Internet Edition and BlackBerry Enterprise Edition.

BlackBerry Internet Edition

BlackBerry Internet Edition is designed to allow individual mobile users access to an Internet mailbox. The service is sold through third-party Internet service providers, and includes the hardware, sync software, flat-rate airtime, and an email account that stores a copy of all the emails sent and received from the BlackBerry handheld.

BlackBerry Enterprise Edition

BlackBerry Enterprise Edition is a corporate wireless email solution designed specifically for corporate environments using Microsoft Exchange or Lotus Domino. This edition integrates with users' existing corporate email accounts to provide a wireless extension of their regular email mailboxes. Users can read, compose, forward, reply, delete, or file messages from the palm of their hand while maintaining a single email address and mailbox. They can also control which messages they receive on their wireless handhelds by setting email filters that monitor keywords and message fields.

BlackBerry Enterprise Edition incorporates Triple DES encryption. That means that email messages remain encrypted at all points between the BlackBerry wireless handheld and the corporate email account, ensuring data integrity and security.

Many third-party solutions under development will add to the BlackBerry functionality, such as business intelligence, Internet content services, middleware, and system management.

Figure 3.12 shows the BlackBerry 5810 handheld.

Figure 3.12   BlackBerry 5810 Handheld.
(Courtesy, Research In Motion Limited)

BlackBerry ISPs

BlackBerry Internet email services users must subscribe to one of several ISP's plans to use the system. BlackBerry Internet Edition is currently available from the following service providers in the United States:

- Aether
- EarthLink
- GoAmerica
- Handango

And in Canada, from:

- Bell Mobility
- Pagenet
- Rogers AT&T

Figure 3.13 shows the current U.S. BlackBerry coverage area for a single ISP.

Figure 3.13 Current BlackBerry coverage area.

(Courtesy, Research In Motion Limited)

Wireless Applications

The widespread strategic reliance on networking among competitive businesses, concomitant to the meteoric growth of the Internet and online services, attest to the benefits of shared data and shared resources. Wireless LANs make it possible for users to access shared information without looking for a place to plug in, and network managers can set up or augment networks without installing or moving wires.

Wireless Technologies in the Home

Wireless technologies are beginning to find widespread acceptance in the home market, for two compelling reasons: ease of installation and the desire to avoid punching holes in a house to pull cable. Also, the small office/home office (SOHO) market is expanding rapidly, and wireless networks scale very well with demands in this category of users.

Some common applications of wireless computing in the home are:

- Broadband (cable, DSL) sharing for multiple Internet access
- Printer and hard-drive sharing
- Multiplayer games

Wireless Technologies in the Office

Wireless technologies were originally intended for use in corporate and government agency environments, so it is not surprising to find wireless networks
implemented in numerous configurations in these arenas, for example:

- Quick setup for mobile workgroups, such as accounting audit teams, or
  trade-show workers

- Installation of networks in older buildings where it would not be cost-
  effective to pull cable

- Warehouse access to central databases of inventory information

- Business continuity for critical applications in disaster-recovery
  schemes

- Real-time customer service information systems at car rentals or
  airports

Wireless Technologies in Public Spaces

A third wireless application arena is public spaces, called hot spots. This is a
rapidly growing area of wireless implementation, as cafes, restaurants, airports, railway stations, and other common-use areas are being provided with
these services. The ability to surf the Internet or receive email while enjoying,
for example, a grande caramel macchiato seems to be gaining popularity.
Internationally, many infrastructure providers are wiring public areas, and,
soon, most airports, conference centers, and many hotels will provide 802.11b
access for visitors.

And, notably, since the events of September 11, 2001, airport wireless systems are coming under intense security scrutiny. Matching bags to passengers
using wireless LANs is under consideration as an option to assist airline and
airports meet the federal requirement to screen every checked bag on every
flight. Currently, the airlines are testing wireless 802.11 WLANs to match bags
with passengers.

Over the course of Part I, you've become fully versed in computer and wireless technical fundamentals. As you enter Part II, you will first encounter
Chapter 4, an examination of basic security methodologies. Wireless technology will change, and each generation of devices evolves, but the goals of security remain constant.

Security Essentials

"Security is a process, not a product... If you think technology can solve your security problems, then you don't understand the problem and you don't understand the technology."

BRUCE SCHNEIER, SECRETS AND LIES

"Wonder is the foundation of all philosphy, inquiry its progress, ignorance its end."

MICHEL EYQUEM DE MONTAINGE, ESSAYS

CHAPTER

4

Security Concepts and Methodologies

Part 1, Technology, comprising Chapters 1 through 3, discussed computer architecture, network technologies, wireless technologies, and devices as a necessary prelude to the book's primary focus: security. This chapter, which opens Part II, introduces fundamental security methodologies and processes.

Why should you care about security methodologies? Probably, your company has a firewall, and someone (you assume) in IT is looking at the logs. When a denial-of-service (DoS) is received, the servers are reset and explanations are issued to upper management. But is that enough? To answer that question, consider a number of other questions, whose answers will make it clear why you need to understand security methodologies:

- Has a minimal risk analysis been performed to give you an idea as to where you should be spending your security dollars?

- How much downtime can the business stand?

- What level of business continuity should you have?

- Do you need a hot site to maintain constant data-processing fault tolerance, or can a warm or cold site suffice? Do you need a full-fledged disaster recovery plan?

- What is the value of data to your business, your customers, your shareholders, your staff?

- What would be the impact on you and/or your business of loss of credibility and public exposure of trade secrets, proprietary business information, or staffing information? Do you, for example, deal in medical, financial, or other private information?

- Do you operate a child-oriented Web site that would suffer if pornography were posted on it?

- Do you know where all your portables are, and do you have a process to sanitize data from media and laptops before being reissued?

- Does your backup system work properly; are you testing the tapes frequently; and do you have a procedure to secure the tapes from unauthorized viewing?

The list could go on and on, but you get the picture. In the hierarchy of policies, procedures, and standards, the technical solution, the firewall, is actually pretty far down the stream. By the time you get the firewall installed, you should have an idea of what data or systems you are trying to protect based upon their value to the organization, either continuity- or privacy-wise. You should have an idea of what you are trying to protect the organization *from*. You should have policies and procedures in place to: protect the company legally, to alert you when you're being violated either internally or externally, to enable you to recover from an invasion incident.

To give you a real-life example of the seriousness of this issue, I'll relate a situation with one of my clients. This client had received $40 million to start up their Web project, which was very much in the news. It wasn't until a week before going online that they realized they had better check their security, especially since they had a special trade secret in the way they used information. That's when I got involved: They contacted me to arrange security audits. Obviously, in that short a period, there was not a lot I could do to perform levels of assurance on their processes; however, I was able to get a very good external penetration testing firm to run tests overnight for a week. We would examine the results in the morning, and engineers would make the configuration changes in the afternoon.

The results of just this surface examination horrified the client. In addition to the common vulnerabilities often found, Trojan horses were everywhere, many of them the common wild varieties unintentionally left by staff and consultants. But we discovered something more disturbing: covert scripts, placed by one or more of the consultants, were sending internal private information to competitors. Needless to say, at the time, the company had no policy in place for managing security of consultants, engineers, or maintenance. And needless to say, this company *now* does full internal and external testing and auditing, and has back-engineered its policies and procedures to make security a full-time practice.

The obvious point is: If you think a technology solution alone is going to protect your company's interests, you're wrong.

In examining security methodologies, the following concepts will be introduced: certification and assurance, information classification, polices, and the tenets of confidentiality, integrity, and availability, known as C.I.A. We begin with the latter.

The Concepts of C.I.A.

Confidentiality, integrity, and availability, C.I.A., are three fundamental tenets of the information systems security process. This triad (shown in Figure 4.1) is the standard by which all security methodologies and remediation processes are judged, answering such questions as: Is there a threat to confidentiality? Does the security process in place remedy it? Do threats to integrity and availability exist, and, if so, are steps being implemented to protect them? Let's look at the properties of each concept in turn.

NOTE The absence of C.I.A. is sometimes called D.A.D., short for disclosure, alteration, and destruction.

Confidentiality

The concept of confidentiality is the assurance that sensitive data is being accessed and viewed only by those who are authorized to see it. Whether the data contains trade secrets for commercial business, secret classified government information, or private medical or financial records, confidentiality implies that data is protected from breaches from unauthorized persons and the damage that would be done to the organization, person, governmental body by such breaches.

Obviously, the tenet of confidentiality is important when it comes to information belonging to, for example, the U.S. Department of Defense, but it comes into play as well in other organizations, whether private, nonprofit, or commercial. Confidentiality is vital to a modern business, especially now with

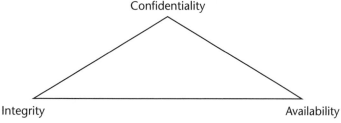

Figure 4.1   The C.I.A. triad.

privacy laws, the Health Insurance Portability and Accountability Act (HIPAA),[1] and the requirement for businesses and organizations to protect their trade secrets and employee information. Though breaches to confidentiality are not as well-publicized as denial-of-service (DoS) attacks (which are primarily aimed at compromising availability), they can have serious implications to a business's competitiveness, a mission's success, and/or personal privacy and safety. Espionage, whether industrial or governmental, is the attempt to compromise confidentiality.

The prevention of an unauthorized disclosure of information, either intentionally or unintentionally, is inherent to the concept of confidentiality. Loss of confidentiality (sometimes called *disclosure)* can occur many ways, for example, by a disgruntled employee's intentional release of sensitive company information; or, probably most commonly, through the misapplication of network system rights, that is, allowing unauthorized employees to view private company data (such as salaries). Every organization has horror stories to tell resulting from the loss of confidentiality.

Integrity

The concept of integrity ensures that the content of data or correspondences are preserved intact through the transfer from sender to receiver. Integrity embodies the guarantee that a message sent is the message received, that is, it was not altered either intentionally or unintentionally during transmission.

Unlike confidentiality, a breach to integrity (often referred to as *alteration)* is usually initiated for the benefit of a competing organization or a government agency. It is usually done in two ways: by the intentional alteration of the data for vandalism or revenge (such as Web site defacement) or by the unintentional alteration of the data caused by operator input, computer system, or faulty application errors.

In the database realm, integrity means that the database has preserved "internal and external consistency" meaning that programming flaws or operator errors have not compromised the quality of the data, and the organization can rely on the data's accuracy.

Assuring integrity is a three-part endeavor:

- Prevent modification of information by unauthorized users.

- Prevent unauthorized or unintentional modification of information by authorized users.

- Preserve the internal and external consistency of databases.

---

[1]The U.S. Kennedy-Kassenbaum Health Insurance Portability and Accountability Act (HIPAA-Public Law 104-191), effective date August 21, 1996, addresses the issues of health care privacy and plan portability in the United States.

Availability

Availability doesn't come to mind as a security tenet as quickly as do confidentiality and integrity because availability can encompass issues that don't, at first, bring to mind security needs: backup tapes, fault tolerance, and downtime, for example.

But the assurance of availability is very much a security issue. Downtime for a business and loss of credibility with customers can injure a corporation or governmental body as seriously as a failure of confidentiality. Long-term DoS attacks can severely hinder a company's ability to continue. In fact, denial of service is often a successful tactic of information warfare. The opposite of availability can, then, be thought of as *destruction*. Moreover, the processes required to prevent or mitigate the effects of loss of availability are very much within the realm of security methodology, because the basic concept of availability assures that authorized persons have uninterrupted access to the information in the system at hand.

In networking, availability refers to those elements that create reliability and stability in networks and systems, assuring that connectivity is functioning as needed so that authorized users have access to the network systems. Obviously, availability is affected by how well a network's controls function to ensure an organization's level of fault tolerance and its ability to recover from failure.

Threats, Vulnerabilities, and Risk

Many information system security methodologies address threats to, vulnerabilities of, and risk level of a system. But before we can discuss these issues, definitions of these three terms must be established:

Threat.   An event or activity that has the potential to cause harm to information systems or networks.

Vulnerability.   Weakness or lack of a safeguard that enables exploitation and the ability to cause harm to information systems or networks.

Risk.   The potential for harm or loss to an information system or network; that is, the probability that a threat will materialize.

Certification and Accreditation

Information systems, particularly those that handle sensitive data, must have processes in place to assure that the procedures for handling the data preserve its C.I.A. These formal methods are applied to ensure that the appropriate information system security safeguards are in place and functioning. In addition, a designated authority must have final responsibility for putting the system into operation. These actions are known as *certification* and *accreditation*, defined, respectively as:

Certification.   The comprehensive evaluation of the technical and nontechnical security features of an information system and other safeguards, made in support of the accreditation process, to establish the extent to which a particular design and implementation meets a set of specified security requirements.

Accreditation.   A formal declaration by a *designated approving authority* (DAA) that an information system is approved to operate in a particular security mode using a prescribed set of safeguards at an acceptable level of risk.

After a defined period of time, or when changes are made to the system and its environment, the certification and accreditation of a system must be recertified and reaccredited. This helps to ensure that the systems maintain their level of accreditation throughout the system's life cycle.

Policies and Procedures

An information system policy can mean several things. There are security polices on firewalls, which refer to the packet-filtering lists. In the information security world, policies refer to the standards, procedures, and guidelines a company adopts to identify risks and focus its security posture.

A well-written policy is an essential element of sound security practice and can be a lifesaver during a disaster. It may be a requirement of a governmental agency, or support some compliance function, like HIPAA. It may provide protection from liability due to an employee's actions, or form the basis for control of trade secrets.

Specifically, the term *policy* refers to a document that defines the overall strategy and goals of the information security process, relative to the goals of the organization. It often lays out how information security will assist the company in its business model.

The first policy usually developed is the high-level Senior Management Statement of Policy. This policy that may contain these elements:

- Acknowledgment of the importance of the computing resources to the business model.

- Statement of support for information security throughout the enterprise.

- Commitment to authorize and manage the definition of lower-level standards, procedures, and guidelines.

Normally, the higher-level policies are created before the lower-level documents, which contain the tactical procedures, standards, and guidelines the

Figure 4.2   Policy hierarchy.

company should follow in its operations. Technological security solutions are determined later in the process. Figure 4.2 shows a sample hierarchy of polices.

For example, what is a firewall? In the world of information systems security, a firewall is a network device implemented to enforce the established policy. If the policy has not been created, and the organization hasn't done due diligence to determine which information should be protected, what the information is worth to the continuity of the organization, and from what defined threat the firewall is intended to protect the organization, the firewall is not being implemented properly. A well-written policy should do all that.

Business Continuity and Disaster Recovery

Two other concepts are inherent to a full understanding of security methodologies: *business continuity planning* (BCP) and *disaster recovery planning* (DRP). Although often overlooked by security professionals, BCP is an important early step in determining an organization's security posture. It is the process of making the plans that will ensure that critical business functions can withstand a variety of emergencies.

There are four main steps to the BCP process:

1. *Initiate scope and plan.* In this first step, the scope of the plan is determined, along with the other elements needed to define the parameters of the plan.
2. *Assess business impact.* A business impact assessment (BIA) and/or vulnerability assessment is done prior to creating a document that can be used to help business units understand the impact of a disruptive event.

3. *Develop recovery strategy plan.* The BIA created in step 2 is used to develop a draft of a business continuity plan. The draft plan may include implementation, testing, and ongoing updating of the plan.

4. *Implement plan approval.* The final step in the BCP process consists of senior management sign-off, implementing enterprisewide awareness of the plan, and establishing a maintenance procedure for updating the plan as needed.

Similar to business continuity, disaster recovery also involves making preparations for an interruption of business, but is focused on the procedures to be followed during and after a loss. The BCP process should create a DRP, which needs to be tested regularly.

Alternative Processing Sites

When a disaster strikes, it may be of such magnitude that the company hit can't function or, at least, process data at its usual location. In this case, it's important for the organization to have an alternate means and location of operation, that is, another processing center to which to it can relocate.

There are basically three types of alternative processing sites a company can implement when a disaster strikes, list and briefly discussed here:

Hot site.   A fully configured computer facility with electrical power; heating, ventilation, and air conditioning (HVAC); and functioning file/print servers and workstations. All systems have been installed and are operating prior to need due to the disaster.

Warm site.   Like a hot site, the warm site is a computer facility with readily available electrical power, HVAC, and computers, but the applications and data may not be loaded. This site will need some work before it can start processing after a disaster.

Cold site.   A cold site differs from the other two in that it is available for equipment installation during an emergency, but no computer hardware, servers, or workstations reside at the site. The cold site is, essentially, a room with electrical power and HVAC, but equipment must be brought on-site when needed, and communications links may or may not be ready.

RISK MITIGATION

Risk to an organization can never be totally eliminated. The term *risk mitigation* means two things: understanding the risks inherent in doing business and minimizing the company's exposure to those risks. This entails determining the risk boundary that, if crossed, will cause the company to incur such losses as to make it cease to be a viable enterprise.

Wireless Disaster Recovery

Wireless ad hoc or infrastructure networks can greatly assist in disaster recovery. Some organizations have disaster recovery plans that incorporate off-premises wireless systems to assist in their business continuity should a disaster strike. Being able to set up a wireless network and begin working anywhere, even in a parking lot, can offer distinct advantages. For this to be possible, however, the wireless systems must be tested regularly, including the performance of simulation drills. These systems must also be stored or located in an area that is far enough away from the original processing site, yet not so far as to make it inconvenient to access them.

Information Classification Concepts

The concept of *information classification,* though its roots are in government, is commonly adopted by business as part of a total security plan.

During the creation of an information classification scheme, the information produced or processed by an organization is classified according to its sensitivity to loss or disclosure. This allows the security controls to be implemented properly according to its classification scheme. In other words, resources, time, and dollars are spent where they are needed most, as determined by the sensitivity and value of the data to the organization.

Both private businesses and government use forms of information classification, although the classification levels are a little different. Government traditionally uses a five-level scheme, ranging from not sensitive (information that can be made freely available to the public) to highly secret information (information that should only be made available on a need-to-know basis to authorized and security-cleared individuals). These levels are:

1. Unclassified
2. Sensitive but unclassified (SBU)
3. Unclassified
4. Secret
5. Top secret

Businesses, on the other hand, may employ a simpler three- or four-level approach, similar to this:

1. Public
2. Sensitive
3. Private
4. Confidential

Table 4.1   Three-level Information Classification Scheme

DEFINITION	DESCRIPTION
Public Use	Information that can safely be disclosed publicly.
Internal Use Only	Information that can safely be disclosed internally, but not externally.
Company Confidential	The most sensitive information intended for access only by specific individuals.

Table 4.1 gives an example of a very simple business approach to information classification, which would suffice for many organizations.

The Ten Domains of the International Information Systems Security Certification Consortium

As the result of cooperation among a number of North American professional societies, the International Information Systems Security Certification Consortium (ISC)^2 was established in 1989. The (ISC)^2 is a nonprofit corporation that has defined a common body of knowledge (CBK) called the Ten Domains of Information Systems Security. Currently, the domains, in alphabetical order, are:

- Access Control Systems and Methodology
- Application and Systems Development Security
- Business Continuity and Disaster Recovery Planning
- Cryptography
- Law, Investigation, and Ethics
- Operations Security
- Physical Security
- Security Architecture and Models
- Security Management Practices
- Telecommunications and Networking Security

The (ISC)^2 developed the Certified Information Systems Security Professional (CISSP) certification as an attempt to guarantee that information systems security professionals meet a standard criteria of knowledge and continue to upgrade that knowledge in the field of information systems security. The ten domains constitute a very wide range of subject matter, from legal to engineering to cryptography and more. Although it is not expected that one security practitioner should be expert in every domain, the CISSP is expected to have a minimum level of knowledge of each domain.

The (ISC)^2 conducts review seminars and administers examinations for information security practitioners seeking the CISSP certification. More information on the CISSP program and the ten domains can be found at: www.isc2.org.

TCSEC and the Common Criteria

The Trusted Computer System Evaluation Criteria (TCSEC) was developed by the National Computer Security Center (NCSC) in 1985 to provide guidelines for evaluating vendors' products for the specified security criteria. These include a series of guidelines called the Rainbow Series, so called because each has a distinct-color cover, two of which are described here, the Orange and Red Books.

The Orange Book

The basic control objectives of the TCSEC document called the Orange Book are security policy, assurance, and accountability. The Orange Book defines major hierarchical classes of security identified by the letters D through A, which are defined in Table 4.2.

The Orange Book defines several levels of assurance requirements for secure computer operations. Assurance refers to a level of confidence that the security policy of a trusted system computing base (TCB) has been implemented correctly and that the system's security features accurately implement that security policy.

Table 4.2 TCSEC Evaluation Classes

CLASS	DESCRIPTION
D	Minimal protection
C	Discretionary protection
C1	Discretionary security protection
C2	Controlled access protection
B	Mandatory protection
B1	Labeled security protection
B2	Structured protection
B3	Security domains
A1	Verified protection

The Orange Book defines two types of assurance: *operational assurance* and *life-cycle assurance*. Operational assurance focuses on the basic features and architecture of the system, while life-cycle assurance focuses on the controls and standards needed for building and maintaining the system.

The Red Book

The U.S. Department of Defense's Trusted Network Interpretation (TNI), called the Red Book, is analogous to the Orange Book, but addresses confidentiality and integrity in trusted computer/communications network systems. The TDI addresses trusted database management systems. The product or system to be evaluated is defined as the target of evaluation (TOE.) The TOE must have a security target, which includes the security enforcing mechanisms and the system security policy.

The Common Criteria

The Trusted Computer System Evaluation Criteria (TCSEC), the European Information Technology Security Evaluation Criteria (ITSEC), and the Canadian Trusted Computer Product Evaluation Criteria (CTCPEC) have evolved into a single evaluation entity, the Common Criteria (CC). The CC for Information Technology Security Evaluation is the result of a five-year international project involving NIST and the National Security Agency (NSA), on behalf of the United States and security organizations in Canada, France, Germany, the Netherlands, and the United Kingdom. These countries have worked in close cooperation with the International Organization for Standardization (ISO) and have assisted in generating the International Standard (IS) 15408.

The CC is a standard for specifying and evaluating the security features of computer products and systems, and is intended to replace previous security criteria such as the TCSEC. This evaluation process establishes a level of confidence that the security functions of such products and systems, and the assurance measures applied to them, must meet.

The CC defines a *Protection Profile* that specifies the security requirements and protections of the product to be evaluated.

The Three Parts of the CC

The Common Criteria comprises three distinct parts:

Part 1: Introduction and General Model.   Defines constructs for expressing IT security objectives, for selecting and defining IT security requirements, and for writing high-level specifications for products and systems. These constructs are called protection profiles (PPs), security targets (STs) and packages.

Part 2: Security Functional Requirements.   Contains a catalog of well-defined and understood security functional requirements that are intended to be used as a standard way of expressing the security requirements for IT products and systems. The catalog is organized into classes, families, and components, as follows:

- Classes are high-level groupings of families of requirements, all sharing a common security focus (e.g., identification and authentication).

- Families are lower-level groupings of requirement components, all sharing specific security objectives but differing in rigor or emphasis (e.g., user authentication).

- Components are the lowest selectable requirements that may be included in PPs, STs, or packages (e.g., unforgeable user authentication).

Part 3: Security Assurance Requirements.   Contains a catalog that establishes a set of assurance components that can be used as a standard way of expressing the assurance requirements for IT products and systems. This catalog has the same class and family component structure as Part 2. Part 3 also defines evaluation criteria for PPs and STs and presents the seven *evaluation assurance levels* (EALs), which are predefined packages of assurance components that make up the CC scale for rating confidence in the security of IT products and systems.

The EALs have been developed with the goal of preserving the concepts of assurance drawn from the source criteria (TCSEC, ITSEC, and CTCPEC) so that the results of previous evaluations remain relevant. For example, EALs levels 2 through 7 are generally equivalent to the assurance portions of the TCSEC C2-A1 scale.

The CC is used in two general ways:

- As a standardized way to describe security requirements, for example, PPs and STs for IT products and systems.

- As a sound technical basis for evaluating the security features of these products and systems.

- More information the Common Criteria can be found at: csrc.nist.gov/cc.

DITSCAP and NIACAP

Two U.S. defense and government certification and accreditation standards have been developed for the evaluation of critical information systems: the Defense Information Technology Security Certification and Accreditation

Process (DITSCAP) and the National Information Assurance Certification and Accreditation Process (NIACAP).

DITSCAP

The DITSCAP establishes a standard process, a set of activities, general task descriptions, and a management structure to certify and accredit IT systems that will maintain the required security posture. The process is designed to certify that the IT system meets the accreditation requirements, and that the system will maintain the accredited security posture throughout the system's life cycle.

There are four phases to the DITSCAP:

Phase 1: Definition.   Focuses on understanding the system's mission, environment, and architecture to determine the security requirements and level of effort necessary to achieve accreditation.

Phase 2: Verification.   Verifies the evolving or modified system's compliance with the information agreed on in the System Security Authorization Agreement (SSAA). The objective is to use the SSAA to establish an evolving yet binding agreement on the level of security required before the system development begins or changes to a system are made. After accreditation, the SSAA becomes the baseline security configuration document.

Phase 3: Validation.   Validates compliance of the fully integrated system with the information stated in the SSAA.

Phase 4: Post-Accreditation.   Includes those activities necessary for the continuing operation of the accredited IT system in its computing environment and addresses the changing threats a system faces through its life cycle.

NIACAP

The NIACAP establishes the minimum national standards for certifying and accrediting national security systems. This process provides a standard set of activities, general tasks, and a management structure to certify and accredit systems that will maintain the information assurance and security posture of a system or site. The NIACAP is designed to certify that the information system meets documented accreditation requirements and will continue to maintain the accredited security posture throughout the system's life cycle.

There are three types of NIACAP accreditations:

- A *site* accreditation evaluates the applications and systems at a specific, self-contained location.

- A *type* accreditation evaluates an application or system that is distributed to a number of different locations.

- A *system* accreditation evaluates a major application or general support system.

The NIACAP also is composed of four phases—definition, verification, validation, and post-accreditation—that are, essentially, identical to those of the DITSCAP.

Using the NIACAP methodology, the Commercial Information Security Analysis Process (CIAP) is being developed for the evaluation of critical commercial systems.

INFOSEC Assessment Methodology (IAM)

In May of 1998, Presidential Decision Directive 63 resulted in the formation of the National Infrastructure Protection Center. Subsequent to the directive, the National Security Agency (NSA) began to offer a limited number of Information Systems Security (INFOSEC) Assessment Methodology (IAM) classes to facilitate the transfer of government-developed technology into the private sector. The IAM course was originally developed by the NSA to train U.S. Department of Defense (DoD) organizations to perform their own INFOSEC assessments to improve their security posture.

The IAM, developed by experienced NSA INFOSEC assessors, is a detailed and systematic way of examining cyber-vulnerabilities. NSA has attempted to use the IAM to assist both INFOSEC assessment suppliers and consumers requiring assessments. NSA has developed specialized knowledge with regard to information systems security assessments through its completion of INFOSEC assessments for its U.S. government customers over the past 15 years.

The IAM class is a two-day course for experienced information systems security analysts who conduct, or are interested in conducting, INFOSEC assessments of U.S. government information systems. The course teaches NSA's INFOSEC assessment process, a high-level, nonintrusive process for identifying and correcting security weaknesses in information systems and networks.

The IAM certification courses are conducted a few times each year. A security practitioner must satisfy a fairly stringent experience requirement to be considered for the training. These include:

- U. S. citizenship.
- Five years of demonstrated experience in the field of INFOSEC, COMSEC or computer security, with two of the five years of experience directly involved in analyzing computer system/network vulnerabilities and security risks.

To qualify for an IAM certificate of completion, students must:

- Attend all of the two-day class.
- Demonstrate an understanding of the IAM through group exercises and class discussions.
- Obtain a passing grade (at least 70 percent) on the IAM test.

The IAM Process

The IAM process is described as a level I assessment: a nonintrusive standardized baseline analysis of the information systems security posture of an automated system. A level II assessment commonly defines a more hands-on evaluation of the security systems (both levels I and II are considered cooperative, that is with the permission and/or initiated by the assessee). A level III evaluation is a red team assessment, possibly noncooperative, and may include external penetration testing. The IAM process also provides recommendations for the elimination or mitigation of the vulnerability.

The IAM process is conducted in three phases:

Preassessment phase.   The assessment team defines the customer's needs and begins to identify the system, its boundaries, and the criticality of the information, and begins to write the assessment plan. This phase normally takes about two to four weeks.

On-site phase.   The team explores and confirms the conclusions made during phase I, gathers data and documentation, conducts interviews, and provides an initial analysis. This phase takes about one to two weeks.

Post-assessment phase.   The team finalizes the analysis, prepares and distributes the report and recommendations. This phase can take anywhere from two to eight weeks.

At the heart of the IAM is the creation of the Organizational Criticality Matrix (see Table 4.3). In this chart, all relevant automated systems are assigned impact attributes (high, medium, or low) based upon their estimated effect on confidentiality, integrity, and availability and criticality to the organization. Other elements may be added to the matrix, such as nonrepudiation, or authentication, but the basic three tenets of IINFOSEC remain.

For more information on the IAM program, visit www.nsa.gov/isso/iam/index.htm.

Table 4.3 Sample IAM Organizational Criticality Matrix

SYSTEM	CONFIDENTIALITY	INTEGRITY	AVAILABILITY
Criminal Records	M	H	M
Informants	H	M	M
Investigations	M	M	M
Warrants	L	H	M

BS7799

Considered by some as the leading Information Security Management System (ISMS), the Code of Practice for Information Security Management (BS7799) has been developed by the British Standards Institute.

A group of leading companies joined, first, to develop the Code of Practice for Information Security Management, now known as BS7799 Part 1, *Code of Practice*, then, in 1998, to develop BS7799 Part 2, *Specification for Information Security Management Systems.* The United Kingdom Department of Trade and Industry commissioned the BS 7799 certification scheme in 1998.

BS7799 is geared to assuring integrity, availability, and confidentiality of information assets. Assurance is attained through controls that management creates and maintains within the organization. BS7799 requires that company management address 10 specific areas:

- Security policy
- Security organization
- Assets, classification, and control
- Personnel security
- Physical and environmental security
- Computer and network management
- System access control
- System development controls
- Business continuity planning
- Compliance and auditing

The scheme requires that participating certification bodies be accredited by recognized national accreditation bodies. The United Kingdom Accreditation Service has accredited six bodies under ISO Guide 62 (EN 45012) to perform certification to BS7799:

- BSI Quality Assurance
- Bureau Veritas Quality International Ltd.
- Det Norske Veritas Quality Assurance Ltd.
- Lloyd's Register Quality Assurance Ltd.
- National Quality Assurance Ltd.
- SGS Yarsley International Certification Service Ltd.

A drive to gain worldwide acceptance of BS7799 has been the primary thrust of the Joint Information Technology Committee of the International Standards Organization (ISO) and the International Electrotechnical Commission (IEC). These organizations are transitioning BS7799 into an international standard known as ISO 17799.

For good information on BS7799, visit: www.ukas.com or www.bsi-global .com/index.html.

A Short History of Cryptography

The science and history of cryptography are fascinating. This section reveals a few historical examples that have affected the way we use secure computing systems today.

The Early Days of Secret Writing

Although cryptography, secret writing, can be traced back more than 5000 years, to the Egyptians, who used hieroglyphics to conceal messages, the first known example of a cryptographic *device* was one used by the Spartans in about 400 BC. Military cryptographers there wrapped a strip of papyrus around a wooden rod. The message was encoded by being written lengthwise down (or up) the rod on the wrapped material. Then, the material was unwrapped for transport to the recipient. In its unwrapped form, the writing appeared to be random characters. When the material was rewound on a rod of the same diameter and length the message could be deciphered.

Around 50 BC, Emperor Gaius Julius Caesar of Rome used a substitution cipher to transmit messages to Marcus Tullius Cicero. In this cipher, letters of the alphabet were substituted for other letters of the same alphabet. Since only one alphabet was used, this cipher is known as a monoalphabetic substitution. It involves shifting the alphabet three letters and making the substitution.

Early Disk Use

Disks, though not as we know them today, have played an important part in cryptography for at least the past 500 years. In Italy, around 1460, Leon Battista Alberti developed cipher disks for encryption. His system was based on printing press technology and consisted of concentric disks. Each disk had an alphabet around its periphery; by rotating one disk with respect to the other, a letter in one alphabet could be transformed into a letter in another alphabet.

In 1790, Thomas Jefferson developed an encryption device using a stack of 26 disks that could be rotated individually. A message was assembled by rotating each disk to the proper letter under an alignment bar that ran the length of the disk stack; then the alignment bar was rotated through a specific angle, A; the letters under the bar comprised the encrypted message. The recipient would align the enciphered characters under the alignment bar, rotate the bar back through the angle A and read the plaintext message. Figure 4.3 shows the Jeffersonian system.

Disk systems were used extensively during the Civil War in the United States. A federal signal officer even obtained a patent on a disk system, similar to the one invented by Alberti and used it to encode and decode flag signals among units.

Figure 4.3   Jeffersonian disks.
(Courtesy of the National Cryptologic Museum)

The 1920s

A mechanical cryptographic machine called the Hagelin Machine was developed in 1920 by Boris Hagelin in Stockholm, Sweden. In the United States, the Hagelin Machine is known as the M-209.

Also in the 1920s, Herbert O. Yardley was in charge of the secret MI-8 organization, also known as the "Black Chamber." Thanks to the work of MI-8, which cracked the codes of a number of nations, during the 1921-1922 Washington Naval Conference, the United States had an edge in the Japanese negotiations. MI-8 was supplying the Secretary of State with the Japanese negotiating plans, which it had successfully intercepted.

Rotor Systems

Rotor systems, also referred to as Hebern Machines, the German Enigma, the Japanese Purple Machine and the American SIGABA "Big Machine" were rotor machines.

The German military used a polyalphabetic substitution cipher machine, called the Enigma, as its principal encipherment system during World War II. A Dutchman, Hugo Koch, developed the machine in 1919, and it was produced for the commercial market in 1923 by Arthur Scherbius. Scherbius obtained a U.S. patent on the Enigma machine for the Berlin firm of Chiffriermaschinen Aktiengesellschaft.

Polish cryptanalysts, working with the French from 1928 to 1938 solved the wiring of the three-rotor system used by the Germans at the time, and created a card file that could anticipate the $6 \times 17,576$ possible rotor positions. The Germans changed the indicator system and the number of rotors to six in 1938, thus tremendously increasing the difficulty of breaking the Enigma cipher.

In 1938, the Poles and French constructed a prototype machine called the Bombe for use in breaking the Enigma cipher. The name was derived from the ticking sounds the machine made as it worked.

The work on the Enigma cipher-breaking system was then taken over by the British at Bletchley Park in England, led by many distinguished scientists, including Alan Turing. The Turing prototype Bombe appeared in 1940; and in 1943, high-speed Bombes were developed by the British and Americans.

NOTE For more information on these code-breaking devices and systems, visit: www.nsa.gov/museum/. I also recommend Simon Singh's *The Code Book: The Science of Secrecy from Ancient Egypt to Quantum Cryptography* (Anchor Books, August 2000) , a very fascinating description of the use of cryptography and cryptanalysis.

Identification and Authorization

Identification, authorization, and access control are very important concepts in the world of Information Systems Security. As will be explained later, wireless systems security is largely based upon the identification schemes for authorization of access control. While encryption and virtual private networks (VPNs) are very important fundamental components of wireless security, access authorization is the main vulnerability of wireless security systems.

When talking and thinking about security for any system, but especially wireless, it is essential to understand the concepts of access control, identification, and authorization. These concepts are especially important in wireless technology, because perhaps the most serious concern about wireless security is the problem of identification: How is it possible to know who is accessing a network, and from where? What points of access are exposed in a network?

The identification problem with wireless emerged as networking evolved. Previously, when it was possible to actually see who was sitting in the chair and logging in to the centralized mainframe, obviously, maintaining security was easier. With the advent of distributed computing; client/server technologies; Internet, intranet, and extranet connectivity; and, now, wireless connectivity, more complex means and methods have to be employed to assure an organization that the users accessing the network really are who they say they are.

No longer is it just the wired terminals that need to be secured, or the Internet router access point; the wireless access area forms a circle of radiation emanating from any device that accepts wireless communications. And with enhancements to antennae on the intruder's side, that circle of radiation is much larger than was previously thought.

Clearly, then, a good understanding of the concepts of access control, identification, and authorization is important. In particular, identification and authentication, which are at the heart of access control systems, must be understood as separate, yet linked.

Identification and Authentication

Identification is the concept of user a stating his or her identity to the system in the form of a logon ID. Identification establishes accountability for the user's actions on the system. The next step, authentication, is the action of verifying the identity claimed by the user. Authentication is usually implemented through the user password at logon.

Authentication is based on the following three factor types:

Type 1: Something you know (PIN, password)

Type 2: Something you have (ATM card, smart card)

Type 3: Something you are (fingerprint, retina scan)

Sometimes a fourth factor, something you do, is added to the list. Something you do may be typing your name or other phrases on a keyboard. However, something you do may also be considered something you are, such as your job role.

Two-factor authentication refers to requiring that two of the three factors be used in the authentication process. For example, withdrawing funds from an ATM machine requires two-factor authentication in the form of the ATM card (something you have) and your PIN number (something you know).

Passwords

Passwords may be required to be changed monthly, quarterly, or at another predetermined interval depending on the criticality of the information to be protected and how frequently the password is used. Obviously, the longer a password is used, the greater the chance of its being compromised.

A *passphrase* is a sequence of characters, usually longer than that allotted for a password. The passphrase is converted into a virtual password by the system. *Tokens*, in the form of credit-card-size memory cards, or smart cards resembling small calculators, are used to supply static and dynamic passwords. A tokens is an example of "something you have."

Four types of smart cards are:

Static password tokens.   The token authenticates the owner to the information system.

Synchronous dynamic password tokens.   The token generates a new unique password value at fixed time intervals, then the unique password is entered into the system or workstation along with the owner's personal identification number (PIN). The authentication entity in the system or workstation knows the owner's secret key and PIN and verifies that the password entered is valid and if it has been entered during the valid time window.

Asynchronous dynamic password tokens.   Similar to the synchronous dynamic password scheme except that the new password is generated asynchronously and does not have to fit into a time window for authentication.

Challenge-response tokens.   A workstation or system generates a random challenge string, which the owner enters into the token along with the proper PIN. The token then generates a response that is entered into the workstation or system. The authentication mechanism in the workstation or system then determines whether the owner should be authenticated.

In all these schemes, a front-end authentication device, a back-end authentication server that services multiple workstations, or the host itself can perform the authentication.

Access Control Models

Controlling access by a *subject* (an active entity such as individual or process) to an *object* (a passive entity such as a file) involves setting up access rules. These rules can be classified into three categories of models: *mandatory access control*, *discretionary access control*, and *nondiscretionary access control*.

Mandatory Access Control

Mandatory access control refers to the authorization of a subject to access an object; it is dependent upon labels that indicate the clearance of the subject and the classification or sensitivity of the object. For example, the U.S. military classifies documents as unclassified, confidential, secret, and top secret. Similarly, an individual can receive a clearance of confidential, secret, or top secret, and based on that level, can have access to documents classified at or below his or her clearance level.

Thus, an individual cleared for secret can access secret documents, confidential documents, and unclassified documents with a restriction. This restriction is that the individual must have a need-to-know relative to the classified documents involved. That is, the documents must be necessary for the individual to complete the assigned task. Even if the individual is cleared for the information in question, unless he or she needs to know it, the individual should not access the information.

Discretionary Access Control

Discretionary access control means that the subject has authority, within certain limitations, to specify which objects can be accessed. For example, access control lists can be used. This type of access control is used in local, dynamic situations where subjects must have the discretion to specify which resources certain users are permitted to access.

When a user, within certain limitations, has the right to alter access control to certain objects, this is termed *user-directed discretionary access control*. Identity-based access control is a type of discretionary access control that is based on the identity of the individual. In some instances, a hybrid approach is used that combines features of user-based and identity-based discretionary access control.

Nondiscretionary Access Control

In nondiscretionary access control, a central authority determines which subjects can access certain objects based on the organizational security policy. The access controls may be based on the role of an individual in the organization (role-based) or the responsibilities and duties of the subject (task-based). In an organization where there are frequent changes in personnel, nondiscretionary access control is useful since the access controls are based on the role or title of the individual in the organization and need not be changed whenever a new person takes over that role.

Controls

Information system security processes need and use controls. Controls are implemented to mitigate risk and reduce the potential for loss. Controls are commonly categorized into the three ways they are used: *preventive, detective,* or *corrective.*

Preventive controls.   These are put in place to inhibit harmful occurrences. Preventative controls are designed to achieve two things: lower the amount and impact of unintentional errors entering the system, and prevent unauthorized intruders accessing the system either internally or externally.

Detective controls.   These are established to discover harmful occurrences. Detective controls are used to detect an error once it has occurred. These controls operate after the fact, as opposed to preventative controls. For example, these controls can be used to track an unauthorized transaction for prosecution, or lessen an error's impact on the system by identifying it quickly. An example of this type of control is an audit trail.

Corrective controls.   These are used to restore systems that are victims of harmful attacks. Corrective (or recovery) controls are implemented to help mitigate the impact of a loss event through data recovery procedures. They can be used to recover damage, such as restoring data inadvertently erased from floppy diskettes, getting the system back on line after a denial-of-service attack.

Based upon how the controls are implemented, controls can also be administrative, logical, or physical.

Administrative controls include policies and procedures, security awareness training, background checks, work habit checks, review of vacation history, and increased supervision.

Logical or technical controls involve restriction of access to systems and the protection of information. Examples of these types of controls are encryption, smart cards, access control lists, and transmission protocols.

Physical controls incorporate guards and building security in general: locking doors, securing server rooms, securing laptops, protecting cables, separating duties, and backing up files.

Accountability

Controls provide accountability for individuals accessing sensitive information. Accountability is accomplished through access control mechanisms requiring identification and authentication and through the audit function. These controls should be in accordance with, and accurately represent, the organization's security policy discussed previously.

In this chapter, you have examined the basic goals of security and the various methodologies used to achieve them. Moving on to Chapter 5, you will see how security is implemented in various wireless systems.

CHAPTER 5

Security Technologies

This chapter describes security technologies that directly affect wireless security, including cryptographic technologies and public key infrastructure (PKI), Wired Equivalent Privacy (WEP), WTLS, and Bluetooth security. Next the chapter gives some examples of wireless tools, such a wireless VPN, packet sniffer, and an access point with advanced security features. The chapter concludes with a discussion of why it is important to implement security monitoring and testing.

Cryptographic Technologies and Public Key Infrastructure

There are two main types of cryptographic technologies: symmetric key (secret key, private key) cryptography and asymmetric (public key) cryptography. In symmetric key cryptography, both the receiver and the sender share a common secret key. In asymmetric key cryptography, the sender and receiver share public keys and private keys. These public and private keys are related mathematically, and a person's private key cannot be derived from his or her public key.

Because of the amount of computation involved in public key cryptography, computation of private keys is around a thousand times faster than public key cryptography. This means that most wireless devices lack the computational power necessary to handle encryption algorithms. For example, in a benchmark study conducted by Ericsson, Web-enabled mobile phones took as long as 15 minutes to handle a Rivest, Shamir, and Adleman (RSA) handshake necessary for WTLS connections. Elliptic-curve cryptography (ECC) algorithms are much less processor-intensive than other algorithms, and some designers say they are more secure. To understand all this, the following subsections offer definitions of a number of symmetric and asymmetric key crypto systems.

Secret Key Cryptography (Symmetric Key)

Most computer users are more familiar with secret key cryptography than with public cryptography. In secret key cryptography, the sender and receiver both know a secret key. The sender encrypts the plaintext message with the secret key and the receiver decrypts the message with the same secret key. Obviously, there is a challenge in making the secret key available to both the sender and receiver without compromise. For increased security, the secret key should be changed at frequent intervals; in fact, ideally, a specific secret key should be used only once.

An important property of any secret key cryptographic system is that the same key can encipher and decipher the message. If large key sizes (greater than 128 bits) are used, secret key systems are very difficult to break. These systems are also relatively fast, hence are used to encrypt large volumes of data. Because of this feature there are many symmetric key algorithms available.

There's a problem with using a symmetric key system, however: because the sender and receiver must share the same secret key, the sender requires a different key for each intended receiver. A commonly used solution to this problem is to use public key cryptography to transmit a symmetric session key that can be used for a session between the sender and receiver. Time stamps can be associated with this session key so that it is valid only for a specified period of time. Time-stamping is a counter to replay, wherein a session key is somehow intercepted and used at a later time. Symmetric key systems, however, do not provide mechanisms for authentication and nonrepudiation.

Data Encryption Standard

The Data Encryption Standard (DES) is probably the best-known symmetric key system. DES is a symmetric key cryptosystem and was devised in 1972 as a derivation of the Lucifer algorithm developed by IBM. DES is used for commercial and non-classified purposes. DES describes the Data Encryption Algorithm (DEA) and is the name of the Federal Information Processing Standard

(FIPS) 46-1 adopted in 1977. DEA is also defined as ANSI Standard X9.32. The National Institute of Standards and Technology (NIST) recertified DES in 1993, but DES will not be recertified again, as it will be replaced by the Advanced Encryption Standard (AES).

DEA uses a 64-bit block size and uses a 56-bit key. It begins with a 64-bit key and strips off 8 parity bits. DEA is a 16-round cryptosystem and was originally designed for implementation in hardware. With a 56-bit key, one would have to try 2^{56} or 70-quadrillion possible keys in a brute force attack. Even though the number is huge, large numbers of computers cooperating over the Internet could try all possible key combinations. Because of this vulnerability, the U.S. Government has not used DES since November 1998. Triple DES, three encryptions using the DEA, has replaced DES and will be used until the AES, described next, is adopted.

It has been proven that encrypting plaintext with one DES key and then encrypting it with a second DES key is no more secure than using a single DES key. R. C. Merkle and M. Hellman showed that a known-plaintext meet-in-the-middle attack could break the double encryption in 2^{n+1} attempts. Therefore double DES was quickly discarded in favor of Triple DES. Triple DES obtains a stronger encryption by encrypting the message three times. Triple DES and DES are specified in Federal Information Processing Standard (FIPS) 46-3.

Advanced Encryption Standard

Announced in January 1997 by the National Institute of Standards and Technology (NIST), the AES is a block cipher intended to replace DES (though it's likely that Triple DES will remain an approved algorithm for U.S. government use). And after soliciting candidate encryption algorithm submissions, on October 2, 2000, NIST announced the selection of the Rijndael Block Cipher as the proposed AES algorithm. The new FIPS publication will specify the cryptographic algorithm for use by the U.S. government, to protect sensitive but unclassified information.

Rijndael, developed by Belgian cryptographers Dr. Joan Daemen and Dr. Vincent Rijmen, is expected to be adopted by other private and public organizations in the United States and around the world. AES has been approved by NIST as FIPS-197, and vendor adoption is expected to begin shortly.

Public (Asymmetric) Key Cryptosystems

Unlike secret key cryptosystems, which make use of a single key known to sender and receiver, public key systems employ two keys, a public key and a private key. The public key is made available to anyone who wants to encrypt a message before sending it; the private key is used to decrypt the message.

One-Way Function

Public key cryptography is possible through the application of a one-way function, which is easy to compute in one direction but difficult to compute in the reverse direction. For such a function, if $y = f(x)$, it would be easy to compute y given x, but very difficult to derive x given y. A good analogy is the telephone directory: whereas it is easy to find a number if you have the name, trying to find name if you only know the number is a daunting task.

For a one-way function to be useful in the context of public key cryptography, however, it needs to have a *trapdoor,* a secret mechanism that allows the user to easily accomplish the reverse function in the one-way function. Thus, if you know the trapdoor, you can easily derive x in the previous example, given y. In the context of public key cryptography, it is very difficult to calculate the private key from the public key unless you know the trapdoor.

Public Key Algorithms

A number of public key algorithms have been developed, some of which algorithms are applicable to digital signatures, encryption, or both. But because there are more calculations associated with public key cryptography, it is 1,000 to 10,000 times slower than secret key cryptography. Thus, hybrid systems have evolved that use public key cryptography to safely distribute the secret keys used in symmetric key cryptography.

Some of the important public key algorithms that have been developed include RSA, the Diffie-Hellman key exchange protocol, and Elliptic Curve Cryptography.

RSA

The RSA algorithm was invented in 1978 by Ronald L. Rivest, Adi Shamir, and Leonard Adleman. RSA is derived from the last names of its inventors, Rivest, Shamir, and Adleman. This algorithm is based on the difficulty of factoring a number, n, that is the product of two large prime numbers. Each number may be something like 200 digits long.

Thus, the difficulty of obtaining the private key from the public key is a hard, one-way function equivalent to the difficulty of finding the prime factors of n. RSA can be used for encryption, key exchange, and digital signatures.

Diffie-Hellman Key Exchange

The Diffie-Hellman Key Exchange enables users to exchange secret keys over an insecure medium without exposing the keys. The protocol allows two users to exchange a secret key over an insecure medium without an additional session key. The method was described by Dr. W. Diffie and Dr. M.E. Hellman in 1976, which subsequently provided the basis for additional public key cryptography development.

Elliptic-Curve Cryptography

Elliptic-curve cryptography (ECC) is another approach to public key cryptography. Elliptic curves are usually defined over finite fields such as real and rational numbers, and implement an analog to the discreet logarithm problem.

Though elliptic-curve algorithms are similar to the RSA or Diffie-Hellman algorithms commonly used in the so-called handshake between two ends of a transaction or digital signature, proponents of elliptic-curve cryptography say its algorithms are as secure, but faster, than RSA and Diffie-Hellman due to a shorter encryption key. This is because the mathematical problem a hacker has to solve to crack the encryption is more difficult: Instead of factoring an unknown number, a hacker must find an undefined point on a theoretical curve. And because the encryption key does not have to be as long, it runs faster.

Furthermore, because it is more difficult to compute elliptic curve discreet logarithms than conventional discreet logarithms or factoring, smaller key sizes in the elliptic curve implementation can yield higher levels of security. The development of the ECC algorithm reduces the conversion memory requirement, which is good news to the PDA world, since PDAs have less processing power than a conventional desktop computer.

Therefore, elliptic-curve cryptography is suited to hardware applications such as smart cards and wireless devices. Recently, ECC has been incorporated into the WTLS in the WAP. It is called WTLS Plus 1.1, which will make it possible for WAP-enabled PEDs to incorporate PKI.

Public Key Infrastructure

A point of compromise in a public key cryptographic system is an individual, A, who is posting a public key under the name of another individual, B. In this scenario, people who are using this public key to encrypt messages intended for B will actually be sending messages to A. Since A has the private key corresponding to the posted public key, A can decrypt the messages intended for B. To counter this type of attack, a certification process can be used to bind an individual to his or her public key.

ELLIPTIC-CURVE DIGITAL SIGNATURE ALGORITHM

Elliptic-Curve Digital Signature Algorithm (ECDSA) is currently an FIPS-approved algorithm for generating and verifying digital signatures. In contrast, ECC is not FIPS-approved for data encryption. The cryptographic strength of the ECC algorithm is currently the subject of much debate in the cryptographic community, and further research into this area is warranted.

A certificate authority (CA) acts as notary to verify a person's identity; it issues a certificate vouching for a public key of the named individual. The certification agent signs the certificate with its own private key. It is verified as the sender if its public key opens the data. The certificate contains the name of the subject, the subject's public key, the name of the certificate authority, and the period of time for which the certificate is valid.

To verify the CA's signature, its public key must be cross certified with another CA. The X.509 standard defines the format for public key certificates. The certificate is then sent to a repository that holds the certificates and certificate revocation lists (CRLs) that list revoked certificates.

The integration of digital signatures, digital certificates, and other services required for e-commerce comprise what's called the public key infrastructure. These services provide integrity, access control, confidentiality, authentication, and nonrepudiation for electronic transactions.

Department of Defense Wireless PKI Initiative

In January 1999, the Department of Defense (DoD) PKI initiative established the facilities, specifications, and policies needed by the DoD to use public key-based digital certificates for information system security, workflow processing, electronic commerce, secure communications, and email within the agency, as well as with organizations of other branches of the federal government. Standards provide the basis for the services provided by the PKI. Standards that influence the PKI include those of the ISO, the IETF, and the NIST.

The DoD PKI provides the services necessary to receive requests for certificates, issue certificates, and otherwise respond to requests for certificates, revoke certificates, publish the CRLs, and maintain a directory service that enables users to retrieve certificates, CRLs, and subscriber contact information. Utilization of the DoD PKI, with certificates bound to an individual user, will enable wireless devices to implement strong identification, authentication, and nonrepudiation procedures.

Many of the current security products, such as wireless VPNs for 802.11 WLANs and mobile VPNs for handheld PEDs, are being designed to use the standard X.509v3 certificate that is supported by the DoD PKI initiative. Compatibility with the DoD PKI is a requirement for products that use encryption technology involving public and private key pairs.

NOTE Implementation of the DoD PKI is still evolving; the most current information is available from the Defense Information Systems Agency, at: http://www.disa.mil/infosec/pki-int.html.

Unfortunately, most wireless PEDs lack secure storage for digital certificates. One question regarding the use of certificates (DoD, PKI, or commercial) with wireless PEDs is how they will actually interface with devices. The answer may lie in a current DoD initiative regarding the *common access card* (CAC), a smart card to be used for storage of a user's individual certificate. However, the CAC and reader were originally designed to interface with desktop and laptop PCs connecting to a wired network. Another option, Web-enabled mobile phones supporting the WAP version 1.2 standard and the use of a WIM smart card to store user certificates should become standard in the United States soon.

At the time of this writing, however, authentication vulnerabilities continue to exist for the use of smart cards, primarily caused by loss or theft of mobile devices with their smart cards still embedded. Therefore, to guard against the risk of unauthorized use, current smart card implementation should require users to enter a separate PIN for access to their certificates.

Mobile PKI

PKI for mobile applications provides encryption of communications and mutual authentication of the user and application provider. Concern associated with "mobile PKI" relates to the possible time lapse between the expiration of a public key certificate and the reissuance of a new valid certificate and associated public key.

This dead time may be critical in disasters or time-sensitive situations. One solution to this problem is to generate one-time keys to use for each transaction. Authentication and authorization can be performed in the mobile device using smart cards to execute PKI-enabled transactions.

Wired Equivalent Privacy

The IEEE 802.11b standard defines an optional encryption scheme called Wired Equivalent Privacy (WEP), which includes a mechanism for securing wireless LAN data streams. WEP was part of the original IEEE 802.11 wireless standard. This standard's algorithms enable RC4-based, 40-bit data encryption to prevent an intruder from accessing the network and capturing wireless LAN traffic.

Originally intended only to supply privacy-type security on par with a wired network, the objective of WEP is to provide an equivalent level of security and privacy comparable to a wired Ethernet 802.3 LAN. WEP uses a symmetric scheme wherein the same key and algorithm are used for both encryption and decryption of data.

The features of WEP include:

- Access control, to prevent users without the correct WEP key (who are, therefore, unauthenticated) from gaining access to the network.
- Privacy, to protect wireless LAN data streams by encrypting them and allowing decryption only by users who have the correct WEP keys.

Although any support for WEP in a mobile device is optional, support for WEP with 40-bit encryption keys is a requirement for Wi-Fi certification by the Wireless Ethernet Compatibility Alliance (WECA), so its members invariably support WEP.[1] Some vendors implement their encryption and decryption routines in software, while others use hardware accelerators to minimize the performance degradation inherent in encrypting and decrypting the data stream.

Let's examine how WEP encrypts and decrypts the data stream.

WEP Encryption

When WEP encrypts data, two processes are applied to the plaintext data: one to encrypt the plaintext, the other to protect against unauthorized data modification. Here's the procedure:

1. The 40-bit secret key is concatenated with an 24-bit initialization vector (IV), resulting in a 64-bit total key size.

2. The resulting key is input to the pseudo-random number generator (PRNG).

3. The PRNG (RC4; described below) outputs a pseudo-random key sequence based on the input key.

4. The resulting sequence is used to encrypt the data by doing a bitwise XOR.

The result: encrypted bytes equal in length to the number of data bytes that are to be transmitted in the expanded data, plus 4 bytes. This is because the key sequence is to protect the integrity check value (ICV, 32-bits) as well as the data. To protect against unauthorized data modification, an integrity algorithm (CRC-32) operates on the plaintext to produce the ICV.

Figure 5.1 shows the WEP encryption algorithm.

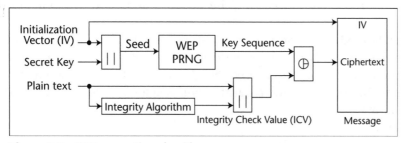

Figure 5.1 WEP encryption algorithm.

[1] For the latest information on Wi-Fi or WECA, visit www.wi-fi.org.

WEP Decryption

To decrypt the data stream, WEP follows this process:

1. The IV of the incoming message is used to generate the key sequence necessary to decrypt the incoming message.

2. The ciphertext, combined with the proper key sequence, yields the original plaintext and ICV.

3. The decryption is verified by performing the integrity check algorithm on the recovered plaintext and comparing the output ICV^1 to the ICV transmitted with the message.

4. If ICV^1 is not equal to ICV, the received message is in error, and an error indication is sent back to the sending station. Mobile units with erroneous messages are not authorized.

Figure 5.2 shows the WEP decryption algorithm.

WEP RC4

WEP is implemented using the RC4 encryption engine, a stream cipher that takes a fixed-length key and produces a series of pseudo-random bits that are XOR'ed with the plaintext to produce ciphertext, and vice versa. RC4 is used in the popular Secure Sockets Layer (SSL) Internet protocol and many other cryptography products.

The WEP RC4 PRNG is the critical component of the WEP process, as it is the actual encryption engine. The IV extends the useful lifetime of the secret key and provides the self-synchronous property of the algorithm. The secret key remains constant, while the IV changes periodically.

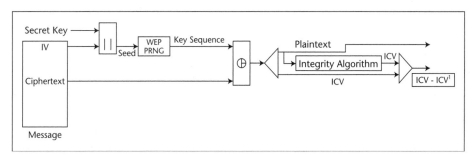

Figure 5.2 WEP decryption algorithm.

Since there is a one-to-one correspondence between the IV and the output, the data in higher-layer protocols like IP is usually predictable. An eavesdropper can readily determine portions of the key sequence generated by the key-IV pair. Using the same pair for successive messages may reduce the degree of privacy. Thus, changing the IV after each message is a simple method of preserving the effectiveness of WEP; but, note, several new products that use different algorithms, such as 3DES and ECC, are becoming available, and they will provide better communications security.

Also, RC4 will likely be dropped in favor of the aforementioned Advanced Encryption Standard (AES). It's believed that a block cipher such as AES will better protect traffic from attacks that attempt to modify data in transit. The first AES-based security systems should be available on the market by the end of 2002.

WEP Authentication Methods

A client cannot participate in a wireless LAN until that client has been authenticated. The authentication method must be set on each client, and the setting should match that of the access point with which the client wants to associate. The IEEE 802.11b standard defines two types of authentication methods: *open* and *shared key*.

Open System Authentication

Open system authentication is the default authentication protocol for 802.11. As the name implies, open system authentication authenticates anyone who requests authentication. With open authentication, the entire authentication process is done in cleartext, and a client can associate with an access point even without supplying the correct WEP key.

The open system authentication is considered a null authentication; that is, the station can associate with any AP and listen to all plaintext data that are sent. It is usually implemented where ease of use is the main issue and the network administrator does not want to deal with security at all. In open system mode, stations and APs are essentially using WEP as an encryption engine only.

Shared Key Authentication

Shared key authentication involves a shared secret key to authenticate the station to the AP. It uses a standard challenge and response, along with a shared secret key, to provide authentication to the station that's attempting to join the network. It allows a mobile station to encrypt data using a common key.

WEP allows an administrator to define a shared key for authentication. Access is denied to anyone who does not have an assigned key. The shared key used to encrypt and decrypt the data frames is also used to authenticate the station, but this is considered a security risk. However, the shared key authentication approach provides a better degree of authentication than the open system approach. For a station to use shared key authentication, it must implement WEP.

Four frames are exchanged in the authentication process:

1. The new station sends an authentication frame to the access point with the WEP bit = 1.

2. The AP returns an authentication frame with challenge text.

3. The new station uses the shared key and initialization vector to encrypt the challenge text, and generates an integrity check value. This frame is sent to the AP with the IV and ICV. The AP decrypts the text and compares its ICV with the one it received.

4. If they match, it sends an authentication frame to indicate success. If it does not match, it returns an authentication frame indicating the reason for failure.

Figure 5.3 illustrates the operation of shared key authentication.

With shared key authentication, the access point sends the client a challenge text packet that the client must encrypt with the correct WEP key and return to the access point. If the client has the wrong key or no key, it will fail authentication and will not be allowed to associate with the access point.

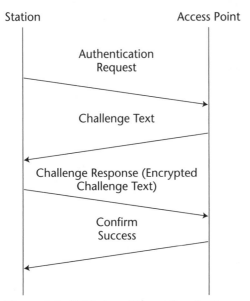

Figure 5.3 WEP shared key authentication.

> ### SECURE SOCKETS LAYER
>
> The Secure Sockets Layer (SSL) has been used for many years to secure communications between Web sites and Web browsers. Recent advancements in CPU power and speed, and increased available memory in the smaller PDAs, has led to a renewed interest in this proven protocol to protect wireless communications, although other standards are challenging its use.

A more detailed description of the shared key authentication procedure is as follows:

1. The requesting mobile device, the initiator, sends an authentication request management frame, indicating that it wants to use shared key authentication.

2. The recipient of the authentication request, the responder, responds by sending an authentication management frame containing 128 octets of challenge text to the initiator.

3. The challenge text is generated by using the WEP pseudo-random-number generator (PRNG) with the shared secret and a random initialization vector.

4. Once the initiator receives the management frame from the responder, it copies the contents of the challenge text into a new management frame body.

5. This new management frame body is then encrypted with WEP using the shared secret, along with a new IV selected by the initiator.

6. The encrypted management frame is then sent to the responder.

7. The responder decrypts the received frame and verifies that the 32-bit CRC integrity check value is valid and that the challenge text matches that sent in the first message.

8. If they match, the authentication is successful; then the initiator and the responder switch roles and repeat the process to ensure mutual authentication.

It's important to remember that it is stations being authenticated here, not users. This authentication method can only verify that particular users belong to a certain group with access rights to the network; it cannot distinguish one mobile user from another.

WEP Key Management

The secret shared key resides in each station's management information database. Though the IEEE 802.11 standard does not specify how to distribute the keys to each station, it does provide two schemes for managing the WEP keys on a wireless LAN:

- A set of four default keys is shared by all stations, including the wireless clients and their access points.
- Each client establishes a key mapping relationship with another station.

The first method provides a window with four keys. When a client obtains the default keys, that client can communicate securely with all other stations in the subsystem. A station or access point can decrypt packets encrypted with any one of the four keys. Transmission is limited to one of the four manually entered keys. The problem with this scheme is that when the default keys become widely distributed, they are more likely to be compromised.

In the second scheme, each client establishes a key-mapping relationship with another station, called a key mappings table. In this method, each unique MAC address can have a separate key; hence, this is thought to be a more secure form of operation because fewer stations have the keys.

Having a separate key for each user helps reduce the chance of cryptographic attacks, but enforcing a reasonable key period remains a problem, because the keys can only be changed manually, and distributing keys becomes more difficult as the number of stations increases.

Wireless Application Protocol Security

As described in Chapter 2, the Wireless Application Protocol (WAP) is widely used by mobile devices to access the Internet, as it's designed for mobile systems with small displays and limited bandwidth, primarily cell phones and personal digital assistants (PDAs). WAP is also used for television Internet browsing and in automotive displays. WAP is similar to TCP/IP, IP, and HTML in the wired world, but it has less overhead than TCP/IP, which is why it's so useful on mobile devices.

MEDIA ACCESS CONTROL AUTHENTICATION

In certain implementations, WLAN vendors support authentication based on the Ethernet physical address, or media access control (MAC) address, of a client. An access point will allow association by a client only if that client's MAC address matches an address in an authentication table used by the access point. Each access point can limit the clients of the network to those using a listed MAC address. If a client's MAC address is listed, then he or she is permitted access to the network. If the address is not listed, then access to the network is prevented.

> **WEP2**
>
> The IEEE 802.11i working group is developing a series of patches addressing WEP's vulnerable encryption methodology. Changes include modifying the way systems create and use the initialization vector (IV) and key used in encrypting network traffic, which have become the basis for widely publicized WEP cracks.[2]
>
> Other modifications are aimed at protecting the system against replay attacks, forged packets, and IV collision attacks. Additional changes to both WEP and the overall 802.11 security framework are expected over the long term. RSA Security has released a patch that can be used in current WEP implementations. The technology, known as *fast-packet keying*, reduces the similarity of WEP keys used to encrypt successive packets, a flaw that is widely exploited to crack WEP-encrypted traffic. The IEEE approved the patch in December 2001.

The purpose of this discussion is to address the WAP security layer, the Wireless Transport Layer Security protocol (WTLS), so let's begin by reviewing the entire WAP protocol stack (shown in Figure 5.4):

- Wireless Markup Language (WML) and Script
- Wireless Application Environment (WAE)
- Wireless Session Protocol (WSP)
- Wireless Transaction Protocol (WTP)
- Wireless Transport Layer Security Protocol (WTLS)
- Wireless Datagram Protocol (WDP)

Wireless Transport Layer Security

The Wireless Transport Layer Security Protocol (WTLS), is WAP's communications security protocol. It operates above the Transport Protocol layer and provides the upper-level layer of the WAP with a secure transport service interface. The interface preserves the transport interface below it and presents methods to manage secure connections. The primary purpose of the WTLS is to provide privacy, data integrity, and authentication for WAP applications, to enable safe connections to other clients.

The WTLS supports a group of algorithms to meet privacy, authentication, and integrity requirements. Currently, privacy is implemented using block ciphers, such as DES-CBC, IDEA, and RC5-CBC. RSA- and Diffie-Hellman-based key exchange suites are supported to authenticate the communicating parties. Integrity is implemented with SHA-1 and MD5 algorithms.

---

[2]In addition to the WEP cracks referred to in the book, recent URLs for WEP crack activity can be found at: http://lists.anti-dmca.org/pipermail/dmca_discuss/2001-August/000044.html, http://www.lava.net/~newsham/wlan/, and http://sourceforge.net/projects/wepcrack.

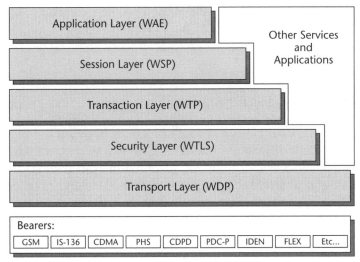

Figure 5.4   The WAP protocol stack.

For secure wireless communications, the client and the server must be authenticated and the connection encrypted. WTLS provides three classes of security:

Class 1: Anonymous Authentication.   In this mode, the client logs on to the server, but neither the client nor the server can be certain of the other's identity.

Class 2: Server Authentication.   The server is authenticated to the client, but the client is not authenticated to the server.

Class 3: Two-Way Client and Server Authentication.   The server is authenticated to the client and the client is authenticated to the server.

WTLS is based on the Transport Layer Security (TLS) security layer used on the Internet, but with a number of modifications to accommodate the nature of wireless networks. For one, it has been optimized for low-bandwidth networks with relatively long latency. And because of the limited processing power and memory of mobile devices, fast algorithms are implemented in the algorithm suite. In addition, restrictions on export and the using of cryptography must be observed. The WTLS is the first attempt to provide a secure

HDML AND C-HTML

The Handheld Device Markup Language (HDML) is a simpler alternative to WML, and actually preceded WML. It contains minimal security features, however. A direct competitor to WAP is the Compact HTML (C-HTML.) C-HTML is essentially a stripped-down version of HTML, making display on a standard Internet browser possible. C-HTML is used primarily in Japan through NTT DoCoMo's i-mode service.

end-to-end connection for the WAP. The most common protocols, such as TLS v1.0 and SSL v3.0, were adopted as a basis of the WTLS. WTLS incorporates features such as datagram support, optimized packet size and handshake, and dynamic key refreshing.

End-to-End Security via the WAP Gateway

The WAP, by means of WTLS, provides end-to-end security between the two WAP endpoints, the mobile terminal and the WAP gateway, to prevent data being modified during transfer by, for example, so-called man-in-the-middle attacks. When the WAP gateway makes the request to the origin server, it uses the SSL below HTTP to secure the request. This means that the data is decrypted and encrypted at the WAP gateway. In addition to performing the conversion from WTLS to SSL, the WAP gateway also compiles applets and scripts, because most mobile devices do not have the capacity to incorporate interpreters in their browsers.

Two popular vendor implementations of WAP gateways are the Captaris Infinite WAP Gateway 2.0 and Nokia's WAP Server version 1.1. The Infinite gateway incorporates the Baltimore Telepathy WAP Security Toolkit (WST). The Nokia WAP Server 1.1 is WAP 1.1-compliant and runs on Windows NT and Unix. The Nokia WAP Server Security Pack includes SSL and supports two encryption versions, 56-bit and 128-bit. Other vendors that offer WAP 1.1 compliant gateway and server products include Ericsson, Motorola, CMG, and Openwave. Figure 5.5 shows a common WAP gateway configuration.

Filling the WAP Gap

It's important to point out a security issue associated with WAP, referred to as the WAP gap. Here's what causes the gap: The wireless session's data stream has to change security protocols, from WTLS to SSL, at the carrier's WAP gateway to continue on over the wired network. At the WAP gateway, the transmission protected by WTLS is decrypted and then reencrypted for transmission using SSL. This results in the data being temporarily in the clear on the gateway, hence subject to compromise if the gateway is not adequately protected.

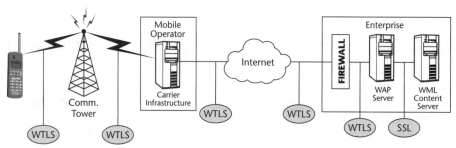

Figure 5.5 Common WAP gateway configuration using WTLS.

To fill the gap, two improvements to WAP have been suggested: one, use a client-side proxy server to transmit authentication and authorization information to the server of the wireless network; two, encrypt the data at the application layer above the transport layer of WTLS and maintain encryption throughout the transmission.

However, the safest implementation of a WAP gateway is for service providers to install the gateway in their own networks. Then the entire connection between the client and the service provider can be trusted, because the decryption will not take place until the transmission has reached the service provider's own network, not in the mobile operator's network.

The WTLS Record Protocol

The WTLS Record Protocol is a layer protocol that accepts raw data from the upper layers for transmission and applies the selected compression and encryption algorithms to the data. Moreover, the Record Protocol takes care of the data integrity and authentication. Received data is decrypted, verified, and decompressed, and then passed to higher layers.

The Record Protocol establishes secure communications via a three-step handshake process: first, a handshake protocol opens a connection; second, a change cipher spec protocol reaches agreement on a cryptographic protocol; and, third, an alert protocol sends error messages. These three protocols work as follows:

- *Handshake Protocol.* All the security-related parameters are agreed upon during the handshake. These parameters include protocol versions, cryptographic algorithms, and information on the use of authentication and public key techniques to generate a shared secret.

- *Change Cipher Spec Protocol.* The Change Cipher Spec is sent to its peer either by the client or the server. When the change cipher spec message arrives, the sender of the message sets the current write state to the pending state, and the receiver sets the current read state to the pending state.

- *Alert Protocol.* There are three types of alert messages: warning, critical, and fatal. Alert messages are sent either using the current compressed and encrypted secure state or under a null cipher spec without compression or encryption.

  Fatal.   If the alert message is labeled as fatal, both parties terminate the secure connection. Other connections using the secure session may continue, but the session identifier must be invalidated, so that the failed connection is not used to establish new secure connections.

  Critical.   A critical alert message results in termination of the current secure connection. Other connections using the secure session may continue, and the session identifier may also be used for establishing new secure connections.

Warning.   A warning alert message does not require a termination of the current secure connection. The receiving side has the option to close the connection, usually by sending a fatal alert message as a response.

Bluetooth Security Architecture

Bluetooth's security architecture provides a flexible security framework that dictates when to involve a user (e.g., to provide a PIN) and which actions the underlying Bluetooth protocol layers should follow to support the desired security checks. The Bluetooth security architecture is built on top of the link-level security features of the Bluetooth system.

The key component of the Bluetooth security architecture is the security manager, which is responsible for carrying out the following tasks:

- Storing security-related information on services and devices.
- Responding to access requests by protocol implementation or application.
- Enforcing authentication and/or encryption before connecting to the application.
- Initiating or processing input from an External Security Control Entity (ESCE), the device user, to set up trusted relationships at the device level.
- Initiating pairing and query PIN entry by the user. PIN entry might also be performed by an application.

The ESCE just mentioned has the authority and knowledge to make decisions on how to proceed in a manner consistent with the Bluetooth security architecture. The entity could be a device user or a utility application executed on behalf of the user and based on preprogrammed security policies. In the latter case, the utility could reside within or outside a particular device using Bluetooth wireless technology.

The Security Manager

During connection establishment, the Bluetooth security manager is queried and grants access based on the trust level of the device and the security level of the service. Both of these levels are taken from internal databases. A centralized security manager allows for easy implementation of flexible access policies because the interfaces to protocols and other entities are kept simple and are limited to query, response, and registration procedures.

The policies for access control are encapsulated in the security manager, so that the implementation of more complex policies does not affect the implementation of other policies. Implementations may determine whether the registration task is performed by the application itself or by a general management entity responsible for setting the path in the protocol stack and/or registering the service at the time of service discovery. The security manager maintains security information for services in security databases. Applications must register with the security manager before becoming accessible.

Link-Level Security Features

Link-level security features are available to implement authentication and encryption. Authentication prevents spoofing and unwanted access to critical data and functions, while encryption protects link privacy. In addition to these link-level functions, the frequency-hopping scheme used with the spread spectrum signal, as well as the limited transmission range of devices using Bluetooth wireless technology, make eavesdropping difficult.

However, enforcing security at only this level inhibits user-friendly access to more public-oriented usage models, such as discovering services and exchanging virtual business cards. Because of these different demands on user models, applications and devices must have more flexibility in the use of link-level security. To meet these demands, the Bluetooth specification defines three security modes that cover the functionality and application of devices:

Mode 1.   Refers to the *absence* of security, and is used when devices have no critical applications. In this mode, the devices bypass the link-level security functions, making them suitable for accessing databases containing nonsensitive information, such as business cards and calendars.

Mode 2.   Provides service-level security, allowing for more versatile access procedures, especially for running parallel applications, which may each have a different security requirement.

Mode 3.   Provides link-level security, whereby the link manager (LM) enforces security at a common level for all applications at the time of connection setup. Although less flexible, this mode enforces a common security level, and it is easier to implement than Mode 2.

Modes 2 and 3 are described more fully.

Mode 2: Service-Level Security

In Mode 2, it is possible to define security levels for devices and services. Devices are either trusted or untrusted, and their status determines the level of access to services:

- A trusted device is one that has a fixed relationship with another Bluetooth device and enjoys unrestricted access to all services. This is commonly referred to as being paired with the device.

- An untrusted device is one that has no permanent fixed relationship, and therefore cannot be trusted.

- A possible variation on this scheme is to set the trust level of a device so that it can access a specific service or a group of services. In this scenario, the requirement for authorization, authentication, and encryption are set independently, according to the type of service access the device must have. For example, for services that require authorization and authentication, automatic access is granted only to trusted devices, while all other devices must undergo manual authorization.

Determining Security Level of a Service

As described in the Bluetooth specification, the security level of a service is defined by three attributes:

- *Authorization required.* Access is granted automatically to trusted devices only—for example, those devices marked as such in the device database—or untrusted devices after an authorization procedure. Authorization always requires authentication to verify that the remote device is the correct one.

- *Authentication required.* The remote device must be authenticated before connecting to an application.

- *Encryption required.* The link must be changed to encrypted mode before access to the service is permitted. This attribute information is stored in the service database of the security manager.

If no registration has taken place, a default security level is used. For an incoming connection, the default is to require both authorization and authentication. For an outgoing connection, the default is to require authentication.

Mode 3: Link-Level Security

All link-level security functions are based on the concept of *link keys*, 128-bit random numbers stored individually for each pair of devices. Authentication requires no user input. It involves a device-to-device challenge and response scheme that employs a 128-bit common secret link key, a 128-bit challenge, and a 32-bit response. Consequently, this scheme is used to authenticate devices, not users.

The first time two devices attempt to communicate, an initialization procedure called *pairing* is used to create a common link key in a safe manner. The standard way of doing this assumes that the user has access to both devices at the same time. For first-time connection, pairing requires the user to enter a Bluetooth security code of up to 16 bytes (or 128 bits) into the paired devices. (Note: When this is done manually, the length of the code will usually be much shorter.)

Although the Bluetooth security code is often referred to as a personal identification number (PIN), it is not a code the user must memorize and keep secret, since it is only used once. If, for some reason, a link key is deleted and the initial pairing must be repeated, any Bluetooth security code can again be entered by the user. Where security requirements are low, it is possible to have a fixed code in devices having no user interface to allow pairing.

The authentication pairing procedure is as follows:

1. A common random number initialization key is generated from the user-entered Bluetooth security code in paired devices; it is used once and then discarded.

2. Through authentication, the Bluetooth security code is checked to see if it is identical to that in the paired devices.

3. A common 128-bit random-number link key is generated; it is stored temporarily in the paired devices. As long as this current link key is stored in both devices, no repetition of pairing is necessary, in which case only the normal procedure for authentication is implemented.

Encryption

Encryption for the baseband link requires no user input. After successful authentication and retrieval of the current link key, a new encryption key is generated from the link key for each communication session. The encryption key length ranges between 8 and 128 bits, depending on the level of security desired. The maximum encryption length is limited by the capacity of the hardware.

Each time the same two devices communicate via Bluetooth transceivers, the link key is used for authentication and encryption, without regard for the specific piconet topology. The most secure type of link key is a combination key, derived from the input of both devices.

For devices with low data-storage capabilities, there is also the option of choosing a unit key, which may be used for several remote devices. For broadcasting, a temporary key is required, which is not used for authentication, but for preventing eavesdropping from outside the piconet. Only members of the piconet share this temporary key.

Other Bluetooth Security Architecture Features

Security for legacy applications.   A default security level is available to serve the needs of legacy applications, that is, applications that are unable to make calls to the security manager on their own. On behalf of the legacy application, an adapter application that can use the Bluetooth specification is required to make security-related calls to the Bluetooth security manager. In such cases, the default policy will be used unless other settings are found in a security database related to the service. The settings in the database will take precedence over the default policy.

Flexible access.   The Bluetooth security architecture allows for selective access to services, meaning that access can be granted to some services and denied to others. The architecture supports security policies for devices that have some services communicating with changing remote devices for applications, such as file transfer and business card exchange. Access granted to a service on these devices does not open access to other services on the device and does not automatically or in an uncontrolled way grant future access to services on the device.

Limited user intervention.   User intervention is needed only to allow devices limited access to services or to set up a trusted relationship with devices, allowing unlimited access to services.

External key management.   The Bluetooth security architecture does not preclude the use of external key management procedures. Such key management applications might be able to directly distribute PINS or the link keys, for example.

Bluetooth security is not intended to replace existing network security features. For extremely sensitive requirements, such as e-commerce, or specialized requirements, such as personal instead of device-oriented authorization, additional application-level security mechanisms can and should be implemented.

Wireless Tools

The objective in this section is to examine three representative wireless tools, including a wireless VPN, a packet analyzer, and an access point with security features. Though hardly a complete list (the number of these products being rushed to market is expanding rapidly) these descriptions will give some idea of the features these products support.

Wireless VPNs

Virtual private networks (VPNs), discussed briefly in Chapter 1, are evolving to include not only mobile devices like laptops, but also wireless handheld devices like PDAs and smart phones, transmitting data in the clear to and from a secure corporate network is forbidden by most enterprise security policies, so transmission of enterprise data across wireless networks has not been widely deployed.

Traditionally, secure wireless transmission has required special technology, therefore interoperability with existing wired VPN infrastructures continues to be an obstacle to wireless VPN deployment. However, several companies are addressing the need for VPNs in the wireless environment, such as Avaya's Wireless VPN, Bluesocket's WG-100 Wireless Gateway, Certicom's movianVPN, Columbitech's Wireless VPN, Fortress Technologies' AirFortress, and NetMotion's Mobility. Let's take a look at Certicom's movianVPN product as a representative example.

movianVPN

Certicom's movianVPN software client provides end-to-end security from wireless handheld devices to the corporate intranet. movianVPN is a software VPN client that supports the VPN security standard, IPSec, to securely extend corporate intranet connectivity to mobile devices using a VPN infrastructure. The product is specifically designed for wireless handheld devices and inter-operates with multiple VPN gateways through an Internet connection established either through a wireless network that supports data services or through a wired connection to an ISP.

movianVPN establishes a secure IPSec tunnel to encrypt all traffic between the device and the gateway, decreasing the risk of eavesdropping, interception, or tampering. An Internet key exchange (IKE) negotiation is performed once the session has been established with the gateway, to negotiate the parameters for securing all of the ensuing communications.

All communication between the client and the VPN gateway is encrypted at Layer 3, thus securing all applications communicating over an IP connection from the device. movianVPN can implement either symmetric or asymmetric encryption algorithms to support legacy VPN systems. Elliptic curve cryptography (ECC) provides fast IKE negotiations where the gateway supports it.

movianVPN incorporates Certicom's 163-bit elliptic curve Diffie-Hellman (ECDH) algorithm for fast performance, as well as 768-bit and 1024-bit Diffie-Hellman (DH) algorithms for interoperability with the legacy base of enterprise VPN products.

In addition, movianVPN features:

- Is interoperable with various vendors' wired gateways.

- Establishes a secure tunnel to supply end-to-end encryption of all traffic between the device and the VPN gateway on the corporate intranet.

- Supports two-factor authentication, including SecurID, Cisco, Hewlett-Packard, Intel, Lucent, Nortel Networks, and Secure Computing gateways.

- Is compatible with a variety of IP-enabled wireless devices running Palm OS 3.5 and above or Microsoft Windows CE Handheld PC 2000, Pocket PC 3.0, or Pocket PC 2002. Future releases will support Symbian and other operating systems.

In addition to connectivity with a wired modem, Certicom strives to provide interoperability with all IP-based wireless WAN services such as CDPD, CDMA, iDEN, GPRS, GSM, and TDMA, and provides support for 802.11b and Ethernet LAN via NDIS. Connections over infrared (IR) are also supported; and support for Bluetooth is planned in the near future. movianVPN supported protocols and algorithms include IPSec Tunnel mode ESP SHA1, MD5, DES-CBC, 3DES-CBC, and IKE Aggressive Mode negotiation DH768, DH1024, and ECDH163 for key exchange.

Wireless Packet Sniffers

Wireless packet analyzers, or *sniffers*, basically work the same way as wired network packet analyzers: They capture packets from the data stream and allow the user to open them up and look, or decode, them. Several companies are offering wireless extensions to their wired-based packet sniffers, including WildPackets, the maker of EtherPeek. Also, Sniffer Technologies, a business unit of Network Associates, has an 802.11 protocol analysis module for its popular Sniffer Pro analyzer. We'll take a brief look at the AiroPeek product here; Appendix B describes the use of AiroPeek in detail.

NOTE A demo copy of, AiroPeek, WildPackets' wireless packet analyzer, is included on the website associated with this book.

AiroPeek

AiroPeek is a comprehensive packet analyzer for IEEE 802.11b wireless LANs, supporting all higher-level network protocols such as TCP/IP, AppleTalk, NetBEUI, and IPX. AiroPeek contains all of the network troubleshooting features of EtherPeek, its Ethernet packet analyzer. AiroPeek is used to isolate security problems by decoding 802.11b WLAN protocols, and analyzing wireless network performance with an identification of signal strength, channel. and data rates.

AiroPeek version 1.1.1 performs these functions:

- Decodes all 802.11b wireless protocols as well as all higher-level network protocols.

- Scans and selects channels by frequency (channel number), BSSID, or ESSID.

- Supports Symbol, Nortel, 3Com, Cisco Aironet 340 and 350, Intel, and Lucent adapters.

- Captures all 802.11b control, data, and management frames.

- Supports real-time and postcapture WEP decryption.

- Displays data rate, channel, and signal strength for each packet.

- Troubleshoots complex WLAN setups, including multiple base stations and wireless distribution systems.

- Identifies rogue transmitters including access points and users.

- Analyzes statistics for all traffic and for filtered sets of captured packets.

- Sets alarms, triggers, and notifications, all of which are user-definable.

- Outputs customized statistics (HTML, XML, text).

System Requirements

AiroPeek requires Windows 98, Windows ME, Windows NT 4.0 (service pack 3, or later), or Windows 2000. To optimize AiroPeek's overall performance, a Pentium 266 MHz or faster processor with 128 MB RAM is recommended. AiroPeek requires the installation of a special NDIS driver for packet capture and to control a supported network adapter.

AiroPeek version 1.1.1 supports the following wireless adapters:

- 3Com AirConnect 11 Mbps DSSS WLAN PC card

- Cisco Systems 340 Series WLAN adapter

- Cisco Systems 350 Series WLAN adapter

- Intel PRO/Wireless 2011 LAN PC Card

- Nortel Networks e-mobility 802.11 WLAN PC card

- Symbol Spectrum24 11 Mbps DS WLAN PC card

- Lucent/Agere ORiNOCO Wireless NIC adapter

NOTE As this book went to press, WildPackets was preparing to release a new expert version, AiroPeek NX, of its wireless LAN analyzer. The 802.11 expert network analyzer provides real-time NX expert diagnostics, in addition to its real-time frame decoding. WildPackets' NX technology includes powerful troubleshooting tools such as latency and throughput analysis, a graphical host and conversation map (*peer map*), and dozens of contemporary network problem diagnoses, including several specific to wireless LANs. AiroPeek NX also adds powerful site survey and security audit features, including a new signal strength meter, postcapture decryption, WEP ICV error tracking, data rate, channel, and average signal strength statistics, and a host of other wireless LAN statistics on the improved Nodes tab.

Cisco Systems' Wireless Products

Cisco's Aironet 350 series of wireless products includes some of the most advanced on the market, as far as features and security. The 350 access point is a wireless LAN transceiver that serves as the centerpoint of a stand-alone wireless network or as the connection point between wireless and wired networks. It has a host of features and enhancements, some of which are discussed here.

Aironet 350 Features

The Aironet access point uses a browser-based management system, but can also be configured by using a terminal emulator, a Telnet session, or the Simple Network Management Protocol (SNMP). Cisco has built in very advanced security features built to the Cisco IOS through LEAP, Cisco's wireless authentication method, and its support for WEP encryption, the Extensible Authentication Protocol (EAP) and MAC-based authentication, and RADIUS server support (see the "RADIUS" sidebar).

The 350 supports multiple authentication types, and implements three WEP key security features: message integrity check (MIC), WEP key hashing, and broadcast WEP key rotation. Also, it can use EAP to authenticate repeater access points, allowing the user to set up repeater access points to authenticate to the network like other wireless client devices. After the user provides a network username and password for the repeater, it authenticates to his or her network using LEAP, and receives and uses dynamic WEP keys.

The 350 can also block interclient communication by using publicly secure packet forwarding (PSPF). This feature prevents client devices associated to a bridge or access point from inadvertently sharing files with other client devices on the wireless network. PSPF provides Internet access to client devices without providing other LAN capabilities. With PSPF enabled, client devices cannot communicate with other client devices on the wireless network. This feature is useful for public wireless networks such as those installed in airports or on college campuses.

Network control features do the following:

- *Trace packets.* The packet-tracing feature can be used to view packets sent and received by the access point and by other wireless devices on your network. Users can view packets to and from a single wireless device, view packets to and from several wireless devices, or view all the packets sent and received through the access point's Ethernet and radio ports.

- *Assign ports.* The Port Assignments page can be used to assign specific network ports to repeater access points to maintain consistent network topology.

- *Collect data on wireless devices.* This feature enables accounting on the access point to send accounting data about wireless client devices to a RADIUS server on the user's network.

- *Limit associations.* This feature makes it possible to set a limit on the number of associations the access point accepts.

Aironet 350 Management Options

The Aironet 350 access point management system can be used through the following interfaces:

- A Web-browser interface
- A command-line interface (CLI)
- Simple Network Management Protocol (SNMP)

The access point's management system pages are organized the same way for the Web-browser interface and the CLI. The Cisco Discovery Protocol (CDP) can be enabled on the access point to improve network monitoring and browse, monitor, or configure other wireless devices on the network.

Other Aironet 350 management features include:

- *Carrier test tool.* The carrier test tool measures the amount of radio activity on each frequency available to the access point. The carrier test determines the best frequency for the access point to use.

- *Protocol filtering.* Protocol filters prevent or allow the use of specific protocols through the access point, and control packet forwarding from the access point to specific network devices with unicast and multicast filtering.

- *Hot standby.* An access point can act as a backup for another access point to provide uninterrupted network connectivity in case an access point malfunctions.

- *Automatic load balancing.* The access point automatically directs client devices to an access point that provides the best connection to the network, based on factors such as number of users, bit error rates, and signal strength.

Figure 5.6 shows a sample screen from the Aironet 350 system's parameters configuration page.

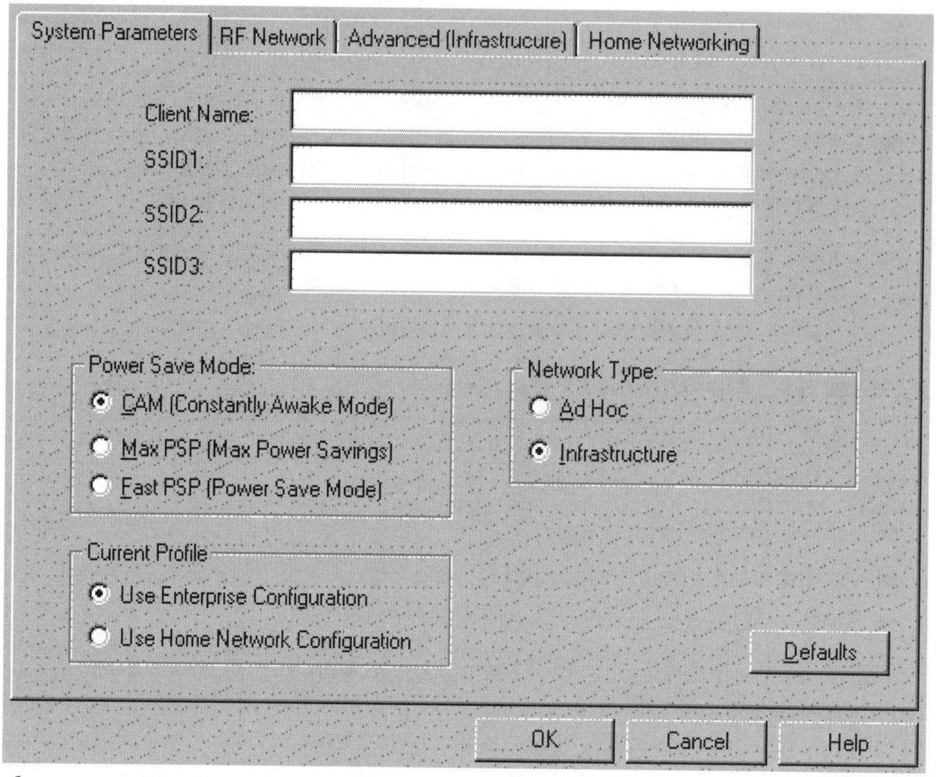

Figure 5.6 Aironet 350 system parameters configuration page.
(Courtesy, Cisco Systems Inc.)

One of the advantages of the Cisco Aironet 350 access point is the ability to align the antennae with the antenna alignment test. The antenna alignment tool displays constantly updated information on the strength and quality of signal between the access point and other wireless networking devices. Cisco offers a large selection of wireless antennae.

Security Monitoring and Testing

This chapter concludes with a brief discussion of two elements of security that are important to any well-rounded and successful security initiative: *monitoring* and *testing*. Together, monitoring and testing provide the enterprise with two resources to greatly improve its security posture and risk exposure. Although

RADIUS

The Remote Authentication Dial-in User Service (RADIUS) was adopted as a standard protocol by the Internet Engineering Task Force (IETF) to provide user authentication, including the use of dynamic passwords and password management. RADIUS is a distributed client/server system wherein the clients send authentication requests to a central RADIUS server that contains all the user authentication and network service access information (network access control lists). RADIUS is a fully open protocol, is distributed in source code format, and can be modified to work with any security system currently available on the market. It also can be used with TACACS+ and Kerberos, and provides CHAP remote node authentication.

these concepts are described here specific to wireless technologies, their impact on security overall is well documented.

The primary goal of monitoring is twofold: problem identification and problem resolution. Monitoring embodies the mechanisms, tools, and techniques that enable the identification of security events that could impact the operation of the company. It also includes the actions to identify the important elements of the events and report that information appropriately. Monitoring can also include watching for illegal software, checking the hardware for faults and error states, and tracking operational events for anomalies.

Obviously, monitoring entails many tasks, but we'll discuss only two elements here:

- Intrusion detection
- Penetration testing

Intrusion Detection Systems

Intrusion detection systems (IDS) monitor computer systems for evidence of an intrusion or inappropriate usage. This includes notifying the appropriate parties to take action to determine the extent of the severity of the incident and, subsequently, remedying the effects of the incident.

An IDS is a useful tool to assist in detective analysis of intrusion attempts. An IDS is used not only to identify intruders, but to create a sampling of traffic patterns. By analyzing activities occurring outside of normal clipping levels, the security practitioner can find evidence of events, such as covert in-band signaling or other abuses of the system.

An IDS is commonly used to monitor network traffic to determine if any violations of an organization's security policy have taken place. The IDS can detect intrusions that have circumvented or passed through a firewall or that are occurring within the local area network behind the firewall. A truly effective IDS will detect common attacks as they are occurring, including distributed attacks. This type of IDS is called *network-based* since it monitors network traffic in real time. Conversely, a *host-based* IDS is resident on centralized hosts.

Network-Based IDS

A network-based IDS usually provides reliable, real-time information without consuming network or host resources; it is passive while acquiring data. Since a network-based IDS reviews packets and headers, denial-of-service attacks can be detected. Also, since the IDS is monitoring the attack in real time, it can respond to an attack in progress to limit damage.

These systems commonly reside on a discrete network segment and monitor the traffic on that network segment. They usually consist of a network appliance with a network interface card (NIC) operating in so-called promiscuous mode, intercepting and analyzing the network packets in real time.

A problem with a network-based IDS system is that it will not detect attacks against a host by an intruder logged in at the host's terminal. If the network IDS, with some additional support mechanism, determines that an attack is being mounted against a host, usually it will not able to determine the type or effectiveness of the attack being launched.

Host-Based IDS

A host-based IDS can review system and event logs to detect an attack on the host and determine if the attack was successful. It is also easier to respond to an attack from the host. These systems use small programs called *intelligent agents* that reside on the host computer, monitor the operating system, continually write to log files, and trigger alarms. They detect inappropriate activity only on the host computer; they do not monitor the entire network segment. Detection capabilities of host-based ID systems are limited by the incompleteness of most host audit log capabilities.

IDS Detection Methods

An IDS detects an attack through two primary mechanisms: signature-based (sometimes called knowledge-based) systems, or statistical anomaly-based (sometimes called behavior-based) systems.

Signature-Based ID

In signature-based ID, signatures or attributes that characterize an attack are stored for reference. Then, when data about events is acquired from host audit logs or network packet monitoring, the data is compared with the attack signature database. If there is a match, a response is initiated. These systems use a database of previous attacks and known system vulnerabilities to look for current attempts to exploit these vulnerabilities; they trigger an alarm if the attempt is found. This IDS mechanism is more common than behavior-based ID.

This approach does have a weakness, however: the failure to characterize attacks that are slow and extend over a long period of time. To identify these types of attacks, large amounts of information must be held for extended time periods.

Another issue with signature-based IDS is that they only detect attack signatures that are stored in their database. A new type of attack will not be in the signature database and, therefore, will not be detected.

IDS VENDORS

Several companies make intrusion detection products. An excellent source for information regarding these products and vendors is Michael Sobirey's Intrusion Detection Systems page at:

www-rnks.informatik.tu-cottbus.de/~sobirey/ids.html;

currently it lists 92 host-and network-based intrusion detection (and response) systems.

This book's companion CD includes a demo version of an Internet security systems IDS product called RealSecure. RealSecure is an integrated host-based and network-based intrusion detection platform that uses a standards-based approach, comparing network traffic and host log entries to the known and likely methods of attackers. Suspicious activities trigger administrator alarms and other configurable responses.

Statistical Anomaly-Based ID

With this method, the IDS acquires data and defines a normal usage profile for the network or host being monitored. This characterization is accomplished through taking statistical samples of the system over a period of normal use. Typical characterization information used to establish a normal profile includes memory usage, CPU utilization, and network packet types. The assumption with this approach is that new attacks can be detected because they should produce abnormal system statistics.

These systems dynamically detect deviation from learned patterns of user behavior; they trigger an alarm when activity considered intrusive (i.e., outside of normal system use) occurs. This mechanism has two disadvantages: it will not detect an attack that does not significantly change the system operating characteristics; or it may falsely detect a nonattack event that caused a momentary anomaly in the system.

Penetration Testing

Penetration testing is the process of challenging the network's defenses by attempting to access the system from the outside using the same techniques that an external intruder, such as a cracker, would use. This testing gives the organization a better snapshot of its security vulnerabilities.

Among the techniques used to perform a penetration test are:

- *Scanning and probing*. Various scanners, like a port scanner, can reveal information about the network infrastructure and allow an intruder to access unsecured ports.

- *Demon dialing*. Demon (or war) dialers automatically test every phone line in an exchange to try to locate modems attached to the network. Information about these modems can then be used to attempt external unauthorized access.

- *Sniffing*. A protocol analyzer can be used to capture data packets that are later decoded to collect information such as passwords or infrastructure configurations.

Other techniques that are not solely technology-based may be used to complement the penetration test. These could include:

- *Dumpster diving*. Searching paper disposal areas for unshredded or otherwise improperly disposed of reports.

- *Social engineering*. The most commonly used technique, it includes getting information (such as passwords) just by asking for it.

WHITE-HAT HACKING

Due to the increasingly sensitive conflict-of-interest issues, many companies are initiating penetration testing programs using external, nonaffiliated companies called *white-hat hackers*. It has been found that such hacking organizations, which do not have an interest in hiding security flaws, more reliably give an impartial accounting of the state of the organization's security. An excellent source of information on white-hat, or ethical, hacking can be found at: www.tigertesting.com.

In Chapter 5 you saw how security fundamentals are applied to wireless systems. In Chapter 6, you will apply the knowledge you have gained to counter real-life wireless threats.

CHAPTER

6

Threats and Solutions

All computer systems and communications channels face security threats that can compromise the systems themselves, the services they provide, and/or the data stored on or transmitted between them. So, here, as we begin the last chapter in our journey to understand computer technology, wireless technology, and security methodologies, it comes down to two questions:

- What are the security issues with wireless systems?
- What can we do to address them?

This chapter is divided into two major sections: *threats* and *solutions*. We begin by addressing the first, threats, from two directions: threats to PEDs, and threats to WLANs. The solutions are divided into three categories: *standards and policies*, *software*, and *hardware*.

Security Threats to Personal Electronic Devices

As you're no doubt aware by now, the personal electronic device (PED) communications arena is expanding rapidly, with new products and technologies being proposed and introduced seemingly every day. Consider, for example: PDAs with wireless modems such as Palm wireless handhelds, Web-enabled cellular phones, and two-way pagers.

A PED uses one of the following for communications: serial cable (with or without cradle), infrared transceiver, wired modem, wireless modem, wired networking card, or wireless networking card. Wired network devices are generally considered more secure than their wireless counterparts, for the latter are usually implemented by subscribing to a commercial Internet or message service provider that is not under the direct control of the organization for maintenance or security. And although companies are spending billions of dollars to reduce the external threats to their networks, the simple fact is, PDAs make it easier for external and internal threats to bypass the companies' security measures. Wireless PDAs, due to their physical size and network connectivity, make it difficult for a security administrator to determine whether a PDA is being used internally.

The more widespread PDA use become, the higher the risk level will rise for corporations. The increase in PDA sales, in conjunction with PDA integration to wireless devices, means it is only a matter of time before malicious users start targeting PDAs to launch widespread, sophisticated attacks. Take, for example, the recently revealed exposure by Philip Hannsen of FBI information. According to the FBI's affidavit,[1] Hannsen often used a PalmPilot to breach the confidentiality of the FBI. Hannsen's PalmPilot was so essential to accomplishing his mission that he even requested the Russians upgrade his Palm III to a Palm VII so that he could encrypt and transmit data faster and more securely.[2]

With that in mind, let's look at the ways PDAs can be a threat to secure computing.

Vulnerability of PDA Operating Systems

PDAs have many of the same OS vulnerabilities found with PCs, but are much less secure than the standard desktop computer used in most organizations. Why? Because most desktop computers deployed in organizations have at least a minimal set of OS security features, which, typically, are installed and controlled in accordance with physical security guidelines, and where appropriate, use the appropriate level of communication security protection.

PEDs have not necessarily been designed to the same standards nor exposed to the same rigorous examination as desktop operating systems. OS security requirements for military systems are derived from AR 380-19 and DoD 5200.28-STD of the Orange Book (which was discussed in Chapter 4). Techniques to evaluate and test products against security functional requirements are spelled out in the ISO standard 15408, usually referred to as the Common Criteria. When compared against the OS against security requirements

---

[1]http://www.fas.org/irp/ops/ci/hanssen_affidavit.html.

[2]http://www.wired.com/news/print/0,1294,41950,00.html.

described in these standards, most PEDs receive a very poor rating. PED operating systems do not have provisions to separate one user's data from another (which is how they support discretionary access control, DAC); they lack audit capabilities; they have no support for object reuse control through the implementation of identification and authentication (I&A); and they do not provide data integrity protection. And even if a PDA is password-protected, a malicious user can retrieve the password of a target PDA by using the Palm debug mode. The password can then be decoded using simple tools such as the PalmCrypt tool. Another problem is that, even when the OS is password-locked, applications can still be installed onto the Palm OS without the owner's knowledge.

Obviously, the result is compromise of the integrity of the data. Once the password has been bypassed, all the information on the PDA is fully readable by the malicious user. Security administrators currently do not have the ability to determine if this type of attack has occurred, nor do they have any method to determine who was responsible for the attack. In short, such an attack is not traceable.

PDA Vulnerability Caused by Physical Loss

Probably the most common threat to a PDA is caused by the physical loss of the device. Though some technical solutions are available to protect against some of the OS security deficiencies just mentioned, none provide a countermeasure to the physical security concerns associated with the use of PDAs. The devices are so small and portable that loss of the device—hence, any information contained on it— is common. Simply put, users frequently lose their PDAs. Thus, PDAs inherently face a greater physical security risk than desktop computers. They are smaller, lighter, and have fewer connections to the physical environment. In addition, their mode of use puts them at greater risk, since they are generally used in open—as opposed to controlled—environments.

Once a device has been lost or appropriated by the wrong party, little stands between the appropriator and the data contained in the device. Should a wireless network device be lost or stolen, the person in control of the device could potentially access the network without authorization and without the knowledge of the security administrator. In extreme cases, it's possible that the data

LINUX PDAS

Since Linux OS PDAs were introduced in 2001, the threat to these devices is no longer limited only to desktops operating on a Windows platform; it now includes Unix and Linux machines. Malicious users can now launch attacks by developing or modifying Linux hacking tools, or use Linux-based PDAs as a launching platform for attacks against the network.

compromise could be so severe as to require that the entire network be recon-figured. The point is, if the device has any sensitive information on it, the information must be considered to have been compromised. For example, offi-cial government documents, marked "For Official Use Only, /SBU"[3] are some-times permitted to be sent via email over a government network. If such a message were received by a stolen PDA while it was connected to the network, it would be available to the thief of the device.

Identification and Authentication

I&A is required to provide a means of identifying who is authorized to use a particular system and to validate that the individual accessing the system is who he or she claims to be. A very basic, common method of I&A is to require a user ID and password to access a system. But many PDAs do not support user I&A for access to information stored on the device. In fact, most PDAs do not come with strong I&A features or with the security mechanism enabled. Factory default settings on most PDAs do not include enabling passwords or other I&A mechanisms. Therefore, it may be necessary to implement third-party software in order to obtain a reasonable level of control.

Vendors are attempting to provide third-party implementation of such I&A mechanisms. For example, the Navy currently uses a security software pack-age called the PDA Restrictor from IS/Complete with Palm OS mobile devices. It requires a user logon I&A password, to protect sensitive information on the computers.

Catching PDA Viruses

The majority of PDAs do not have antivirus software installed on them; nor does most desktop antivirus software scan for viruses during the HotSync process (which is when viruses are most often transferred to the PDA). Most PDAs do not have third-party software installed to detect, protect from, and remove malicious code. A survey reported in *Information Security Magazine* in January 2002, showed that 98 percent of all PDAs do not have any antivirus protection.

Currently, there are very few viruses in the wild to infect the Palm OS or other PDA operating systems. Perhaps this is a limitation of the OS, or perhaps it is because, as just mentioned, to transfer the virus to the handheld it is necessary to go through the HotSync procedure. But with wireless devices, this is going to be easier. If it becomes possible to transmit a virus via a PAN or near-field transmission, we may start to see the incidence of PDA and PED

---

[3]SBU stands for "Sensitive But Unclassified" a fairly low-level data classification rating. See Chapter 4 for more information on data classification ratings.

viruses grow. Of those known to exist already, we'll look at the details of three viruses that were written specifically for PDAs: Phage.963, Vapor.741, and LibertyCrack.

Phage.963

Phage.963 was the first virus designed for the Palm OS. Its symptoms are as follows: When an infected application is run, first, the screen is filled in dark gray, then the program terminates. This virus infects all third-party applications on the PDA device and overwrites the first section in the host .PRC file. When a new program is copied to the Palm system via IR transfer, this program will execute normally. If another application that is already infected is run, the newly transferred file will also become infected.

Phage.963 was released from an IRC chat room, and from there directly infected other Palm OS applications. Fortunately, it's easy to remove and doesn't do much damage. It also is known as Palm.Virus, Phage.Dropper, and Phage 1.0, and has a variant called Phage.1325.dr.

Vapor.741

Vapor.741, also released from an IRC Chat Room, works a little differently from Phage.963. Vapor.741 is a Trojan horse also designed for the Palm OS. When first run, it causes all third-party application icons to disappear, making it seem as if the programs had been deleted. But the files still exist, only their icons are missing. When this virus is run, it turns on the hidden bit for all applications, making them look as if they have been removed. Recovery requires a hard reset and HotSync. Vapor.741 is also called Vapor 666.

LibertyCrack

LibertyCrack is another Trojan horse that does a little more damage than the other two. This one also infects handheld devices running the Palm OS. It arrives masquerading as a crack for an application called "Liberty," which allows a Palm OS device to run Nintendo GameBoy games. The crack claims to convert the freely available shareware version of Liberty into the full registered version. When run, however, the Trojan attempts to delete all applications from the handheld and then reboot it.

On a Palm OS device, the LibertyCrack will appear in the launcher with the same icon as the Liberty application under the name Crack 1.1. On a PC, the Trojan will appear as a file named liberty_1_1_crack.prc, with a size of 2,663 bytes. The Trojan is generally installed to a Palm OS device from a host computer during a HotSync operation. It can also be beamed from one Palm device to another via infrared (more on infrared vulnerabilities in the next section).

OmniSky wireless Internet users may receive this Trojan via an email attachment. Liberty Crack is also known as liberty_1_1_crack.prc, Palm.Liberty.A, and Trojan.Palm.Liberty

Tapping Infrared Vulnerabilities

All Palm OS PDAs available today have the capability to pass data between them using an infrared (IR) port. The default setting typically requires both the person sending the data and the person receiving the data to confirm the data transfer. Nonetheless, there is the possibility that future OS versions could change this default or allow for serendipitous transfer of data.

Most PEDs do not come with encryption capabilities to protect sensitive information stored on them. PEDs that do provide encryption of stored data usually do not support a FIPS-approved encryption algorithm, such as DES and 3DES. Even if PDA users encrypt their data on their PDAs, when beaming data to and from other PDAs, often the data is not encrypted. During the transmission between two IR ports, encrypted data becomes just as vulnerable as plain data.

Another vulnerability of the IR port is the capability of the PDA to record IR signals. This enables a malicious user to control devices that operate via IR signals or spoof a device into thinking that the IR signal is coming from a legitimate source. For example, PDAs can record the IR signal used by auto alarms to lock and unlock vehicles. Once the signal has been recorded on the PDA, the signal can be retransmitted from the PDA to unlock the vehicle and disable the vehicle alarm. This technique has already been used by car thieves on the East Coast of the United States.

Users of PDAs should be aware of the promiscuous modes of their PDAs, some of which leave them open to beaming at their infrared ports. Also, a great deal of PDA hacking software is becoming available on the Internet.

Opening PED Network Backdoors

Some Palm PDAs have wireless connections that allow the downloading of email; and wireless modems are available as accessories for other makes of PDAs. If the wireless feature is used while the PDA is connected to a networked PC through the synchronization cradle, a backdoor into the network could be opened.

This vulnerability stems from the fact that PDAs are often used to connect to commercial servers on networks outside the organization. If they are also simultaneously connected to internal systems, they become a backdoor entry point into the installation network. For example, a PDA that is used to surf the Web via a wireless modem while connected to a desktop PC on a company network for file synchronization purposes could be used in this way.

PDA Transmission Interception

Any wireless PDA is at risk of having its communications monitored, interrupted, or even taken over if data is transmitted in the clear, that is, unencrypted. In a common session hijacking exploit, a third party could replace or augment communications from one or both of the original communicating parties.

Just as with a wired WAN connection, the data passes through many uncontrolled paths between the two communicating elements. The major difference is that the AP(s) and their associated servers are usually under the management and control of a commercial service provider, and not the implementing organization.

Wireless Network Threats

In the traditional wired LAN world, access to network resources is via a connection to an Ethernet port, therefore access to the LAN is governed by the physical access to the LAN ports. In contrast, in a WLAN environment, the data is transmitted by another medium using radio frequency (RF). Since RF has the capability to penetrate walls and ceilings, any WLAN client can receive it, intentionally or unintentionally, if it is within range.

With wireless signals clearly not limited by walls, wireless networks lend themselves to a host of attack possibilities and risks. And because wireless networks provide a convenient network access point for an attacker, potentially beyond the physical security controls of the organization, there is a significant and long-term security problem. For any network manager, these are serious concerns that have to be considered before introducing WLANs to an organization.

BLUETOOTH INTERFERENCE

As covered earlier, Bluetooth operates in the unlicensed 2.4-GHz band currently shared by other wireless communication standards such as 802.11b, HomeRF, and various home telecommunications systems. Eventually, as the number of open channels decreases, these devices start to interfere with one another. Also, the 2.4 GHz frequency is the operating frequency for microwave ovens, which can effectively jam radio transmissions. In an attempt to limit the impact of interference and fading, the Bluetooth radio uses a fast acknowledgment and frequency-hopping transceiver, which hops faster and uses shorter packets than other systems with the same frequency.

802.11 Vulnerabilities

The 802.11 standard provides only limited support for confidentiality through the Wired Equivalent Privacy (WEP) protocol, whose design contains significant flaws. The IEEE standards committee for 802.11 failed to address many of the difficult security issues, such as key management and a robust authentication mechanism.

WEP Weaknesses

To understand the problem caused by the 802.11 standard deficiencies, let's review the WEP construct. WEP was designed as a security option that sits on top of the IEEE 802.11b standard and adds privacy and authentication to wireless LANs. The 802.11b wireless technology uses WEP as a method of encrypting and decrypting wireless communications between a client and an access point connected to a wired LAN. WEP depends on the use of a secret key to encrypt and decrypt packets traveling between the wireless network card and access point. This encryption and decryption takes place using the Rivest Code 4 (RC4) algorithm. RC4 was developed in 1987 by Ronald Rivest and kept as a trade secret by RSA Data Security. On September 9, 1994, the RC4 algorithm was posted anonymously on the Internet on the Cyperpunks "anonymous remailer" list.[4]

The concept behind WEP is that, using encryption, the protocol could protect the data being transmitted with the same robustness as a wired LAN would. But WEP was not designed to withstand a directed cryptographic attack. In fact, it uses a hashing algorithm for its encryption, and most products implement a 64-bit shared key, 40 bits of which are used for the secret key and 24 bits are used for the initialization vector. The key is installed at the wired network AP and must be entered into each client as well. However, WEP does not use a FIPS-approved data encryption algorithm required for use in a military environment. The point is, WEP has well-known flaws in the encryption algorithms used to secure wireless transmissions.

Published WEP Attacks

A number of researchers have investigated attacks on the WEP. Here are brief overviews of the results of these investigations.[5,6]

---

[4]An excellent source for RC4 can be found at www.ncat.edu/~grogans/algorithm_history_and_descriptio.htm.

[5]Those interested in more on WEP vulnerabilities should refer to the following paper: "Your 802.11 Network Has No Clothes" at www.cs.umd.edu/~waa/wireless.pdf.

[6]Bill Arbaugh has a Web page which summarizes many 802.11 security problems at: www.cs.umd.edu/~waa/wireless.html.

- University of California, Berkeley, and Zero-Knowledge Systems researchers released a paper outlining the vulnerability of key stream reuse caused by the mismanagement of IVs. In their paper titled "Intercepting Mobile Communications: The Insecurity of 802.11,"[7] it was noted that all possible IVs could be exhausted in as little as five hours. This would permit an attacker to capture two encrypted packets using the same key stream, allowing the attacker not only to decrypt the contents of an encrypted packet, but also to insert or change traffic, redirect decrypted traffic to an alternate IP address, or even develop an IV dictionary to be used to decrypt any and all traffic traveling within a wireless network.

- "Weaknesses in the Key Scheduling Algorithm of RC4," a paper written in 2000 by Scott Fluhrer, Itsik Mantin, and Adi Shamir, exposed two significant weaknesses of RC4 in the key scheduling algorithm (KSA).[8] These researchers found that a small portion of the secret key determines a large portion of the initial KSA output. They also found an inherent flaw in WEP: the secret key can be easily derived by looking at the key stream used with multiple IVs. The authors discovered that this vulnerability is present not only in the current implementation of WEP but also in the proposed future standard, WEP2. Both the key and IV size made little difference in the time required to compromise the key.

- Rice University and AT&T Lab researchers put the aforementioned Fluhrer theory into practice by cracking encrypted packets and successfully demonstrating the severity of the flaw. While the researchers did not release the code necessary to mount the attack, it wasn't long before others did.

- In 2001, Nikita Borisov and a group of researchers from University of California, Berkeley, published a paper regarding weaknesses in the WEP RC4 stream cipher called "Security of the WEP algorithm."[9] They found that if two messages used the same key stream it might reveal information about both messages. Further, XOR'ing two ciphertexts that use the same key stream would cause the key stream to cancel out, and the result would be the XOR of the two plaintexts.

- Adam Stubblefield, an intern at AT&T Labs, was the first person to implement the Fluhrer attack mentioned previously (see Appendix D). He noted that an extra 802.2 header is added in IP traffic, making the attack easier, as every IP packet has the same first plaintext byte. In order for the attack to be successful, during the early phase of the attack, the first few key bytes must be guessed correctly.

[7]www.isaac.cs.berkeley.edu/isaac/wep-draft.pdf.

[8]www.securityfocus.com/cgi-bin/library.pl?cat=154&offset=10.

[9]www.isaac.cs.berkeley.edu/isaac/wep-faq.html.

Currently, there are two programs capable of exploiting the RC4 vulnerability: AirSnort, and WEPCrack. Both run under Linux, and require a relatively small amount of captured data, anywhere from 100MB to 1GB. AirSnort is a free open source program that collects encrypted network traffic then breaks the encryption so that data on the wireless network can be viewed.[10]

An IEEE task force, called Task Group E, is working on upgrading WEP to WEP2 with the intention of separating encryption and authentication functions so that the same static key does not need to be shared within a WLAN. However, the IEEE recognizes that WEP2 will not be the ultimate solution to WLAN's security problems, so it has also approved a draft to establish a stronger authentication and 128-bit key management system, tentatively called Enhanced Security Network (ESN). ESN's encryption will augment the weaker RC4 PRNG algorithm with the Advanced Encryption Standard (AES). ESN is not expected to be finalized until late 2002.

Service Set Identifier Problems

The service set identifier (SSID) is an identification value programmed in the access point or group of access points to identify the local wireless subnet. This segmentation of the wireless network in multiple networks is a form of an authentication check. If a wireless station does not know the value of the SSID, access is denied to the associated access point. When a client computer is connected to the access point, the SSID acts as a simple password, which provides a measure of security.

The wireless access point is configured to broadcast its service set identifier (SSID). When enabled, any client without a SSID is able to receive it and have access to the access point. Users are also able to configure their own client systems with the appropriate SSID, because they are widely known and easily shared. A problem caused by the fact that most access points broadcast the SSID in their signals is that several of these access points use default SSIDs provided by the manufacturers, and a list of those default SSIDs is available for download on the Internet. This means that it's very easy for a hacker to determine a network's SSID and gain access to it via software tools. Figure 6.1 shows an attack using the SSID.

---

[10]AirSnort is a play on Apple's trademarked name for its 802.11b implementation, AirPort. For more information on AirSnort, please visit airsnort.schmoo.com. For more information on WEPCrack, visit sourceforge.net/projects/wepcrack.

Target WLAN Network

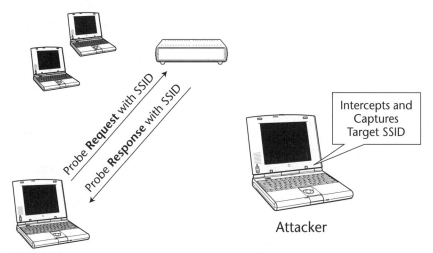

Figure 6.1 An SSID attack.

In summary then, implementing an SSID as a primary security feature is not a good idea, especially in a large network. SSID security alone is very ineffective for three reasons: The value is known by all network cards and access points; the value is easily accessibly through air and radio waves; and no encryption is provided. Moreover, use of WEP is optional, so often the only barrier preventing access to the network is the knowledge of the SSID, a very insecure practice.

Eavesdropping

Wireless technology is also vulnerable to eavesdropping, especially because intruders do not have to physically tap into a network. Whether on a different floor, across the room, or outside the building, as long as the intruder has a WLAN network card that has a promiscuous mode (that is, has the capability to capture every packet on the segment of the LAN), he or she can passively "sniff" your network traffic without gaining physical access. True, this can also happen on a wired LAN, but requires that the person use sensitive listening equipment, which has to be held close to the cable to listen to the electromagnetic waves. A wireless LAN is at risk of invasion *unless* the WLAN is set up to not accept signals from outside a specified user group; if it is not set up in this way, a third party could set up a communication device within the range and join in the network.

Also consider the following:

- Eavesdropping, or interception, constitutes a failure of the INFOSEC tenet of confidentiality, and is a threat to identification and authentication (I&A). All WLANs risk having communications monitored, interrupted, or hijacked. Many currently available commercial WLAN devices transmit all data unencrypted. With these devices, stray but useable signals are not uncommon as far as half a mile away.

- Covert monitoring of wireless LANs is simple. Unless specifically configured to prevent another WLAN device from joining the network, a WLAN device will accept communications from any device within its range. Some businesses are even setting up WLAN transmitters that will continuously broadcast messages that will be received and displayed on any compatible WLAN devices that come within range.

- The wired network is vulnerable to MAC or IP spoofing, which means an intruder can monitor unencrypted communications using a network sniffer. The wireless world is susceptible in the same way, the only difference being that the intruder doesn't need physical access in order to attempt the connection; he or she only has to be within signal range.

Eavesdropping over the Broadcast Bubble

The radio broadcast waves that are used to connect wireless network devices do not simply stop once they reach a wall or the boundary of a business; they continue to travel—into parking lots, other businesses, and elsewhere, in an expanding circle from the broadcast point, creating a so-called bubble of transmission radiation. The risk caused by the bubble should be obvious: Intrusive parties can eavesdrop on network traffic from wherever they can set up a laptop to intercept the signals. Though 802.11b standards specify that the broadcast range is only 150 to 300 feet, in reality, the signal travels much farther.

The point is, eavesdropping is very easy in the radio environment. When a message is sent over radio transmission, anyone and everyone equipped with a suitable transceiver in the range of the transmission can listen in. Keep in mind that the 802.11 standard uses frequency hopping spread spectrum (FHSS), direct sequence spread spectrum (DSSS), or infrared radio transmission types (described in Chapter 2), and that FHSS and DSSS operate in the 2.4GHz range, which can be easily transmitted through walls at distances of roughly a few hundred feet.

Furthermore, the 802.11 protocol inherently leaves the physical layer header unencrypted, providing critical information to the attacker. Therefore, data encryption is the critical layer of defense, but often data is transmitted unencrypted. Using wireless packet sniffers, an attacker can passively intercept wireless network traffic and, through packet analysis, determine login IDs and passwords, as well as collect other sensitive data.

MASQUERADING

Masquerading is the act of an adversary posing as a legitimate user in order to gain access to a wireless network or a system served by the network. For example, a user with inappropriate access to a valid network authenticator could access the network and perform unacceptable functions such as access a server and plant malicious code. Strong authentication is required to avoid masquerade attacks.

Transmission Alteration and Manipulation

Alteration and manipulation constitute a failure of the INFOSEC tenet of *integrity* of either the data transmission or on the data stored on a system. Alteration and manipulation means that data has been inserted, deleted, or otherwise modified on a system during transmission. An example would be the insertion of a Trojan horse program or virus on a user device or to the network. Protecting against illegal access to the network and its attached systems is one means of avoiding manipulation, using some form of communications protection, such as VPNs. As already noted, WEP can be used to protect information for privacy, but the encryption method implemented with WEP is not a strong, FIPS-approved algorithm.

Denial-of-Service Attacks

A denial-of-service (DoS) attack is an example of the failure of the tenet of *availability*. A DoS attack occurs when an adversary causes a system or a network to become unavailable to legitimate users, or causes services to be interrupted or delayed. Consequences can range from a measurable reduction in performance to the complete failure of the system. An example from the wireless world could be an external signal jamming the wireless channel. There is little that can be done to keep a determined adversary from mounting a DoS attack, because, as noted, wireless LANs are susceptible to interference and interception, hence often can be easily jammed.

Wireless networks are vulnerable to DoS attacks due to the nature of the wireless transmission medium. If an attacker makes use of a powerful transceiver, enough interference can be generated to prevent wireless devices from communicating with one another. DoS attack devices do not have to be next to the devices being attacked, either, they must be *within range* of the wireless transmissions.

Examples of techniques used to deny service to a wireless device are:

- Requests for authentication at such a frequency as to disrupt legitimate traffic.

- Requests for deauthentication of legitimate users. These requests may not be refused according to the current 802.11 standard.

- Mimicking the behavior of an access point and convincing unsuspecting clients to communicate with it.

- Repeatedly transmit RTS/CTS frames to silence the network.

The 2.4-GHz frequency range, within which 802.11b operates, is shared with other wireless devices such as cordless telephones, baby monitors, and Bluetooth-based devices. All these devices can contribute to the degradation of and interruption to wireless signals. In addition, a determined and resourceful attacker with the proper equipment can flood the frequency with artificial noise and completely disrupt wireless network operation.

War Driving

War driving (also *war walking*) is a term used to describe a hacker, who, armed with a laptop and a wireless adapter card, and traveling via a car, bus, subway train, or other form of transport, goes around sniffing for WLANs. Currently, two tools are freely available on the Internet that make it possible to carry out such an attack (they are described next).

The concept of war driving is simple: Using a device capable of receiving an 802.11b signal, a device capable of locating itself on a map, and software that will log data from the second when a network is detected by the first, the hacker moves from place to place, letting these devices do their job. Over time, the hacker builds up a database comprising the network name, signal strength, location, and ip/namespace in use. Via SNMP, the hacker may even log packet samples and probe the access point for available data.

To determine how effective war driving can be, computer security researcher and consultant Peter Shipley combined GPS equipment, an external antenna, his laptop, and his car to map wireless networks throughout the San Francisco Bay Area and Silicon Valley. In less than an hour he had collected vital information on nearly 80 wireless networks, including their network names, signal strengths, latitude and longitude, and a host of other data.

Common war driving exploits find many wireless networks with WEP disabled and using only the SSID for access control. And, as noted earlier, the SSID for wireless networks can be found quickly. This vulnerability makes these networks susceptible to what's called the "parking lot attack," where at a safe distance from the building's perimeter, an attacker gains access to the

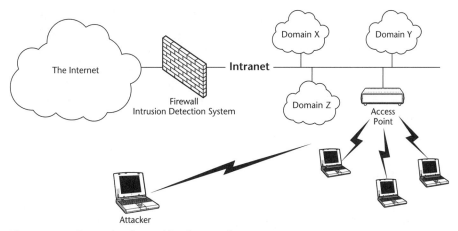

Figure 6.2   Example of a parking lot attack.

target network. Figure 6.2 shows an example of a parking lot attack into a network. Using such information, a war driver can determine which company was probed and the value of information contained in the network.

The two tools mentioned previously are Netstumbler[11] and IBM's Wireless Security Auditor.[12] They can provide a war driver with vital information, such as SSID and access point name, signal strength, the vendor of the access points, the firmware version of the access point, the encryption method, and the authentication method. It's also important to point out, however, that these tools are useful to network administrators as well: they can help NAs determine whether any rogue access points have been installed inside the network.

Going through WLAN Network Backdoors

We've already discussed backdoors to PEDs. It's also necessary to be aware that wireless solutions may create backdoors into LANs. Backdoors can make it possible to bypass all perimeter and host-based security mechanisms. Therefore, plans for wireless solutions must include implementation behind network perimeter access control devices, and connection through an approved wireless network AP or gateway. The wireless network AP or gateway solution selected should protect against vulnerabilities such as unauthorized network access and the "WAP gap" discussed in Chapter 5.

[11]www.netstumbler.com.

[12]www.research.ibm.com/gsal/wsa/.

Quite often the deployment of a wireless network opens a backdoor into the internal network, which gives an attacker access beyond the physical security perimeter of the organization. Compounding this vulnerability is the fact that the access control mechanisms available with current access points contain serious flaws making it easy for an adversary to subvert them. Furthermore, the wireless AP is essentially a hub, with all the security risks associated with a hub. Thus, all traffic is easy to monitor or intercept when connected to a wireless LAN.

Insertion Attacks

In this type of attack, unauthorized devices are deployed in order to gain access to an existing network. Laptops or PDAs can be configured to attempt access to networks simply by installing wireless network cards and setting up near a target network. If password authentication is not enabled on the network, it's a simple matter to get a connection to an access point and network resources.

Another type of insertion attack is the deployment of rogue access points, either by a hacker or by well-meaning internal employees seeking to enhance wireless coverage. Hacker-controlled access points can be used to entice authorized wireless clients to connect to a hacker's access point rather than to the network's intended access points. In addition, access points not authorized by the network administrator have the potential to be improperly configured and thus vulnerable to outside attack. This raises the risk of the interception of login IDs and passwords for future direct attacks on a network. The risk can be magnified if rogue access points are deployed behind the corporate firewall.

Uncontrolled Access Points

Typically, an access point has one or several methods available to control access to a wireless LAN, typically including use of a common SSID, to allow access based on MAC address, and WEP. Since the default authentication in 802.11 is open authentication, most systems will authenticate any user who requests connection. Shared key authentication is described but not mandated in 802.11, and it can be defeated.

Another important fact to be aware of is that a wireless access point is not necessary for two wireless-enabled clients to communicate. Consequently, each client is at risk of the same file-sharing and TCP/IP attacks as clients on a wired LAN. Even when password authentication is implemented on wireless network access points, unauthorized access is still possible through the use of brute-force dictionary attacks. Password-cracking applications can methodically test passwords in an attempt to break in to a network access point.

Another common issue with 802.11b networks is that the access points have been designed for easy installation. So, though security features may be present, in most cases the default settings are for the features to be turned off so the network can be up and running as quickly as possible. Network administrators who leave their equipment with the default settings intact are particularly vulnerable, as hackers are likely to try known passwords and settings when attempting to penetrate wireless networks.

Standards and Policy Solutions

Security policies must be developed or enhanced to accommodate the new wireless environment. Primary issues to address in these policies will be ownership and control of the wireless network, access control to the network, physical security of access points, encryption, auditing, and procedures for detecting and handling of rogue access points or networks.

Wireless networks are similar to remote access networks in that the end devices are an unknown quantity; for example, the client device may not even belong to the company. Thus, these technologies need a central point of control and will often share some resources with the network, such as switches and authentication servers.

When devising policies for these technologies, it is important to consider the wireless devices as other remote access devices and determine how they may (or may not) fit into existing security policies. The wireless security policy should encompass situations where users may find themselves using wireless access outside the office. For example, every day, more hotels, airports, and conference centers are offering wireless access, opening users to vulnerability from other users on the network and, in some cases, from the Internet. Prescribing consistent use of VPN technology is the best protection against eavesdropping when connecting over public networks; and to guard against interception of wireless signals, the security policy should also call for routine audits of wireless usage. Also, all network cards should be registered, so that activities can be traced back to an individual.

The summary recommendation for a company's use of wireless technologies should relate back to the company's risk management strategy, aided by the computer security certification and accreditation process. That means that all proposed uses of wireless technology for communications should be reviewed as part of a certification and accreditation process before they are placed in an operational environment. Certification and accreditation of these devices, along with the proposed networks that will use the devices, should be initiated during the design phase of the program or project.

A thorough security policy will also restrict all PEDs without strong I&A built in or added to the system to administrative task use only, such as maintaining calendars and nonsensitive contact lists. Under no circumstance should a PED without strong I&A be used to store, process, or transmit official company information. And, as stated earlier, PEDs must always be treated as an automated information system (AIS) and be managed accordingly, meaning that the connection technology changes the context within which the device is assessed for communications security requirements. An individual PED should be designated as part of an unrestricted environment (no SBU data) or as part of a sensitive environment. If a PED is designated for use in a sensitive environment, it should not be connected via wireless connections outside of the sensitive environment.

A starter list of suggested security policies for PEDs would include:

- *Use encryption.* PEDs, PDAs, and PAN devices like Bluetooth should be prohibited from transmitting sensitive data, unless the data is encrypted (using a FIPS-approved algorithm); and/or the area in which the broadcast bubble radiates should be physically and electronically (RF) controlled. Additionally, since the PEDs are so susceptible to loss or theft, the company should initiate a policy to require that all data stored on PEDs be encrypted.

- *Guard shoulder-surfing zones.* As users of desktop and laptop PCs already know, sensitive information can be obtained fairly easily simply by looking over the shoulder of a person working at a computer. The same risk is true for PDAs, and is probably heightened since they are used in so many different surroundings. And, as already noted, they are more susceptible to theft than a desktop, server, or laptop. Security policies, therefore, should instruct users how to be aware of their surroundings when using PEDs (airports, hotel lobbies, training centers, etc.) and how to take appropriate precautions to reduce their exposure to prying eyes and sticky fingers.

- *Develop and use Common Criteria protection profiles.* The first step for any company program or project that is considering the use of wireless technologies and PEDs is to identify the protection requirements of the data to be processed, stored, handled, and communicated in the system. A suggested method of identifying and tracing these requirements is through the development of a Common Criteria protection profile. Such a profile would specify for vendors or integrators the features that are required for successful security implementation of a wireless technology solution. Recognizing that the PED is essentially a miniature PC can help in the development of the security requirements document. (Note: At a meeting of the Common Criteria Working Group sponsored by the Space and Naval Warfare Systems Center, in

Charleston, North Carolina, in November 2000, it was announced that work was beginning on a protection profile for wireless technology.)

PDA Security Policies

Few would deny that PDAs can enhance productivity; unfortunately, they can also introduce security vulnerabilities that should be addressed by PDA policies. Currently, many companies do not have any policies or procedures in place that specifically address PDAs; in fact, many managers aren't even aware of the types of data being stored on PDAs.

Confidentiality will be a major issue companies will have to address when determining how to secure the use of PDAs within the workplace, because currently, many companies do not have any policies or procedures in place to specifically address PDAs, nor are they fully aware of the myriad types of data being stored on PDAs. Users store a wide range of information on their PDAs, from the personal to the professional, including financial data, medical information, prescription numbers, passwords, notes from company meetings, and much more.

Without good security policies in place, confidentiality of this information can be easily breached without the PDA users' knowledge, and generally there is no way to determine who is responsible for the invasion or theft of data. A single policy should be created to specifically address PDAs and wireless communication tools. This will enable the policy to grow with future technologies, for example by incorporating both cellular and PDAs into one device using Bluetooth technology.

A PDA security policy should also address the types of data that will be authorized for storage on PDAs and wireless communication devices; authorized use areas should also be defined. By addressing these concerns, Security administrators can, for example, ban the use of wireless devices within the physical boundaries of the company, thereby enforcing a general security guideline that states, for example, "All connections must go through the firewall." And use care when configuring the access points because the default behavior may not meet the requirements of your security policy.

REPUDIATION

Repudiation refers to the denial by a user that he or she has performed an action on the network; for example, sending a particular message or accessing the network and performing some action. Strong authentication of users, integrity assurance methods, and digital signatures can reduce the incidence of repudiation.

The U.S. Navy has defined what it considers to be the proper and specific usage of PDAs within a command. We'll review those guidelines here because anyone who uses PDAs that synchronize with computers on company networks should adopt or adapt the following security measures and write them into security policies, procedures, standards, and network user agreements:

- Use only commercially produced applications or applications developed by trusted sources.

- Connect PDAs only to unclassified computers.

- Do not enter passwords, combinations, PINs and classified information into a PDA.

- Do not use PDA remote connectivity features while connected to a desktop PC, particularly a networked PC.

- Do not, as a rule, maintain classified data on a PDA. Though some classified (secret-level) programs have been developed for the Palm, it is still advised that these PDAs be controlled as any secret material, which means never connecting them to a computer network—even a classified computer network—because of the risk of introducing a backdoor. The following are additional recommendations concerning security of PDAs holding classified data:

  - Never connect classified PDAs to unclassified computers. Connect classified PDAs only to stand-alone computers of the same classification.

  - Never connect a PDA to a computer on a classified network. This applies even if the network connection is not present at the same time the PDA is connected (such as with laptops).

  - Never share classified PDA data with unclassified PDAs in any fashion (IR port, HotSync, cable).

  - Do not maintain classified data or programs on PDAs with wireless features, such as the Palm VII. Likewise, do no use modems and other accessories with classified PDAs.

As a final note on this topic, be aware that there is no formal guidance on declassifying PDAs, thus physical destruction is currently the only option available for this purpose. Performing a hard reset does not declassify a PDA.

User Security Awareness

Another essential aspect to any security policy is user security awareness training. Such training should focus on the proper control and use of PEDs to help reduce the incidence of loss or theft of the devices. A significant security factor associated with the proper use of wireless technologies (and PEDs in particular) is the acknowledgment by the user that the PED is in fact functioning in the same capacity as a standard PC or workstation. Reinforcing the standard information security training, along with the company's wireless policies, can help raise user awareness to the vulnerabilities associated with these systems.

It is the responsibility of security administrators to make PDA users aware of the dangers that are inherent to use of PDA devices, and training is central to this effort. Simply put, when users understand their responsibilities and the dangers posed by loss of an official PED, loss rates will go down.

Network Solutions

The purpose of this section is to explore the ways that WLANs can be made more secure. We begin with a discussion of the 802.1x standard briefly mentioned in Chapter 3.

802.1x

Recall that a group of vendors is proposing to use the IEEE 802.1x standard for authentication and key distribution. Cisco has implemented it in its Aironet series of cards, and Microsoft has added the feature to its latest OS, WinXP. The goal of 802.1x is to provide a level of authentication comparable to that of the wired network.

Under this plan, any appropriated wireless network interface cards (NICs) no longer pose a threat because the network now authenticates the user, not the hardware. When the user (called the supplicant) wants to use the network service, he or she will connect to the access point (called the authenticator), and a RADIUS server (the authentication server) at the other end will receive the request and issue a challenge. If the supplicant can provide a correct response, it is allowed access.

In the Cisco model, the supplicant and authentication server change roles and attempt mutual communication. Using this method of authentication, the risk of authenticating to a rogue access point is minimized. After authentication, the authentication server and the supplicant determine a WEP key for the session. This gives each client a unique WEP for every session.

MAC Address Filtering

Some 802.11 access point devices have the capability to restrict access to only those devices that are aware of a specific identification value, such as a MAC address. Some access point devices also contain a table of permitted and denied MAC addresses, which enables a device administrator to specify the exact remote devices that are authorized to make use of the wireless service. Client computers are viewed by a unique MAC address of its IEEE 802.11 network card. To secure an access point using MAC address filtering, each access point must have a list of authorized client MAC address in its access control list.

Unfortunately, MAC address filtering is time-consuming because the list of client MAC address must be entered manually into each access point; also, the MAC address list must be kept up to date. For these reasons this method is better suited for use in a smaller network, where the security solution of choice may be 128-bit WEP in conjunction with MAC address filtering and SSID.

By creating access lists of MAC addresses with permission to access the network, an organization can limit the ability of unauthorized clients to connect to the network at will. Unfortunately, if the number of wireless clients is large, using these lists has the potential to create significant administration overhead. In addition, since MAC addresses of wireless NICs are transmitted in cleartext, a sniffer would have little difficulty identifying a known good address that can be spoofed as part of an attack (more on MAC spoofing in a moment). Therefore, the MAC addresses of all NICs should be registered with the LAN administrator; and the base stations should be set to accept only those MAC addresses.

Using Cisco's EAP-aware RADIUS server (Cisco Access Control Server), it is possible to control access to the wireless access point by MAC address. This may represent an added administrative burden, but it is necessary to protect against unauthorized users and rogue access points, especially since many companies allow small purchases, such as wireless cards, to be bought at a departmental or personal level.

One possible approach to managing wireless network cards is to have the security administrator record the wireless card MAC address, have the employee read and sign the appropriate security policy, enter the MAC address into the RADIUS server, and, finally, affix a serial-numbered approval sticker on the wireless card.

MAC Spoofing

Researchers contend that MAC address filtering is not a reliable method to secure a wireless network because legitimate MAC addresses can be easily captured by an attacker using a packet sniffer. The attacker, they maintain, can then alter the MAC address of their card to gain access. Though this is true, it must be pointed out that changing the MAC address of a network card is an extremely difficult process, which requires reflashing the memory on the card; in short, it is not a trivial task.

In contrast, malicious users make short work of accessing MAC addresses on PCMCIA WLAN cards, most of which have their MAC address printed on the card itself. An attacker can simply copy the address and spoof it. MAC addresses are also broadcast in the clear so an attacker can just simply sniff it. This invasion is made even easier when WLAN cards can have their MAC address changed in software. MAC addresses also present scalability problems, because the number of addresses that can be stored by an access point is limited.

SSID Solutions

Wireless equipment manufacturers use a default service set ID (SSID) to identify the network to wireless clients. All access points often broadcast the SSID in order to provide clients with a list of accessible networks. Unfortunately, the SSID also serves to let potential intruders identify the network they have targeted for attack. If the SSID is set to the default manufacturer setting, it often means that the additional configuration settings (such as passwords) are at their defaults as well.

Therefore, a wise addition to any security policy is to make it a requirement to disable SSID broadcasting entirely. If company must broadcast a network listing, it's essential that the default SSID setting be changed. All other default settings should be changed as well to further reduce the risk of a successful attack. The radio SSID should be set to a unique value, and the access point name should not reflect the company's main name, division, products, brand name, or any information that would enable a hacker to determine which company he or she had found. Again, avoid default SSID values such as Cisco's "tsunami." And, if you're using an Aironet, under the AP Radio Hardware Page, respond No to the "Allow Broadcast SSID to Associate" question. This forces client devices to have an exact SSID match. If this option is left enabled, devices can learn the SSID and associate with the access point.

Antenna Selection

The antenna used by a network can greatly affect wireless security. Enterprise and campus networks probably should steer clear of *omnidirectional* coverage, such as that used by hotels, airports, and similar public areas. Rather, any security-conscious organization should probably opt for directional, patch antennas to control the radio footprint.

NOTE Military commands that use 802.11b wireless APs for SBU data have the antennae under line-of-sight watch for the width of the radiation bubble. Studies have shown, however, that this bubble can be much larger than anticipated by standards, due to equipment variations, weather conditions, and the strength of the eavesdropper's antennae and equipment.

It is a also good idea to periodically check the radio footprint using the vendor-supplied signal strength tools. Too often, radio engineers, who may have complete coverage as their goal, perform this task during installation and may encompass public areas, which should *not* be included.

Here are a few additional guidelines to follow regarding antennae installation:

- Be prepared to pay for expert advice on antenna placement and installation.

- Use the vendor-supplied tools for display of signal strength and limit the signal appropriately. For example, Cisco adapters ship with a tool called Link Status Meter, which can be used to spot-check signal quality.

- Know where your wireless signal can be intercepted. This is essential. Be sure that the footprint is under your control. If the signal is detectable outside your property, it may be a good idea to install a surveillance camera to record the activity in that area.

- Place antennae properly, to limit the amount of radio energy available to eavesdroppers outside the company walls. For additional protection, consider installing a chain-link fence. Cisco has posted a notice that "a chain-link fence, wire mesh with one to one and a half-inch spacing, acts as a half-inch [harmonic] wave that will block a 2.4-GHz signal 15 inches."

- As part of the initial site survey to determine placement of wireless access points, consider placing the equipment toward the center of the building to minimize the strength of wireless signals emanating to the outside world. Avoid placing equipment near windows, which will allow the signal to travel farther and possibly reach unintended receivers.

Virtual LANS

It's commonly recommended that access points be placed on their own segment or virtual LAN (VLAN) with a stateful IP filtering firewall separating the restricted wireless LAN and unrestricted internal wired LAN. Further, if VLANs are used to connect the access points, it's recommended to use access lists on the switches and isolate the wireless VLAN from all other VLANs.

The port security feature on switches should be used to specify which wireless access points can be connected to the wired network and where. It has also been suggested that the wireless VLAN be defined in each switch, with one port for each access point, and resist the temptation to define ports for future expansion. One consideration is a *zoned approach,* whereby public areas are disabled and other, more controlled areas are left enabled.

RADIUS Authentication Servers

Several 802.11 access points offer Remote Authentication Dial-In User Service (RADIUS) authentication, whereby clients gain access to the network by supplying a username and password to a separate server. This information is sent over the network securely, eliminating the possibility of passive snooping.

User-based authentication provides a centrally managed method of verifying users who attempt to access the wireless network. A RADIUS server provides this functionality and has the capability to handle VPN client authentication as well. Some RADIUS implementations can allow the user to be authenticated via a digital key system and restrict access to preauthorized areas per user. Cisco's RADIUS server, mentioned earlier in the chapter, even makes it possible to establish access by time and date.

NOTE It is strongly suggested that implementers disable their wireless LANS during off hours where practical.

Virtual Private Networks

Many organizations use virtual private networks (VPNs) to allow employee access to the corporate LAN via the Internet, while providing security against unauthorized users. Wireless LANs can also benefit from VPN use. The wireless portion of the network can be separated from the wired network by a firewall. By configuring the firewall to pass only VPN traffic, all other network activity can be stopped, thus preventing unauthorized clients from gaining access to the main network. All traffic between the wired and wireless network takes place through the VPN tunnel and is encrypted via the IPSec protocol. IPSec thwarts sniffer attacks launched using applications such as the aforementioned AirSnort.

In fact, a VPN is a logical solution for wireless networks seeking to ensure access control: no unauthorized routes to the Internet exist from the wireless network, which obviously protects the network against unauthorized use of costly Internet bandwidth. Moreover, authentication has to be established before traffic to the internal network is acknowledged. Another advantage of deploying VPN technology on an enterprise network is low administration for the client and the access point.

High-security network designers must investigate implementing a VPN solution with wireless access. VPN provides a secure and dedicated channel over an untrusted network, such as the Internet, and wireless networks. The VPN server, which acts as a gateway to the private network, provides authentication and full encryption over the wireless network. IEEE 802.11 wireless access can be established via a secure VPN connection using various tunneling protocols.

A VPN can be used to act as a gateway between the WLAN and the network, and can supplement the WEP's authentication and encryption functions. When VPN clients need to access the network, it will connect to a VPN server, and the server will authenticate the client. Once authenticated, the VPN server will provide the client with an IP and an encryption key. All communications will be carried out through this IP. Every packet that passes through this secure tunnel between the client and server will be encrypted. Consequently, an attacker cannot simply hijack an IP to gain access, because he or she will not possess the encryption key. The VPN server will simply reject all connections from the attacker.

VPN solutions are available in both hardware and software versions; a hardware solution offers the advantage of speed of packet encryption and decryption. With a VPN in place, employees who wish to access the organization's network from an ISP can connect via the VPN.

Other guidelines for VPN implementation include:

- Consider using VPN clients on wireless devices to enforce strong encryption; and require positive authentication via hardware tokens.

- Consider VPN systems for mobile and wireless devices. For application within the company, use a WEP-like or wireless VPN (wVPN) solution that supports a FIPS-approved data encryption algorithm to ensure data confidentiality in a WLAN environment.

- Ensure that each endpoint of the VPN remains under company control. When possible, install WLAN network APs and wVPN gateways behind network perimeter security mechanisms (e.g., firewall, IDS, etc.), so that wireless access to the internal wired network can be controlled and monitored.

- Incorporate VPN technology from the client directly to the access point. Equip the client computers with personal firewalls or intrusion detection systems. Position the intrusion detection system between the access point and the firewall to deny any unauthorized connection.

VPN Products

Several wVPN products are available that support encryption of transmitted data, for example, from F-Secure and Certicom. Wireless VPNs provide encrypted communications from the PED client, via wireless connectivity, to a local server or firewall that serves as the VPN gateway. Certicom's product can use its elliptic curve cryptography (ECC) or 3DES; it was shipping at the time of this writing. Another product, F-Secure's VPN+ is IPSec-compliant and can encrypt data at speeds as high as 24 Mbps with 3DES encryption (168-bit).

Cisco has released VPN clients for Windows, Linux, and PocketPC. Certicom has enhanced its movianVPN product for Palm, WinCE, and PocketPC16. The movianVPN clients are positioned for modem users, as the product's flagship platform is Palm, which currently has no Ethernet capability. The new Palm 500 and 505 have expansion slots, which Palm has stated are for 802.11b and GPS expansion cards.

A common VPN implementation uses SecurID for positive user authentication and IPSec tunnels with triple-DES encryption between the wireless device and the internal network. This implementation uses the Cisco 3030 VPN Concentrator, which has native support for SecurID token authentication. This network had previously deployed SecurID and had upgraded to version 2.6 of Cisco Access Control Server. This same methodology is used for remote access, so there is minimal user impact. An intruder must first obtain access to the wireless LAN with an authorized network card, then authenticate to the VPN server using a SecurID token before attaining any access to the corporate network.

VPN solutions are also available for mobile wireless devices and encrypted messaging services (such as BlackBerry) using commercially available encryption technology. They can be implemented to compensate for the "service in the middle" (recall the "WAP-gap") security vulnerability of the communications process. For basic messaging services, a BlackBerry-enabled system might be appropriate. That said, be aware that a commercial infrastructure that supports such a service would first have to be reviewed, since the location of the distribution server could be in another state or in another country. However, this may not be an issue if the system does not handle extremely sensitive data.

WAP Security

If WAP products with WTLS will be used in the enterprise, the solution should be thoroughly tested, along with other proposed security and application technologies, to ensure system interoperability and data encryption standards. The WAP-gap vulnerability may be countered by running WTLS sessions from a WAP gateway located on an company-controlled network outside a perimeter firewall or, ideally, within the company installation network.

A new standard defined in WAP 1.2 and 2.0 is called the Dynamic Proxy Navigation Model. It enables wireless network service providers to give up control of their WAP gateway to customers, who could then run their own secure, direct connections.[13] In the interim, to provide additional security, a circuit from the customer-controlled network on which the data source resides (typically a Web server) may be leased to connect directly to the wireless network service provider using a dedicated WAP gateway.

---

[13]An interesting proxy navigation model initiative can be found at www.fstc.org/projects/wireless/wireless-security.cfm.

Additional WAP security guidelines to consider include:

- Take special precautions to avoid the compromise of sensitive information caused by the WAP gap. WAP-enabled PEDs should not use commercial wireless network service provider gateways to access company Web servers unless end-to-end data encryption is provided.

- If possible, consider establishing a company WAP gateways in the installation networks, so that wireless access may be controlled by firewalls, and connections may be monitored by IDS. A company WAP gateway reduces the risk of data compromise, because the WTLS-to-SSL conversion required to access company Web servers would occur on a company-controlled and protected network.

- On Web-enabled mobile phones, use WAP version 1.2 support for PKI digital certificates. WAP version 1.2 (released December 2000) addresses the WAP-gap security vulnerability by supporting the use of Wireless/WAP Identification Module (WIM) smart cards that use PKI certificates to ensure continuous encryption throughout the connection. (Note: Unfortunately, it may be awhile before compatible mobile phones are available in the United States that support WAP version 1.2 and WIM smart cards for storage of subscriber identification information and digital certificates.)

Dynamic WEP Keys

To reduce the possibility of key compromise, several vendors, including Cisco and Agere, are offering products that eliminate the use of static keys, and instead implement per-user/per-session keys combined with RADIUS authentication. Clients must authenticate with a RADIUS server using network credentials, and WEP keys are dynamically distributed securely to the client.

There are two main advantages to this method of key distribution: First, dynamic keys carry less administrative overhead, since keys are automatically changed with each user logon; second, dynamic keys eliminate the vulnerabilities described earlier inherent to using WEP and static keys.

There is a drawback to this method, however: Currently, there is no standard for key distribution in the IEEE 802.11b standard. Therefore, interoperability is impossible since each distribution method is vendor-specific. Hopefully this will change with the introduction of 802.11x, which, as already explained, will standardize key distribution and authorization.

According to Cisco, a major security exposure in WLANs is due primarily to static WEP and the tremendous administrative burden it imposes. With the Cisco Aironet solution, session keys are unique to the users; that is, they are not shared among them. Cisco's Aironet solution creates per-user, per-session, dynamic WEP keys tied to the network logon, thereby addressing some of the limitations associated with the shared static key system just described. Also, with LEAP authentication, the broadcast WEP key is encrypted using the session key before being delivered to the end client. By having a session key unique to the user, and by tying it to the network logon, the solution also eliminates vulnerabilities due to stolen or lost client cards or devices.

Denial-of-Service Solutions

Protecting wireless networks from a denial-of-service (DoS) attack can be difficult and expensive. A possible solution is to create a Faraday cage around the boundaries of the wireless network as protection.[14] A Faraday cage isolates the network from electro-magnetic radiation, however, this would cut off other wireless communications devices (such as cellular telephones), and would not prevent someone from entering the cage to activate the DoS equipment.

The current nature of wireless communications makes it difficult to assure that a signal will be available in all situations and locations, whether of critical or of normal importance. Unless additional assurance beyond standard device configurations can be said to prevent DoS attacks and signal loss, current technologies should not be used where consistent connectivity is an absolute requirement.

Monitoring and Intrusion Detection Systems

It is considered good practice to deploy network sniffers on a regular basis in order to identify rogue access points that may be providing unauthorized access to the network. Recall that rogue access points might be deployed either by well-intended employees within the organization or by outside intruders whose goal is to penetrate the system illegally. As an additional precaution, take measurements external to a facility in areas an intruder might be likely to attempt an attack. It is helpful to know just how far wireless network signals travel outside the intended boundaries of a building.

ENABLE WEP!

As mentioned previously, WEP is disabled by default on most wireless network equipment. Despite its proven flaws, enabling WEP is better protection than nothing at all. It adds an additional barrier to access against the casual war driver. The point is, be sure to enable WEP.

---

[14]Simply, a Faraday cage is a room totally encapsulated in metal or metal mesh that makes it impossible for electric fields to enter. It's however extremely difficult to make one that works 100%. And in some cases the cage can actually amplify the unwanted radiation.

Wireless sniffing software is available that can be used to easily find rogue access points on a LAN. These include AiroPeek from WildPackets, Mobile-Manager from Wavelink, Sniffer Wireless from Network Associates, and Network Stumbler from Marius Milner. Using one of these products, do a periodic wireless scan of your network to pick up rogue access points that may have popped up unnoticed. This often happens when someone sets up a wireless network inside the firewall.

Three more guidelines for guarding against unauthorized access include:

- Add or amend your security policy to prevent users from setting up their own wireless network without permission.

- Consider using a network-based intrusion detection system (IDS) on the wireless LAN. During initial deployment, the sensor can be set to log all activity. This can be very helpful when explaining potential vulnerabilities to senior management. Configure the IDS sensors to detect any attempts to scan the wireless network or penetrate the VPN, RADIUS, or DHCP server. To detect unusual traffic going to a wireless device, protect all RADIUS and DHCP servers with host-based intrusion.

- Maintain extensive logs of both the restricted and unrestricted LAN access. These logs are critical when tracing malicious activity on your network.

Access Point Security

The AP provides central management and a connection point to the wired LAN infrastructure. It supports device identification and communications security, and thus increases the general security of a wLAN. IEEE 802.11 devices can be set to respond only to a specific set of other devices, based on a list of MAC addresses. APs can be set to require a secret key that has to be installed in each such device permitted to communicate over a particular wireless segment This is possible if the access point implements Extended Service Set Identification (ESSID).

A list of AP guidelines includes:

- Configure IEEE 802.11 access points with a nondefault, noninformative service set identifier (SSID).

- Use the max WEP algorithm, for some help.

- Use MAC address filtering.

- Manage signal strength by lowering the gain to the minimum required for the system to function.

- Use sniffing tools and IDS.

- Implement port security on the switch.

NOTE On military bases with installed access points, the command has a set time at which a circuit breaker is thrown to cut the power to the AP. This prevents use of the AP for wireless access into the network after-hours. The circuit boxes are located in an area that is under guard.

AP Mode Use

The 802.11b APs should be used in infrastructure mode only (see Chapter 2); do not allow ad hoc networking. Though ad hoc networking can be a useful tool, many corporations choose to disable it because of the unrestricted shared environment it creates.

Cisco's Aironet 350 has a feature that helps in this regard. Called publicly secure packet forwarding (PSPF), it prevents client devices associated to a bridge or access point from inadvertently sharing files with other client devices on the wireless network. PSPF provides Internet access to client devices without providing other capabilities of a LAN.

With PSPF enabled, client devices cannot communicate with other client devices on the wireless network. This is intended to eliminate all interdevice traffic except that which has been encrypted via IPSec tunnels.

The IEEE 802.11 suite of standards indicate that the use of spread spectrum RF technology may reduce the amount of interference between PEDs and serve to reduce the effectiveness of monitoring an attempted service interruption.

To address the problem of session highjacking or intentional service interruption, Cisco recommends a timeout for each user. The timeout should be fast enough so that there is no chance for an attacker to compromise the WEP key. Factors for determining the timeout include: numbers of users per access point, the packet size, and the packet rate.

Another solution to unauthorized intrusion comes from Interlink Networks'[15] Wireless Access Manager. Available as software, it implements the EAP and LEAP protocol used in the 802.1x standard. Using a RADIUS-based solution, it provides the WLAN with the same security features found in the Cisco Aironet series described earlier. Companies with existing access points and wireless cards need not upgrade or change them to new ones as long as the access points are RADIUS-compliant.

When possible, WLAN network APs and wVPN gateways should be installed outside network perimeter security mechanisms so that wireless access to the internal wired network can be controlled and monitored. Ideally, each should be positioned in the installation's top-level architecture (TLA) outside the network's perimeter firewall(s) and IDS. However, usually this will not be feasible because of communication range limitations, unless the TLA location would be in range of all WLAN clients.

[15]www.interlinknetworks.com.

Another common recommendation is that connections to the Web servers inside the organization's network go through SSL, to prevent any information from being sent or received in the clear. It is advisable to use only SSL 3.0, as the 2.0 version is vulnerable to the man-in-the-middle attack.

Software Solutions

This section explores the various encryption technologies available to protect wireless transmissions. It also includes a look at some sample software written specifically for PEDs.

Encryption Technologies

Data encryption is the only sure method of protecting information in transit. Where WLANs are to be implemented, thorough analysis, testing, and risk assessment should be done to determine the risk of information intercept, monitoring, and other threats. An IEEE 802.11x system should be used that supports the spread spectrum technology. In a neutral or safe environment, the WEP implementation can be used to ensure data confidentiality. For application within the company, however, it is recommended that a WEP-like or wVPN solution be used, one that supports a FIPS-approved data encryption algorithm, to ensure data confidentiality in a WLAN environment.

It should be understood that none of these encryption implementations are secure from traffic (packet header) analysis, because only the data payload of the packets is encrypted. Furthermore, protection against interruption of communications through jamming is not provided (although the spread spectrum will help). Interoperability specification and testing should be accomplished prior to investing in equipment.

Besides relying on the WEP for confidentiality, users should implement other available encryption methods. SSH should be use instead of Telnet when connecting to remote hosts. Tunneling features available in SSH can be utilized for providing secure connections to applications that are connected to a remote server. An example is the POP mail, instead of connecting directly over to the POP server. Other SSH user guidelines include:

- Configure the SSH client to create a secure tunnel from the machine to the port on the remote server side.

- Configure the mail reader to the local port that connects to this tunnel.

- When installing SSH, install SSH version 2 to avoid vulnerabilities found in the earlier one.

A number of SSH software programs are available on the Internet for free, such as OPENSSH. This should help make SSH an attractive option.

A technology proposed by NextComm, Inc. (www.nextcomm.com) uses an IC chip that uses MD5 hash to generate the key stream and a key distribution system to change keys rapidly. Called Key Hopping, this distribution system can change keys as fast as every three seconds to prevent hackers from gathering enough packets for analysis. However, to enjoy these benefits, this system requires the access points and client cards to use the IC chip.

WEP Encryption Workarounds

In the case of devices equipped with 802.11 technologies, WEP can be used to encrypt data from one device to another. But as explained, WEP has serious problems. To address WEP algorithm problems, Cisco has implemented several enhanced 802.11b security methods, such as:

Secure key derivation. The original shared secret secure key derivation is used to construct responses to the mutual challenges. It undergoes irreversible one-way hashes that make password-replay attacks impossible. The hash values sent over the wire are useful for one-time at the start of the authentication process, but never again.

Reauthentication policies. Aironet administrators can also set policies for reauthentication at the back-end RADIUS server ACS2000. This will force users to reauthenticate more often and get new session keys. Because the vulnerability window can be configured to be very small, it can minimize attacks where traffic is injected during the session.

Initialization vector changes. The Cisco Aironet wireless security solution also changes the initialization vector (IV) on a per-packet basis so that hackers can find no predetermined sequence to exploit. This capability, coupled with the reduction in possible attack windows, greatly mitigates exposure to hacker attacks due to frequent key rotation. In particular, this makes it difficult to create table-based attacks based on the knowledge of the IVs seen on the wireless network.

PED Data Encryption

All encryption is not created equal. The same considerations that are used in choosing an algorithm and implementation strategy for a traditional computing device are required. This may sometimes require forsaking some ease of use. Assuming a strong encryption algorithm, the protection provided by the encryption also relies on a benign environment, one in which the encryption technique is not circumvented by hostile code, such as a Trojan horse program. Use of encryption for protection of data stored on the PED also requires that all copies of the data to be protected are encrypted, including such things as temporary files if they exist on the system.

A focus of concern for PEDs is the loss or theft of a device. This is particularly true if the PED contains sensitive information and does not support strong I&A. Because of this, encryption of the information stored on the PED should be implemented. Add-on software products are available that can be installed on the PED to maintain all files and messages in an encrypted format, making it more difficult for someone to access and read the data. A variety of encryption algorithms are supported, which provide varying degrees of protection, such as Sentry 2020, which is described below.

Vendors, users, and managers of corporate deployments of PEDs need to ensure that effective cryptography systems are in place for their mobile appliances. ECC has emerged as an effective solution because of its relative lightness for the PDAs weaker processors. As time goes on, these processor strengths will continue to rise, so eventually a stronger system may be needed. For more radio-based systems, frequency hopping may be the ultimate solution, but it is likely that higher-end applications will need additional cryptographic techniques in the future to ensure the highest security.

Federal Information Processing Standards

Department of Defense-level policies and FIPS-specified cryptographic algorithms are maintained and validated through the National Institute of Standards and Technology (NIST) for use in a military environment. Currently, the FIPS-approved algorithms for encryption include the Data Encryption Standard (DES), 3DES, Skipjack, and the new AES. They are available for some PEDs and will soon be available for others.

It's recommended that encryption of stored data be implemented for all PEDs that will be used outside the physical security confines of a user's assigned workspace. A strong, FIPS-approved algorithm should be used for data encryption. Serviceability, ease of use, and proper implementation analyses should be completed on several products before one is selected. Serious consideration must be given to encryption key management techniques and procedures. Also, interoperability testing should be done with these products and others proposed for use in the protection of communications.

PED Security Software

Software exists that specifically addresses the vulnerabilities of PDAs. Companies spend large resources on security software such as antivirus, sniffers, encryption software, and firewalls to protect desktops, servers, and the corporate network. However, very little funding is spent on protecting the PDAs themselves. If companies want to reap the rewards of PDA usage, dedicated resources must be allocated to PDA protection.

This area of security software for PDAs is still relatively new, but many companies are starting to come into the field. The following subsections describe a few entries.

movianCrypt

Certicom's movianCrypt integrates a password-based user login system with strong encryption technology for Palm OS devices. Transparent to end users, applications run unmodified on movianCrypt-enabled devices, encrypting data as it is stored, and decrypting data as it is accessed.

FEATURES

- Utilizes the 128-bit Advanced Encryption Standard (AES).

- Invokes password security. The password is not stored on the device, and it does not get transferred to the desktop during a HotSync.

- Reencrypts data on the fly; fine-tuned for performance on the 68 K processor.

- Is compatible with Certicom's movianVPN and other third-party applications.

SPECIFICATIONS

- Palm PDAs running Palm OS 3.0 or higher (including 4.0).

- Handspring Visor running Palm OS 3.1 or higher.

- 110 Kb of storage memory and 8 Kb of dynamic memory.

- One PRC file is available for all OS versions.

Sentry 2020 for PocketPC

Sentry 2020 provides encrypted virtual volumes. All information (files, folders, file system structures) stored on a Sentry volume is transparently encrypted/decrypted every time an application performs a read/write operation on the volume. Without a correct password, Sentry volume is just a file with encrypted contents. When the correct password is provided, the volume is mounted, and appears as a drive letter (Windows 95/98, Windows NT) or as a folder in the root directory (Windows CE). Any application can then work with the contents of the mounted Sentry volume without noticing the encryption being performed on the fly.

When mounted, a virtual volume looks like an ordinary disk and files can be stored on it. Every read operation on the volume causes decryption of the data and every write operation causes encryption. Each volume is encrypted using a randomly generated key, which itself is encrypted using a user-supplied password. Random-value generation uses parameters like mouse movement, timer, performance counters, and so on, which are scrambled using the SHA-1 hash algorithm. The randomly generated key is stored in a key file, encrypted with a user-supplied password, and a randomly generated salt value is stored in the same file. Volume encryption is performed on each 512-byte block independently. Before encryption, the contents of each block are scrambled, using the number representing the position of the block in the volume. This is done so that two blocks with identical contents (for example, all zeroes) will look totally different after encryption.

Sentry2020 uses the CAST-128 algorithm, which is a symmetric encryption algorithm implemented as an ActiveX component.[16] The CAST-128 code has been validated against the RFC 2144 reference implementation test vectors. Sentry 2020 uses a key length of 128 or more bits, supports all Windows CE media, and is compatible with Sentry for Windows NT/2000/XP. It supports these platforms:

- PocketPC 2002 (Windows CE 3.0)
- PocketPC (Windows CE 3.0)
- Palm-size PC (Windows CE 2.11)
- Handheld PC 2000 (Windows CE 3.0)
- Handheld PC Pro (Windows CE 2.11)
- Handheld PC (Windows CE 2.0)

Pretty Good Protection (PGP) Wireless

Network Associates has developed Pretty Good Protection (PGP) wireless, which is designed to secure information on PDAs and wireless phones, including WAP phones that use the Palm OS, using PGP encryption technology.

PGP encryption technology offers a high level of encryption, decryption, digital signatures, and authentication to secure information stored and transmitted on PDAs using a 256-bit encryption.

F-Secure

F-Secure has greatly expanded its PDA offering from antivirus, to include file encryption programs. The following subsections list the current features of F-Secure's handheld crypto offerings.

F-Secure FileCrypto for Symbian OS

F-Secure FileCrypto for Symbian OS protects confidential and personal information stored on the mobile devices using the Symbian OS, even if the terminal is stolen or lost. This program automatically encrypts all files before storing and decrypts the files again when they are opened, without any need for user intervention. It uses 128-bit Blowfish encryption.

---

[16]"The CAST-128 Encryption Algorithm," Carlisle Adams, May 1997.

F-Secure FileCrypto for PocketPC Personal Edition

F-Secure FileCrypto for PocketPC Personal Edition has been specifically developed to protect stored data in Compaq iPAQ PocketPC handhelds. With the application, Compaq iPAQ PocketPC users can create secure folders for storing confidential and personal information. The product also protects data on removable media, such as memory cards and microdrives.

F-Secure FileCrypto for PocketPC Enterprise Edition

F-Secure FileCrypto for PocketPC Enterprise Edition is a full-featured file encryption application for PocketPC devices. It provides secure user authentication and automatic protection against unwanted data disclosure in corporate environments and demanding personal use.

FEATURES

- *Automatic protection.* Automatically encrypts sensitive data before storing, and decrypts it again when it is needed, without any user intervention. The contents of the folders and the mail messages are encrypted with the 128-bit AES algorithm.

- *Easy encryption of stored mail messages.* The user can encrypt all stored mail messages and lock the inbox of the mail application.

- *Secure user authentication with PIN and passphrase.* Offers two ways of user authentication: a PIN code and a passphrase. When the device is activated, the PIN code is used for easy access to the device. If the PIN code is entered incorrectly, the application will request the user to enter the passphrase. After three failed attempts, the device will be locked and can only be unlocked with the master key created during installation.

- *Support for external memory.* Unprotected information on removable media can usually be accessed with any compatible device. Supports secured folders also on external memory devices, such as memory cards and microdrives.

- *Easy key recovery if passphrase is forgotten.* Offers an easy mechanism for recovering the encrypted data if the passphrase is forgotten. When the main application has been installed, it creates a strong, random master key. In a user forgets the passphrase, the user or an administrator can use the master key to create a new passphrase.

Supported devices include Compaq iPAQ PocketPC handhelds and HP Jornada PocketPC 2002 handhelds.

PED Antivirus Software

Antivirus (and malicious code detection) software is available for most PEDs (except data-enabled cellular phones), as well as for desktops and servers that interact with PEDs. This software tests for and detects known virus implementations and many forms of malicious code. The countermeasure against the threat of viruses and malicious code is to properly install and configure antivirus software and to update the virus signature files as new computer viruses are discovered.

Companies must make the use of antivirus software on PEDs and their associated workstations mandatory. To ensure the level of protection required against viruses, it is important to maintain the database(s) they use to profile and identify viruses, worms, and malicious code. The network infrastructure must accommodate virus software updates for all PEDs and their supporting desktops and servers. Also, companies should have a program for testing and certifying antivirus products for PEDs, and investigate companywide licensing of PED-based antivirus software, as is currently done for desktop antivirus software.

Companies must also ensure that both the support environment (wired network) and the PED always check files passed between the two. For complete protection, both PED-based and desktop-based virus-scanning software should be used. Finjan Software has developed a product (Finjan Antivirus for Palm and PocketPC devices) that monitors PEDs to ensure that malicious code is not transferred to PCs. Finjan is also researching behavior-monitoring products for PEDs, because large, reactive antivirus databases are simply too large to be stored on such a storage/processing-limited device.

The antivirus products for Smartphones, WAP phones, and PDAs continue to enter the marketplace regularly, and this trend is expected to continue. The following subsections highlight just a few of the technologies that are available.

VirusScan Wireless

McAfee's VirusScan Wireless is designed for Smartphones or WAP phones and PDA devices. It provides virus protection for all leading handheld platforms, including Palm OS, Windows CE, and Symbian EPOC devices. McAfee advertises that VirusScan Wireless will safeguard critical data against attacks by viruses, worms, or Trojan horses.

McAfee's "micro engine," designed for Smartphones, is based on the McAfee VirusScan technology. The new micro-scanning engine examines files and applications for viruses and malicious code locally on Smartphones and PDAs. VirusScan Wireless will also have the capability to automatically update virus definition files through a Smartphones Internet connection capability.

F-Secure

F-Secure has produced a software package for the three known viruses that infect only the Palm OS. This product can be downloaded to the user's Palm directly from the F-Secure home page. F-Secure also has a complete handheld software suite that includes antivirus and file crypto for Palm OS, PocketPC, and Symbian OS. The current software suite includes:

- F-Secure Anti-Virus 1.01 for PocketPC
- F-Secure Anti-Virus 2.01 for Palm OS
- F-Secure FileCrypto 1.12 for PocketPC Enterprise Edition
- F-Secure FileCrypto for Symbian OS
- F-Secure Anti-Virus for Symbian OS

F-Secure Anti-Virus for Symbian OS

F-Secure Anti-Virus for Symbian OS is an antivirus application that, together with a virus signature update service, provides fully automatic protection for Symbian-based mobile devices against viruses and other malicious or harmful content.

FEATURES

- Does not require user intervention. All files are automatically intercepted and scanned when they are saved, copied, downloaded, synchronized, or otherwise modified.
- Supports memory cards. Automatically scans files on memory cards and other storage media. When an infected file is detected, it is immediately quarantined in order to protect all other data in the system.
- Automatic antivirus database update. Supports several methods of updating the database. The virus definitions can be received automatically over the air or by downloading the latest database version from a Web server.

F-Secure Anti-Virus for Symbian OS is available as an early-availability program to qualified hardware vendors and operators. Commercial versions of the product will be introduced as new products using the Symbian OS become available.

F-Secure Anti-Virus for Palm OS

F-Secure Anti-Virus for Palm OS (3.5 or later) is an automatic antivirus software solution that runs locally on the Palm OS device.

FEATURES

- *Always-available protection.* Data can be transferred to handheld devices in a number of different ways, including HotSync synchronization and beaming. To properly protect the data on the device, it is essential that the software solution reside locally on the handheld device.

- *Automatic scanning after HotSync.* The Palm OS device is automatically scanned for all known malicious code (such as viruses and Trojans) after each HotSync operation. The application also provides information on the infected files.

F-Secure Anti-Virus for PocketPC

F-Secure Anti-Virus for PocketPC is an antivirus software solution that runs locally on the PocketPC device. It provides up-to-date and always-available protection for these new mobile corporate computing devices. Since the solution runs on the mobile device, it is able to detect and delete also all malicious software that enters the device through wireless connections.

FEATURES

- Always-available protection locally on the handheld device. Data can be transferred to handheld devices in a number of different ways, including ActiveSync synchronization, removable memory cards, and wireless IP connectivity. To properly protect the data on the device, it is essential that the software solution reside locally on the handheld device.

- Automatic antivirus database updates. Updates are automatically pushed to the PocketPC device through the user's host PC.

- Automatic antivirus scanning. Supports automatic scanning at startup and after every virus signature database update. Removable memory, such as Compact Flash cards, and microdrives, can be automatically scanned when inserted.

Supported devices include Compaq iPAQ PocketPC handhelds and HP Jornada PocketPC 2002 handhelds.

Trend Micro PC-cillin for Wireless

PC-cillin for Wireless Version 2.0 for Palm OS provides antivirus security for wireless devices with automatic real-time launch scanning. Real-time launch scanning activates whenever applications on the device are launched and prevents viruses from activating on the device.

PC-cillin for Wireless supports three platforms:

- Palm users: Palm OS 3.1 or above

- EPOC users: Psion Revo or Revo Plus

- PocketPC users: Windows CE 3.0

PC-cillin is a fully resident virus scanner. It can scan any file immediately after receipt, even if it was beamed directly or received over the Internet.

IS/Complete's PDA Restrictor v1.0

IS/Complete's PDA Restrictor v1.0 is not an antivirus program; rather, it allows an administrator to create profile categories for different users as well as a default profile on a single PDA. These profiles limit the applications to which each user has access. With the use of passwords, each profile may only log on to applications or records that the administrator deems appropriate. This function of PDA Restrictor is helpful if the company wants to give many employees PDAs but only wants to train them on a few applications. It also discourages employees from using the device for anything other than business.

These restricted profiles implement their own security both against employees misusing the PDA and others who may try to access private information. Restrictor is also a security application that can automatically lock PDAs and hide records. As a precaution against having private information falling into the wrong hands, Restrictor secures the PDA and will not allow access without proper passwords, even after a soft reset.

As of early 2002, the Restrictor is compatible with the following PDAs:

- 3Com Palm III
- 3Com Palm IIIx, IIIe
- 3Com Palm V
- 3Com Palm Vx
- IBM Workpad Companion
- IBM Workpad C3 PC Companion

As of early 2002, the Restrictor is not compatible with the following PDAs:

- 3Com Palm VII
- Handspring Visor
- Handspring Visor Deluxe

PDA Restrictor requires the Palm Operating System 3.1x, 3.3 and 3.5x.

Physical Hardware Security

If a wireless terminal or storage media is stolen or lost, unauthorized persons may be able to read unprotected confidential or personal information from the device memory. Data on memory cards and microdrives can usually be accessed via any compatible device.

Cabling systems to attach PEDs to work surfaces can reduce the number of lost PEDs, although this also greatly restricts their mobility. Sensitive information could be protected by stronger implementations of encryption, or filtered at a mail or file transfer server. Should the device accidentally receive classified information, destruction of the device is the only authorized form of sanitation.

User security awareness training regarding the proper control and use of PEDs will help to eliminate some loss of the devices. Providing a securing mechanism for a PED that must be left unattended (in a lab or in a hotel, for example) may help prevent theft. Using encryption, as mentioned earlier, will not recover the PED, but will protect the data stored on it from illicit use. The support environment can and should be set up to implement the local policy of SBU data and PED use. Only officially authorized PEDs should be used, since they may have to be destroyed if they become contaminated with classified or unauthorized SBU information.

BIOS Passwords

The BIOS password mechanism is a feature on most laptop computers and some palmtops. It is implemented in the power-up instructions that are initiated when the power is turned on. For this reason it is nearly impossible to circumvent. Unfortunately, the BIOS password mechanism is often not enabled, because if the BIOS password is forgotten, the only way to start the device is to remove and replace the read-only memory (ROM) chip in the device. If a typical user password mechanism is also enabled on the device, the use of a BIOS password requires that the user remember and enter two passwords in order to use the device.

Except in Windows NT, PED operating systems have not been rigorously evaluated and should not be considered secure. If the OS has not been evaluated, it is impossible to consider built-in password mechanisms as secure. As just noted, although BIOS passwords provide an implementation challenge— if you lose them, you cannot use the device—they do protect the device from general snooping.

Biometrics and Smart Cards

Biometrics technologies are automated means of identifying or authenticating the identity of a living person based on physiological or behavioral characteristics. Typical biometric characteristics that are used to uniquely authenticate the identity of an individual commonly are hand parts, such as fingerprints, palm scan, and hand geometry; and eye parts, such as a retina or iris scan.

An issue with biometrics is the remediation procedure for a compromised key. It is much more difficult to change a biometric than, say, a password or smart card.

Biometrics of several types are becoming available for a limited number of PEDs, and promise to be fairly widespread within a year or two. Currently available fingerprint technology can be added to a PED that has a PCMCIA slot; it replaces the native password mechanism. Voice recognition is available on certain phones, but must be purchased with the phone, not as an add-on. Both of these technologies are in their infancy for this application area.

Because, as just stated, PED operating systems are unevaluated, any third-party I&A mechanism (such as smart cards, PCMCIA cards, and biometrics that rely on such cards) must be self-protecting; that is, they cannot rely on the OS in order to function properly. The same is true for third-party authentication servers. Voice recognition, available on some phones, is considered a reasonably high level of I&A assurance for unclassified operations. Additionally:

- Smart cards should be combined with the requirement to separately enter a PIN for access to the user's certificate.

- Additional studies should be conducted to determine if the DoD PKI and proposed CAC smart card would satisfy all the requirements for use with wireless PEDs.

- The ECC encryption algorithm should be validated by NIST prior to its use for data confidentiality within the federal government. It currently is validated for digital signatures only.

Smart Cards

Third-party additions for PEDs are available that use smart cards or Personal Computer Memory Card International Association (PCMCIA) cards to implement a secure challenge/response that takes the place of the basic password mechanism. These devices enforce a two-factor authentication by requiring the user to have the smart card (or PCMCIA card) and to know a passphrase or unlock code, similar to the personal identification number (PIN) used with automated teller machines.

Already popular in Europe, some mobile phone and other mobile device manufacturers' designs allow smart cards to slide directly into the wireless devices. The use of a public key infrastructure (PKI), where digital certificates and keys are bound to the user, is the preferred solution to validate users' identity.

Based on the items just mentioned, it is recommended that PEDs without strong I&A built in or added to the system should be used only for administrative tasks such as maintaining calendars and nonsensitive contact lists. Under no circumstance should a PED without strong I&A be used to store, process, or transmit sensitive company information.

BlackBerry Security

Research in Motions's BlackBerry device is considered very secure for mobile email and messaging. Its rapid success and adoption in the workplace is largely due to its intuitive user interface, and the reliability of its security design. BlackBerry offers complete end-to-end security with 3DES encryption, which is specified for use in FIPS 46-3, as described in ANSI X9.52.

BlackBerry security is derived from an encryption key shared by the hand-held and the desktop. The key used by the handheld is generated on the desktop by extracting random information from mouse movements, then hashing the collected random bits. The key is then exchanged with the handheld through a port connection. This exchange can only be done once, so that the key is available in two places: on the desktop and on the handheld. The advantage of this symmetric key encryption system using a secure key exchange is that the encrypted data exchanged between the handheld and the desktop is guaranteed to be confidential and authenticated, since it comes from a source holding the shared key.

Once this key has been generated, a copy of it is stored on the server, and the other copy is stored on the handheld. For messaging to occur, these keys must match at both the server and the handheld, or the message will be discarded.

In the BlackBerry solution, information transferred between the handheld and the desktop or LAN is not decrypted at any intermediate point. This means that only the desktop and the handheld have access to the information sent between them. In particular, it means that the service provider does not have access to any potentially sensitive information.

Recommendations

While there are serious vulnerabilities inherent to using WLANs and PEDs, taking certain precautions to safeguard the confidentiality and integrity of the data contained on them can make a WLAN as safe as its wired equivalent. Although these precautions may cost more in terms of both effort and money, they are necessary if you have an existing WLAN or intend to implement one. The 802.11 TGi group is working on new ways to replace WEP with schemes such as replacing the RC4 with AES and adding sequence numbers to packets to prevent replay attacks.

Until such schemes are finalized and available (as the 802.11i or 802.1x standards), there will be no complete fix for these existing vulnerabilities. In the meantime, to reduce the unauthorized access to system and other resources, recommended security policy additions can be summarized as follows:

- Change the administrative password that is preset on the access point.
- Change the default SSID values.
- Disable SSID broadcasting.
- Enable encryption.

- Avoid installing access points near external walls or windows where signals might be intercepted.

- Place the WLAN outside the firewall to run a virtual private network (VPN) to the inside of the firewall.

- Implement the Remote Authentication Dial-In User Service (RADIUS) protocol to provide another level of security designed to authenticate remote clients to a centralized server.

- Employ end-to-end encryption on the system.

Conclusion

Through six chapters, you have examined the fundamental structure of computers and networks, the internal protocols of wireless theory, current wireless devices, the fundamental tenets of security methodology, how security is implemented in wireless systems, and common threats and how to counter them.

As we lunge headfirst into the future, only one thing can be guaranteed: computing devices, protocols, and theory will change, sometimes rapidly, sometimes slowly (such as the basic structure of a computing machine). But the need for security, and the eternal struggle to ensure safe data exchange will go on. Warfare will focus more and more on information disruption , and businesses will face ever mounting challenges to confidentiality, integrity, and availability.

Glossary

10Base2   802.3 IEEE Ethernet standard for 10 Mbps Ethernet using coaxial cable (thinnet) rated to 185 meters.

10Base5   10 Mbps Ethernet using coaxial cable (thicknet) rated to 500 meters.

10Broad36   10 Mbps broadband Ethernet rated to 3600 meters.

10BaseF   10 Mbps baseband Ethernet using optical fiber.

10BaseT   10 Mbps UTP Ethernet rated to 100 meters.

100BaseT   100 Mbps baseband Ethernet using twisted pair wire.

1000BaseT   1000 Mbps (1Gbps) baseband Ethernet using twisted pair wire.

3DES   Triple Data Encryption Standard.

3G Third generation of digital phone technology.

802.10 IEEE standard that specifies security and privacy access methods for LANs.

802.11 *1.* IEEE standard that specifies 1 Mbps and 2 Mbps wireless connectivity. Defines aspects of frequency hopping and direct sequence spread spectrum systems for use in the 2.4 MHz ISM (industrial, scientific, medical) band. **2.** The IEEE Committee responsible for setting wireless LAN standards.

802.11a Specifies high-speed wireless connectivity in the 5 GHz band using orthogonal frequency division multiplexing (OFDM) with data rates up to 54 Mbps.

802.11b Specifies high-speed wireless connectivity in the 2.4 GHz ISM band up to 11 Mbps.

802.15 Specification for Bluetooth LANs in the 2.4-2.5 GHz band.

802.2 Standard that specifies the logical link control (LLC).

802.3 Ethernet bus topology using carrier sense medium access control/carrier detect (CSMA/CD) for 10 Mbps wired LANs. Currently the most popular LAN topology.

802.4 Specifies a token-passing bus access method for LANs.

802.5 Specifies a token-passing ring access method for LANs.

Acceptance testing Type of testing used to determine whether the network is acceptable to users.

Access point (AP) A wireless LAN transceiver interface between the wireless network and a wired network. Access points forward frames between wireless devices and hosts on the LAN.

ACESS Acronym for Pitney-Bowes automated customer support system.

ACK Acknowledgment. A short-return indication of the successful receipt of a message.

Acknowledged connectionless service   A datagram-style service that includes error-control and flow-control mechanisms.

ACL   Asynchronous connectionless link, one of the two types of data links defined for the Bluetooth systems. ACL is an asynchronous (packet-switched) connection between two devices created on the LMP level. Not to be confused with access control lists in firewalls or routers.

Active mode   Mode in which the Bluetooth unit actively participates on the channel. The master schedules the transmission based on traffic demands to and from the different slaves.

Adaptive routing   A form of network routing whereby the path data packets traverse from a source to a destination node that depends on the current state of the network. Calculates the best path through the network.

Address Resolution Protocol (ARP)   A TCP/IP protocol that binds logical (IP) addresses to physical addresses.

Ad hoc network   A wireless network composed only of stations communicating with each other in a peer mode, that is, with no access points. *See* Infrastructure network.

AES   Advanced Encryption Standard.

AID   Association identifier, a number assigned by the access point when a mobile station associates with it.

AIS   Automated information system.

ALOHA   The University of Hawaii data radio system that features unconstrained contention access on the inbound side.

AM_ADDR   Active member address, sometimes called the MAC address of a Bluetooth unit. A 3-bit number that is valid as long as the slave is active on the channel.

AMPS   Advanced Mobile Phone System. The U.S. standard for analog cellular service.

AMSC   American Mobile Satellite Corporation. A voice and data, geosynchronous satellite system that now owns ARDIS.

AMTA   American Mobile Telecommunications Association.

Analog cellular   A telephone system that uses radio cells to provide connectivity among cellular phones. The analog cellular telephone system uses frequency modulation (FM) radio waves to transmit voice-grade signals.

Analog signal   An electrical signal with an amplitude that varies continuously.

AOL   America Online. An Internet service provider (ISP).

AP   *See* Access point.

API   *See* Application program interface.

Appliance   The device that runs applications and is the interface between the user and the network (PC, Palm, laptop, etc).

Application layer   The top layer of the OSI model concerned with application programs. It provides services such as file transfer and electronic mail to the end users of the network.

Application process   An entity, either human or software, that uses the services offered by the application layer of the OSI reference model.

Application program interface   A software interface provided between a specialized communications program and an end-user application.

Application software   Software that accomplishes functions such as database access, electronic mail, and menu prompts.

AR   Army regulation.

AR_ADDR   Bluetooth: Access request address. Used by the parked slave to determine the slave-to-master half-slot in the access window in which it is allowed to send access request messages. This address is only valid as long as the slave is parked, and is not necessarily unique.

Architecture   As refers to a computer system, an architecture describes the type of components, interfaces, and protocols the system uses and how they fit together.

ARDIS   Advanced Radio Data Information System. A nationwide, packet-switched, two-way data radio network providing host and third-party connectivity, as well as email and messaging services. Founded in 1990, it is now owned by AMSC and employs Motorola protocols and infrastructure.

ARP   *See* Address Resolution Protocol.

ARQ   *See* Automatic repeat-request.

ARQN   Automatic repeat request number. Used as a 1-bit acknowledgment to inform the source of a successful transfer of payload data with CRC.

Association frame   A frame sent by a mobile unit to associate with an access point. If the mobile station moves out of the home cell, it must associate with a new access point. *See* Association service.

Association service   An IEEE 802.11 service that an enables the mapping of a wireless station to the distribution system via an access point. Allows wireless stations to access the distribution system via an access point.

Assurance   Grounds for confidence that an IT product or system meets its security objectives. *See* DITSCAP.

Asynchronous Transfer Mode   A cell-based connection-oriented data service offering high-speed data communications. ATM integrates circuit and packet switching to handle both constant and burst information at rates up to 2.488 Gbps. Also called *cell relay*.

Asynchronous transmission   Type of communications data synchronization with no defined time relationship between transmission of data frames. *See* Synchronous transmission.

ATIM   Announcement traffic indication message. Used in ad hoc mode to notify a station operating in power save mode that there are frames for it.

ATM   *See* Asynchronous Transfer Mode.

Attachment unit interface (AUI)   A 15-pin interface between an Ethernet network interface card and a transceiver.

AUI *See* Attachment unit interface.

Authentication Generically, the process of verifying "who" is at the other end of a transmission. Specifically, for wireless networks, the process a station uses to announce its identify to another station. IEEE 802.11 specifies two forms of authentication: open system and shared key. In Bluetooth, this is achieved by the authentication procedure based on the stored link key or by pairing with a PIN.

Authentication device A device whose identity has been verified during the lifetime of the current link based on the authentication procedure.

Authentication frame A frame sent by a mobile unit to authenticate with an access point. Security settings for each side must be compatible for successful authentication.

Authentication Service IEEE 802.11 service that allows wireless stations to associate with another station via an access point. WEP uses a series of authentication frames.

Automatic repeat-request A method of error correction where the receiving node detects errors and uses a feedback path to the sender for requesting the retransmission of incorrect frames.

AUX An ACL link packet type for data. An AUX1 packet resembles a DH1 packet except it has no CRC code. As a result it can carry up to 30 info bytes.

AVL Automatic vehicle locator.

Backbone network A network that interconnects other networks.

Bandwidth Specifies the amount of the frequency spectrum that is usable for data transfer. In other words, it identifies the maximum data rate a signal can attain on the medium without encountering significant attenuation (loss of power). Also, the amount of information one can send through a connection.

Baseband A signal that has not undergone any shift in frequency. Normally with LANs, a baseband signal is purely digital. The baseband describes the specifications of the digital signal-processing part of the hardware. Also, a transmission system in which the signals are broadcast one at a time at their original frequency (not modulated).

Base station   In a radio network, where the transceivers and antennae are located.

Basic service set (BSS)   A set or group of 802.11-compliant stations that operate as a fully connected wireless network. Also group of 802.11 stations that operate as a fully connected wireless network in a basic service area (BSA).

Baud rate   The number of pulses of a signal that occur in one second. Thus, baud rate is the speed at which the digital signal pulses travel. Also, the rate at which data are transferred.

BD   Common abbreviation for a Bluetooth device.

BD_ADDR   Bluetooth device address. Each Bluetooth transceiver is allocated a unique 48-bit device address. It is divided into a 24-bit LAP field, a 16-bit NAP field, and an 8-bit UAP field.

BER   Bit error rate.

BIOS   Basic Input/Output System.

Bit   Short for binary digit. A single digit number in binary, 0 or 1.

Bit rate   The transmission rate of binary symbols: 0s and 1s. Bit rate is equal to the total number of bits transmitted in one second.

Block cipher   In cryptography, a block cipher is obtained by segregating plaintext into blocks of n characters or bits and applying the same encryption algorithm and key to each block.

Bluetooth   An open specification for wireless communication of data and voice, based on a low-cost short-range radio link facilitating protected ad hoc connections for stationary and mobile communication environments. The Bluetooth Special Interest Group (BSIG) includes leaders from the telecommunications and computing industries who are driving development of the technology and bringing it to market.

Bluetooth clock   Internal Bluetooth system clock that determines the timing and hopping of the transceiver. It can be implemented as a 28-bit counter, with the LSB ticking in units of 312.5 µs, giving a clock rate of 3.2 kHz.

Bluetooth device class   A Bluetooth parameter that indicates the type of device and the types of services that are supported. The class is received during the discovery procedure.

Bluetooth service type   One or more services a Bluetooth device can provide to other devices. The service information is defined in the service class field of the Bluetooth device class parameter.

Bridge   A network device that provides internetworking functionality by connecting networks. Bridges can provide segmentation of data frames and can be used to connect LANs by forwarding packets across connections at the media access control (MAC) sublayer of the data link layer of the OSI model.

Broadband   A transmission system in which signals are encoded and modulated into different frequencies and then transmitted simultaneously with other signals, having undergone a shift in frequency. A LAN broadband signal is commonly analog.

BSC   Binary synchronous communication.

BSS   *See* Basic service set.

BSS basic rate set   The set rate of data transfer that all stations in a BSS will be capable of using to receive frames. This rate is preset for stations in the WLAN.

BSSID   Basic service set identifier. A 6-byte address that identifies a particular access point. Also known as a network ID in Wi-Fi.

BTAM   Basic telecommunications access method.

Bus topology   A type of network topology wherein all nodes are connected to a single length of cabling with a terminator at each end.

Business card   In this context, the electronic date equivalent to a printed business card. It is treated like a file and can be exchanged between Bluetooth devices.

Byte   A set of bits, usually 8, that represent a single character.

Carrier current LAN   A LAN that uses power lines within the facility as a medium for the transport of data.

Carrier sense multiple access (CSMA) The technique used to reduce contention by listening for contention before transmitting.

Carrier sense multiple access with collision detection (CSMA/CD) Most common Ethernet cable access method.

Category 1 twisted pair wire Used for early analog telephone communications; not suitable for data.

Category 2 twisted pair wire Rated for 4 Mbps, and used in 802.5 token ring networks.

Category 3 twisted pair wire Rated for 10 Mbps, and used in 802.3 10BaseT Ethernet networks.

Category 4 twisted pair wire Rated for 16 Mbps, and used in 802.5 token ring networks.

Category 5 twisted pair wire Rated for 100 Mbps, and used in 100BaseT Ethernet networks.

CBC Cipher block chaining.

CC Common Criteria.

CCITT Comité Consultatif International Télégraphique et Téléphonique; in English, the International Telegraph and Telephone Consultative Committee An organization based in Geneva, Switzerland, established as part of the United Nations International Telecommunications Union (ITU) and later taken over by the ITU. The CCITT is dedicated to establishing effective and compatible telecommunications among members of the United Nations. CCITT develops the widely used V-series and X-series standards and protocols.

CCK Complementary code keying.

CDDI *See* Copper Data Distributed Interface.

CDI Cellular Data Incorporated.

CDLC Cellular Data Link Control. A protocol developed by Racal to transmit data via cellular connections.

CDMA Code division multiple access, a digital cellular communications technology. Each call is identified by an individual code. Multiple calls can be grouped together on a single frequency by sharing radio spectrum in which individual transmissions are separated by encoding. CDMA uses spread spectrum techniques for handling radio communications and marks an improvement on AMPS and TDMA cellular service. Two common means of encoding are frequency hopping or direct sequence spread spectrum. *See also* FDMA and TDMA.

CDPD *See* Cellular digital packet data.

CDRH *See* Center for Devices and Radiological Health.

Cell relay *See* Asynchronous Transfer Mode.

Cellular digital packet data (CDPD) Systems that are able to share cellular spectrum with voice. CDPD overlays the conventional analog cellular telephone system using a channel-hopping technique to transmit data in short bursts during idle times in cellular channels. It operates full duplex in the 800 and 900 MHz frequency bands, offering data rates up to 19.2 Kbps.

Center for Devices and Radiological Health (CDRH) The division of the U.S. Food and Drug Administration (FDA) that evaluates and certifies laser products for public use.

Centronics A de facto standard 36-pin parallel 200 Kbps asynchronous interface for connecting printers and other devices to a computer.

Channel Bluetooth: A logical connection on the L2CAP level between two devices serving a single application or higher-layer protocol. A portion of the media bandwidth used for passing PDUs.

Channel (hopping) sequence A pseudo-random sequence of 79 (23 for the 23-MHz system) frequencies in Bluetooth. Does not show repetitive patterns over a short time interval, but distributes the hop frequencies equally.

Channel agility Option in DSSS that allows the station to use frequency hopping to enable synchronization. *See* Direct sequence spread spectrum.

Chipping code A method for encoding the physical layer signals on DSSS networks.

C/I   Carrier-to-interference ratio, in decibels. C/I refers to interference arising from a nonadjacent identical channel. To satisfy the AMPS quality objective, a system must provide a C/I of 17 dB or greater over 90 percent of its coverage area.

Cipher   Cryptographic transformation that operates on characters or bits.

Ciphertext or cryptogram   Unintelligible encrypted message.

Circuit-switched   The application of a network in which a dedicated line is used to transmit information. Compare packet-switched. Also, for Bluetooth, the application of a network in which a dedicated line is used to transmit Bluetooth data.

Class of device (CoD)   *See* Bluetooth device class.

Clear channel assessment   A function that determines the state of the wireless medium in an 802.11 network.

Client   A computer that accesses the resources of a server.

Client/server architecture   A network system design in which a processor or computer designated as a file server or database server provides services to other client processors or computers. Applications are distributed between a host server and a remote client.

CLK clock   Typically, the master device clock that defines the timing used in the piconet (Bluetooth).

CLKE   Clock estimate, in Bluetooth, a slave's estimate of the master's clock, used to synchronize the slave device to the master.

CLKN   Clock native, the clock of the current Bluetooth device.

Clustering   Situation in which a plaintext message generates identical ciphertext messages using the same transformation algorithm, but different cryptovariables or keys.

C/N   Carrier-to-noise ratio. A power ratio of wanted to unwanted signal, expressed in decibels (dB).

Coaxial cable (coax)   Type of transmission cable consisting of a hollow outer cylindrical conductor that surrounds a single inner wire conductor for current flow. Because the shielding reduces the amount of electrical noise interference, coax can extend to much greater lengths than twisted pair wiring.

Code division multiple access (CDMA)   A spread spectrum digital cellular radio system that uses different codes to distinguish users.

Codes   Cryptographic transformation that operates at the level of words or phrases.

Collision detection   The detection of simultaneous transmission on the communications medium.

Connectable device   An in-range Bluetooth device that will respond to a page message and set up a connection.

Connection-oriented service   Service that establishes a logical connection that provides flow control and error control between two stations needing to exchange data.

Connectivity   A path through which communications signals can flow.

Connectivity software   A software component that provides an interface between the networked appliance and the database or application software located on the network.

Contention-free (C-F)   A wireless media access mode whereby the access point caches all frames for C-F stations, then polls the C-F stations to receive any frames they have queued for delivery, and transmits any frames it has in the buffer for them.

Copper Data Distributed Interface (CDDI)   A version of FDDI specifying the use of unshielded twisted-pair wiring.

CP   Capability provider. A module within the local device that provides a service to other modules. Protocol stack modules (RFCOMM, L2CAP) are capability providers, as are "application interface modules" such as OBEX and ESC-AT. In fact, any module that registers a port that other modules can connect to is a capability provider.

CPU   The central processing unit of a computer.

CRC   *See* Cyclic redundancy check.

CRL   Certificate revocation list.

Cryptanalysis   The process of obtaining the plaintext or key from cipher-text. Cryptanalysis is used to intercept valuable information, and alter it or exchange it for fake messages to deceive the original intended recipient.

Cryptographic algorithm   Step-by-step procedure that is used to encipher plaintext and decipher ciphertext.

Cryptography   Art and science of hiding the meaning of a communica-tion from unintended recipients. The word "cryptography" comes from the Greek, *kryptos,* meaning hidden, and *graphein,* to write.

Cryptology   Field that encompasses cryptography and cryptanalysis

CS-CDPD   Circuit-switched CDPD.

CSMA   *See* Carrier sense multiple access.

CSMA/CA   Carrier sense multiple access with collision avoidance, used in 802.11 Ethernet.

CSMA/CD   Carrier sense multiple access with collision detection, used in 802.3 Ethernet.

CTIA   Cellular Telecommunications Industry Association.

CTP   Cordless telephone profile.

CTS   Clear to send.

CVSD   Continuous variable slope delta modulation.

Cyclic redundancy check (CRC)   A common error-detection process. A mathematical operation is applied to the data when transmitted; its result is appended to the core packet. Upon receipt, the same mathemat-ical operation is performed and checked against the CRC. A mismatch indicates a very high probability that an error has occurred during transmission.

DA   Destination address. Address of the final destination to which the frame is sent.

DAC *1.* Device access code, a code derived from the unit's BD_ADDR, used during page, page scan, and page response substates. *2.* Discretionary Access Control in TCSEC.

Data Encryption Standard (DES) A cryptographic algorithm that protects unclassified computer data. DES is a National Institute of Standards and Technology (NIST) standard that is available for both public and government use.

Datagram service A connectionless form of packet switching whereby the source does not need to establish a connection with the destination before sending data packets.

Data-link layer The OSI level that performs the assembly and transmission of data packets, including error control.

Data-high rate Bluetooth: An ACL- link data packet type for high- rate data.

Data service unit/channel service unit (DSU/CSU) A set of network components that reshape data signals into a form that can be effectively transmitted over a digital transmission medium, typically a leased 56 Kbps or T1 line.

DB-9 A standard 9-pin connector commonly used with RS-232 serial interfaces on portable computers. The DB-9 connector will not support all RS-232 functions.

DB-15 A standard 15-pin connector commonly used with RS-232 serial interfaces, Ethernet transceivers, and computer monitors.

DB-25 A standard 25-pin connector commonly used with RS-232 serial interfaces. The DB-25 connector will support all RS-232 functions.

DCF Distributed coordination function.

DCID Destination channel identifier, used as the device local endpoint for an L2CAP transmission. It represents the channel endpoint on the device receiving the message. *See also* SCID.

DCS Digital Communication System. IBM's field-service system, which was folded into ARDIS in 1990.

DDS   Digital dispatch service.

Deauthentication frame   The frame sent by a station that wants to end an existing authentication relationship.

Decipher   To unscramble the encipherment process to make the message human-readable.

De facto standard   A standard based on broad usage and support; not directly specified by the IEEE.

Default   A value or option that is automatically chosen when no other value is specified.

DES   *See* Data Encryption Standard.

Destination   In the context of Bluetooth, a device receiving an action from another Bluetooth device. The device sending the action is called the source.

Device discovery   In the context of Bluetooth, the mechanism to request and receive the Bluetooth address, clock, class of device, used page scan, and names of devices.

Device name   *See* Bluetooth device name.

Device security level   Determines access to a device. Access can be denied based on the required device security level. There are two levels of device security: trusted and untrusted.

DHCP   *See* Dynamic Host Configuration Protocol.

DIAC   Dedicated inquiry access code, used to inquire for specific types of devices.

DIAD   Delivery information and acquisition device.

Diffused laser light   Type of laser transmission where the light is reflected off a wall or ceiling.

DIFS   Distributed interframe space. The 50-μs interval between data and management frames from the access point.

DII   Defense Information Infrastructure.

Direct sequence spread spectrum (DSSS)   A method used in 802.11b to split the frequency into 14 channels, each with a frequency range, by combining a data signal with a chipping sequence. Data rates of 1, 2, 5.5, 11 Mbps are obtainable. DSSS spreads its signal continuously over this wide-frequency band.

Disassociation frame   A frame sent when a mobile station wants to terminate an existing association for any reason.

Disassociation service   The 802.11 term that defines the process a wireless station or access point uses to notify that it is terminating an existing association.

Discoverable device   A Bluetooth device in the range that allows it to respond to an inquiry message.

Distributed Queue Dual Bus (DQDB)   The IEEE 802.6 standard that provides full-duplex 155 Mbps operation between nodes in a metropolitan area network.

Distributed routing   A form of routing wherein each router on the network periodically identifies neighboring nodes, updates its routing table, then sends its routing table to all of its neighbors. Because each node follows the same process, complete network topology information propagates through the network and eventually reaches each node.

Distribution service   Used by an 802.11 station to send MAC frames across a distribution system.

Distribution system   A component of a 802.11 wireless system that interconnects basic service sets via access points to form an extended service set. Used to forward frames outside of the local BSS.

Distribution System Service   A set of services used by 802.11 to send MAC frames between stations that are not in direct communication through a distribution system.

DITSCAP U.S.   Department of Defense Information Technology Security Certification and Accreditation Process.

DLCI Bluetooth: Data link connection identifier, a 6-bit value representing an ongoing connection between a client and a server application used in the RFCOMM layer.

DM Bluetooth: Data-medium rate. An ACL link data packet type for medium-rate data. Commonly DM1, DM3 and DM5 formats.

DoD U.S. Department of Defense.

DOJ U.S. Department of Justice.

DoS Denial of service.

DQDB *See* Distributed Queue Dual Bus.

DRN Digital Radio Network. Motorola's first public airtime service, launched in 1986 and folded into ARDIS in 1990.

DS Distribution system.

DSMA Digital sense multiple access. The "busy bit" implementation of CSMA.

DSR Data set ready. A device sends an RS-232 DSR signal when it is ready to accept data.

DSSS *See* Direct sequence spread spectrum.

DSU/CSU *See* Data service unit/channel service unit.

DT Data terminal.

DTIM Delivery traffic indication map. The DTIM period is the number of beacon frames between multicast frame deliveries. The DTIM count is an integer value that counts down to zero. It is the number of beacon frames before the delivery of multicast frames.

Dynamic Host Configuration Protocol (DHCP) A protocol that issues IP addresses automatically within a specified range to devices such as PCs when they are first powered on. The device retains the use of the IP address for a specific license period that the system administrator can define.

EAP Extensible Authentication Protocol. Cisco proprietary protocol for enhanced user authentication and wireless security management.

EBCDIC Extended Binary-Coded Decimal Interchange Code. An 8-bit character representation developed by IBM in the early 1960s.

ECC Elliptic curve cryptography.

ECDSA Elliptic curve digital signature algorithm.

ECZ Enhanced cellular control.

EDI *See* Electronic Data Interchange.

EIA *See* Electronics Industry Association.

EIFS Extended interframe space.

EIRP Effective isotropic radiated power.

Electronic Data Interchange A service that provides communications for business transactions. ANSI standard X.12 defines the data format for EDI.

Electronics Industry Association (EIA) A U.S. standards organization that represents a large number of electronics firms.

EMCI Economic and Management Consultants International.

Encipher To make the message unintelligible to all but the intended recipients.

End-to-end encryption Encrypted information sent from the point of origin to the final destination. In symmetric key encryption, this requires the sender and receiver to have the identical key for the session.

ERP Effective radiated power.

ESN Electronic serial number. A unique number for devices, particularly cellular phones. It can be used to trace a phone's location and user.

ESS Extended service set.

ESSID Extended service set identifier An ESSID is configured on each access point in an extended service set.

ETC(2) Enhanced transmission capability. The protocol employed by AT&T Paradyne for cellular data transfer, and licensed by vendors such as U.S. Robotics. ETC(2) offers fast, robust connection at relatively high transmission speeds (14.4 Kbps).

Ethernet repeater A component that provides Ethernet connections among multiple stations sharing a common collision domain. Also referred to as a shared Ethernet hub.

Ethernet switch More intelligent than a hub, has the capability to connect the sending station directly to the receiving station.

Ethernet An industry-standard local area network media access method that uses a bus topology and CSMA/CD. IEEE 802.3 is a standard that specifies Ethernet.

Extension point A base-station two-radio transceiver that bridges the gap between a wireless client and an access point or between a wireless client and another extension point.

ETSI European Telecommunications Standards Institute.

Evaluation Assessment of an IT product or system against defined security functional and assurance criteria, performed by a combination of testing and analytic techniques.

Evaluation assurance level (EAL) One of seven increasingly rigorous packages of assurance requirements from the Common Criteria (CC). Each numbered package represents a point on the CCs predefined assurance scale. An EAL can be considered a level of confidence in the security functions of an IT product or system.

Extended service set (ESS) A collection of basic service sets tied together via a distribution system. Several basic service sets assigned a common extended service set ID (ESSID) to form a larger area that supports frame forwarding.

FCC Federal Communication Commission.

FCS Frame check sequence.

FDDI   *See* Fiber-Distributed Data Interface.

FDMA   Frequency division multiple access. A spectrum-sharing technique whereby the available spectrum is divided into a number of individual radio channels. *See also* CDMA and TDMA.

FDX   Full duplex.

FE   Field engineering.

FEC   *See* Forward error correction.

F-ES   Fixed-end system. The server/host that handles a client device. Used in CDPD.

FH   Frequency hopping.

FHS   Frequency- hopping synchronization. Bluetooth control packet revealing the BD_ADDR and the clock of the source device.

FHSS   *See* Frequency hopping spread spectrum.

Fiber-Distributed Data Interface (FDDI)   An ANSI standard for token-passing networks. FDDI uses optical fiber and operates at 100 Mbps in dual counter-rotating rings.

FIFO   Acronym for first in, first out.

File server   A computer that provides network stations with controlled access to sharable resources. The network operating system (NOS) is loaded on the file server, and most sharable devices, including disk subsystems and printers, are attached to it.

File Transfer Protocol   A TCP/IP protocol for file transfer.

FIPS   Federal Information Processing Standard.

Firewall   A network device that shields the trusted network from unauthorized users in the untrusted network by blocking certain specific types of traffic. Many type of firewalls exist, including packet filtering and stateful inspection.

FLEX   A Motorola protocol employed on existing paging channels transmitting at 6400 bps.

FM   Frequency modulation. A method of transmitting information over a radio wave by changing frequencies.

Forward error correction   Mathematical scheme performed on a wireless packet to repair some damage that occurs during transmission to attempt to reduce the number of retransmissions. Bluetooth has two versions of FEC, 1/3 FEC and 2/3 FEC.

Fractional T-1   A 64-Kbps increment of a T1 frame.

Frame relay   A packet-switching interface that operates at data rates of 56 Kbps to 2 Mbps. Frame relay is minus the error control overhead of X.25, and assumes that a higher-layer protocol will check for transmission errors.

Frequency division multiple access (FDMA)   A digital radio technology that divides the available spectrum into separate radio channels. Generally used in conjunction with time division multiple access (TDMA) or Code division multiple access (CDMA).

Frequency hopping multiple access (FHMA)   A system using frequency hopping spread spectrum (FHSS) to permit multiple, simultaneous conversations or data sessions by assigning different hopping patterns to each.

Frequency hopping spread spectrum (FHSS)   A method used to share the available bandwidth in 802.11b WLANs. FHSS takes the data signal and modulates it with a carrier signal that hops from frequency to frequency on a cyclical basis over a wide band of frequencies. FHSS in the 2.4-GHz frequency band will hop between 2.4 GHz and 2.483 GHz. The receiver must be set to the same hopping code.

Frequency shift keying (FSK)   A modulation scheme for data communications using a limited number of discrete frequencies to convey binary information.

FTP   *See* File Transfer Protocol.

GAP   Generic access profile. Describes the mechanism by which one device discovers and accesses another device when they do not share a common application.

Gateway   A network component that provides interconnectivity at higher network layers. For example, electronic mail gateways can interconnect dissimilar electronic mail systems.

Gaussian frequency shift keying (GFSK)   A frequency modulation technique that filters the baseband signal with a Gaussian filter before performing the modulation. This is the modulation used in the radio layer of the Bluetooth system. A modification to FSK with a low modulation index.

GEOS   Geostationary satellite. A fixed-position satellite that orbits at an altitude of approximately 22,300 miles.

GFSK   *See* Gaussian frequency shift keying.

GIAC   General inquiry access code. The default inquiry code used to discover all devices in range.

Gigabyte (GB, GByte)   A unit of measure for memory or disk storage capacity; 1,073,741,824 bytes.

Gigahertz (GHz)   A measure of frequency; 1 billion hertz.

Global Positioning System (GPS)   A worldwide, satellite-based radio navigation system providing three-dimensional position, velocity, and time information anywhere on or near the surface of the Earth, often within 10 meters of accuracy. The 24 GPS satellites are owned and operated by the U.S. Department of Defense.

Global System for Mobile Communications   A digital cellular communications technology available in both Europe and the United States. GSM offers multiple services for the subscriber, such as short message service (SMS). Also, Groupe Speciale Mobile, a Pan-European standard for digital cellular telephone systems. GSM uses TDMA with eight slots per carrier, with the carriers spaced 200 kHz apart.

GOEP   Generic object exchange profile.

GPS   *See* Global Positioning System.

GSM   *See* Global System for Mobile Communications.

GVTS   Global Vehicle Tracking System.

GW   Bluetooth gateway. A Bluetooth-enabled base station connected to an external network.

Handheld PC   Term adopted by Microsoft and its supporters to describe handheld computers employing Microsoft Windows CE operating system.

Hand-off   The process that occurs when a mobile user travels from one cell, terminating the communications, to another cell, initiating the communications.

HCI   Host Controller Interface. A layer that provides a command interface to the LMP and baseband layers.

HDLC   *See* High-level Data-Link Control.

HDX   Half duplex.

Headset (HS)   A microphone and earpiece used to conduct conversations. Headsets can be connected directly to a cellular device or remotely.

Hertz (Hz)   Unit of frequency measurement; one cycle of a periodic event per second.

Hierarchical topology   A topology wherein nodes in the same geographical area are joined together, then tied to the remaining network as groups. The idea of a hierarchical topology is to install more links within high-density areas and fewer links between these populations.

High-level Data Link Control   An ISO protocol for link synchronization and error control.

HOLD mode   Devices synchronized to a piconet can enter power-saving modes in which device activity is lowered. In Bluetooth, the master unit can put slave units into HOLD mode, where only an internal timer is running. Slave units can also demand to be put into HOLD mode. Data transfer restarts instantly when units transition out of HOLD mode. It has an intermediate duty cycle (medium power efficient) of the three power-saving modes (sniff, hold, and park).

HomeRF Working Group   A group formed to provide the foundation for a broad range of interoperable consumer devices by establishing an open industry specification for wireless digital communication between PCs and consumer electronic devices anywhere in and around the home.

Host   A time-sharing computer accessed via terminals or terminal emulation. A computer to which an expansion device attaches. For example, when a LAN card is installed in a PC, that PC is the host to that adapter.

HR/DSSS   High rate direct sequence spread spectrum.

HS   *See* Headset.

HTTP   Hypertext Transfer Protocol.

HV   High-quality voice. A Bluetooth SCO link voice packet that comes in three formats, HV1, HV2, and HV3. HV packets do not have an CRC or payload header. *See also* Bluetooth packet types.

HiperLAN   A wireless LAN protocol developed by ETSI that provides a 23.5 Mbps data rate in the 5 GHz band.

Hypertext Markup Language (HTML)   A standard used on the World Wide Web for defining hypertext links between documents.

I&A   Identification and authentication.

IAC   Inquiry access code, used in inquiry procedures. The IAC can be one of two types: dedicated , for specific devices, or generic, for all devices.

IAPP   Inter-Access Point Protocol. A proprietary protocol used to forward frames between access points.

IAW   Acronym for "in accordance with...."

IBSS   *See* Independent basic service set.

IBSS network   *See* Independent Basic Service Set Network.

ICV   Integrity check value. In WEP encryption, the frame is run through an integrity algorithm, and the ICV generated is placed at the end of the encrypted data in the frame. Then the receiving station runs the data through its integrity algorithm and compares it to the ICV received in the frame. If it matches, the unencrypted frame is passed to the higher layers. If it does not match, the frame is discarded.

ID   Common abbreviation of Identifier or identity.

Idle mode   A device is in idle mode when it has no established links to other devices; in this mode, however, the device may discover other devices.

IDS Intrusion detection system.

IEEE *See* Institute of Electrical and Electronic Engineers.

IETF Internet Engineering Task Force.

IKE Internet key exchange.

Independent basic service set (IBSS) IEEE 802.11 network that has no access point and consists of two or more wireless stations. *See also* Ad hoc network.

Independent basic service set network IEEE 802.11-based wireless network that has no backbone infrastructure and consists of at least two wireless stations communicating peer-to-peer. *See also* Ad hoc network.

Independent network Vernacular for a network that provides peer-to-peer connectivity without relying on a complete network infrastructure. *See also* Ad hoc network.

Industrial, scientific, and medicine (ISM) bands Radio frequency bands authorized by the Federal Communications Commission (FCC) for wireless LANs. ISM bands are located at 902 MHz, 2.400 GHz, and 5.7 GHz. The transmitted power is commonly less than 600 mwatts, therefore no FCC license is required.

Infrared (IR) light Light waves having wavelengths ranging from about 0.75 to 1,000 microns, which is lower in frequency than the spectral colors but higher in frequency than radio waves.

Infrastructure network A wireless network connected to a wireless access point. In an infrastructure network, the access point provides wireless connectivity to the wired network or LAN and manages its own wireless network traffic.

Inquiry procedure Enables a device to discover which devices are in range, and to determine the addresses and clocks for the devices. After the inquiry procedure has completed, a connection can be established using the paging procedure.

Inquiry (hopping) sequence   Sequence of 32 (16 for the 23-MHz system) frequencies, The frequency is calculated using the GIAC LAP or the DIAC LAP. The phase in the sequence is derived from the native unit's clock. Thirty-two frequencies are calculated, the main center frequency and 31 other frequencies, which have an of offset of 16. A new center frequency is calculated every 1.28 seconds. To handle all 32 frequencies, the inquiry hopping sequence switches between two inquiry trains, of 16 frequencies each.

Inquiry (hopping) response sequence   Covers 32 (16 for the 23-MHz) unique response frequencies that all are in an one-to-one correspondence to the current inquiry hopping sequence.

Inquiry response state   When a device has received an inquiry packet, it can respond with an inquiry reply packet. It will send this using the inquiry response hopping sequence.

Inquiry scan state   When a device wishes to receive inquiry packets it enters the inquiry scan mode. This scanning follows the inquiry hopping sequence.

Institute of Electrical and Electronic Engineers (IEEE)   A United States-based standards organization that participates in the development of standards for data transmission systems. IEEE has made significant progress in the establishment of standards for LANs, namely the IEEE 802 series of standards.

Integrated Services Digital Network (ISDN)   A collection of CCITT standards specifying WAN digital transmission services. The overall goal of ISDN is to provide a single physical network outlet and transport mechanism for the transmission of all types of information, including data, video, and voice.

Integration service   Enables the delivery of media access control (MAC) frames through a portal between an 802.11 system and a non-802.11 LAN.

Integration testing   Process used to verify the interfaces between network components as the components are installed. The installation crew should integrate components into the network one by one and perform integration testing when necessary to ensure proper gradual integration of components.

Interference   Noise or other external signals coming from other devices, such as microwave ovens and other wireless network devices that will result in delay to the user either by blocking transmissions from stations on the LAN or by causing bit errors to occur in data being sent.

Interframe space   The time interval between the end of a transmitted frame and the beginning of the next frame. Defines spacing between different aspects of the IEEE 802.11 Media Access Control (MAC) protocol to enable different transmission priorities. The IEEE 802.11 specification has several interframe spaces that depend on the type of frame last transmitted, the next frame, and the device that is waiting.

Intermediate System-to-Intermediate System Protocol   An OSI protocol for intermediate systems exchange routing information.

International Standards Organization (ISO)   A nontreaty standards organization active in the development of international standards such as the Open System Interconnection (OSI) network architecture.

International Telecommunications Union (ITU)   An intergovernmental agency responsible for making recommendations and standardization regarding telephone and data communications systems for public and private telecommunication organizations.

International Telegraph and Telephone Consultative Committee (CCITT)   *See* CCITT.

Internet   The largest network in the world. Successor to ARPANET, the Internet includes other large internetworks. The Internet uses the TCP/IP protocol suite and connects universities, government agencies, businesses, for-profit and nonprofit organizations, and individuals around the world.

Internet Protocol (IP)   The Internet standard protocol that defines the Internet datagram as the unit of information passed across the Internet. IP provides the basis of a best-effort packet delivery service. The Internet protocol suite is often referred to as TCP/IP because IP is one of the two fundamental protocols, the other being the Transfer Control Protocol.

Internetwork   A collection of interconnected networks. Often it is necessary to connect networks, and an internetwork provides the link to do this. An organization on one network may want to share information with another organization on a different network. The internetwork provides the necessary functionality to enable sharing information between these two networks.

Internetwork Packet Exchange (IPX)   NetWare protocol for the exchange of message packets on an internetwork. IPX passes application requests for network services to the network drives and then to other workstations, servers, or devices on the internetwork.

IP   *See* Internet Protocol.

IPSec   Secure Internet Protocol.

IR   *See* Infrared (IR) light.

ISDN   *See* Integrated Services Digital Network.

ISI   Intersymbol interference.

ISM   *See* Industrial, scientific, and medicine bands.

ISO   *See* International Standards Organization.

Isochronous transmission   Type of synchronization whereby information frames are sent at specific times.

ISP   Internet service provider.

ITA   Industrial Telecommunications Association.

ITU   *See* International Telecommunications Union.

IV   Initialization vector. For WEP encryption.

Joint application design (JAD)   A parallel team design process composed of users, salespeople, marketing staff, project managers, analysts, and engineers. Members of this team are used to simultaneously define requirements.

JTAA   Joint Technical Architecture Army.

Key   Information or sequence that controls the enciphering and deciphering of messages. Also known as cryptovariable.

Kilobyte (KB, Kbyte)   A unit of measurement of memory or disk storage capacity; a data unit of 1,024 bytes.

Kilohertz (kHz)   A unit of frequency measurement, equivalent to 1,000 hertz.

Known device   A device for which at least the BD_ADDR is stored.

LAN   *See* Local area network.

LAP   *1.* LAN access point. *2.* Lower address portion. A 24-bit section of the BD_ADDR. *See also* NAP and UAP. *3.* Link access procedure.

Laser   Acronym for light amplification by stimulated emission of radiation; a device containing a substance where the majority of its atoms or molecules are put into an excited energy state. As a result, the laser emits coherent light of a precise wavelength in a narrow beam. Most laser metropolitan area networks (MANs) use lasers that produce infrared light.

LBT   Shorthand for "listen before talking."

LC   Link controller. Manages the link to other Bluetooth devices. It is the low-level baseband protocol handler.

LC channel   Link Control channel. One of the five logical channels defined for the Bluetooth system. The LC channel is mapped onto the packet header, and controls low-level link control info. The LC is carried in every packet except the ID packet, which has no packet header.

LCD   Liquid crystal display.

LD   Locating device.

LEAH   Law Enforcement Assistance Administration. The funding agent that stimulated the first commercial uses of data radio technology.

LEAP   Extensible Authentication Protocol provided by the firmware on the client adapter and Cisco software. LEAP is used in place of EAP for client adapters whose operating systems do not support EAP.

LEOS   Low Earth-orbiting satellite. These variable-position "birds" are in polar orbits at altitudes of 420 to 1200 nautical miles above the Earth.

LFSR   Linear feedback shift register. Used in Bluetooth to generate the HEC and CRC.

Light-emitting diode (LED)   Used in conjunction with optical fiber, a LED emits incoherent light when current is passed through it. Its advantages include low cost and long lifetime; and they are capable of operating in the Mbps range.

Link Access Procedure   An ITU error-correction protocol derived from the HDLC standard.

Link encryption   Each entity has keys in common with its two neighboring nodes in the chain of transmission. Thus, a node receives the encrypted message from its predecessor neighboring node, decrypts it, then reencrypts it with another key that is common to the successor node. Then, the encrypted message is sent on to the successor node where the process is repeated until the final destination is reached. Obviously, this mode provides no protection if the nodes along the transmission path are subject to compromise.

Link key   The authentication key used to establish a link between wireless devices.

LLC   Logical Link Control. The IEEE layer 2 protocol.

LM   Link manager. Software that carries out link setup, authentication, link configuration, and other protocols.

LM channel   Link manager control channel. One of the five logical channels defined for the Bluetooth system. The LM channel carries control info exchanged between the link managers of the master and the slave(s). It can be carried by either the SCO or ACL link.

LMP   Link Manager Protocol. Used for link setup and control. The LMP PDU signals are interpreted and filtered out by the link manager on the receiving side and are not propagated to higher layers.

LMP-authentication   An LMP-level procedure for verifying the identity of a remote device. The procedure is based on a challenge-response mechanism that uses a random number, a secret key, and the BD_ADDR of the noninitiating device. The secret key used can be a previously exchanged link key or an initialization key created based on a PIN (as when pairing).

LMP pairing   An LMP procedure that authenticates two devices based on a PIN and subsequently creates a common link key that can be used as a basis for a trusted relationship or a (single) secure connection.

Local area network (LAN)   A network that interconnects devices in the same office, floor, or building, or areas inside buildings with areas just outside.

Local bridge   A bridge that connects two LANs within close proximity.

Logical channel   There are five logical channels defined for the Bluetooth system. The LC and LM control channels, and the UA, UI, and US user channels. The LC channel is carried in the packet header; all the other channels are carried in the packet payload.

Logical Link Controller and Adaptation Protocol (L2CAP)   Supports higher-level protocol multiplexing, packet segmentation and reassembly, and quality-of-service information conveyance.

Logical link control layer   The highest layer of the IEEE 802 Reference Model. Provides similar functions to those of a traditional data link control protocol.

LSA   Licensed space arrangement.

LSB   Least significant bit.

MAC   *See* Media access control.

MAC address   A 3-bit address used to distinguish between units participating in a piconet. Within Bluetooth, this is the AM_ADDR .

MAC layer   *See* Media access control layer.

MAC protocol data unit (MPDU)   Unit of data in an IEEE 802 network exchanged by two peer MAC entities across a physical layer.

Mail gateway   A type of gateway that interconnects dissimilar electronic mail systems.

MAN   Acronym for metropolitan area network.

Management information base (MIB)   A collection of managed objects residing in a virtual information store.

MAPI   Microsoft's mail application programming interface.

MASC   Mobitex asynchronous communication.

Master device   A device that initiates an action or requests a service on a piconet. Also the device in a piconet whose clock and hopping sequence are used to synchronize all other devices in the piconet.

MAU   *See* multistation access unit.

MD-BS   Mobile database station. Used to identify CDPD base stations, to differentiate them from their voice cellular counterparts.

MD-IS   Mobile data intermediate system. The CDPD control element above the base station, usually located at the mobile telephone switching office (MTSO).

Media access control (MAC)   IEEE 802 standards sublayer used to control access to a network medium, such as a wireless LAN. Each computer has its own unique MAC address.

Medium   In this context, a physical link that provides a basic building block to support the transmission of information signals. A medium may be composed of metal, glass, plastic, or air.

Medium access   The data-link layer function that controls how devices access a shared medium. IEEE 802.11 uses either CSMA/CA or contention-free access modes. Also, a data-link function that controls the use of a common network medium.

Megabits per second (Mbps)   One million bits per second.

Megabyte (MB, Mbyte)   A unit of measurement for memory or disk storage capacity. Usually 1,048,576 bytes; sometimes interpreted as 1 million bytes.

Megahertz (MHz)   A measure of frequency equivalent to 1 million cycles per second.

M-ES   Mobile end system. The CDPD acronym for a device with a radio modem.

Meteor burst communications   A communications system that directs a radio wave, modulated with a data signal, at the ionosphere. The radio signal reflects off the ionized gas left by the burning of meteors entering the atmosphere and is directed back to Earth in the form of a large "footprint," enabling long-distance operation.

MHX   Mobitex higher (main) exchange. *See also* Mobitex.

MIB   *See* management information base.

Microcell   A bounded physical space in which a number of wireless devices can communicate. Because it is possible to have overlapping cells, as well as isolated cells, the boundaries of the cell are established by some rule or convention.

Middleware   An intermediate software component located on the wired network between the wireless appliance and the application or data residing on the wired network. Middleware provides appropriate interfaces between the appliance and the host application or server database.

MIDI   *See* Musical Instrument Digital Interface.

MIN   Mobile information number.

MIRS   Motorola Integrated Radio System. An all-digital, high-speed (64-Kbps) system for voice and data (including, e.g., paging, facsimile). The first user was Nextel, which brought Los Angeles live in August 1993 and now covers much of the nation.

MNP   Microcom networking protocol. An error-detection/retransmission scheme originally developed for wireline modems. A numbered series of increasingly rich offerings, it includes both data compression and cellular alternatives.

MOA   Mobitex Operator's Association.

Mobile IP   A protocol developed by the Internet Engineering Task Force (IETF) to enable users to roam to parts of the network associated with a different IP address than the one loaded in the user's appliance. Also refers to any mobile device that contains the IEEE 802.11 MAC and physical layers.

Mobility   Capability to continually move or be moved (in the case of PEDs and PDAs) from one location to another.

Mobility requirements   Describe the movement of the users when performing their tasks. Mobility requirements should distinguish whether the degree of movement is continuous or periodic.

Mobitex   An L. M. Ericsson system that permits both voice and digital data over channels organized in a cellular manner. In the United States, the user is BSWD and voice is neither licensed nor employed.

Modulation   The process of translating the baseband digital signal to a suitable analog form. Any of several techniques for combining user information with a transmitter's carrier signal.

MOX   Mobitex area exchange.

MPDU   MAC protocol data unit, exchanged at the physical layer between two WLAN entities.

MRM   Motorola mobile radio modems.

MRNE   Mobile Radio New England. A street-level vehicular system.

MS   Mobile station. Generic term for the mobile device in question (GSM phone, Bluetooth device, etc.).

MSA   Metropolitan statistical area. The broader area surrounding a given city. For example, the New York City MSA embraces Manhattan and portions of Long Island, Westchester, Connecticut, and New Jersey counties.

MSB   Most significant bit.

MSC   Message sequence chart.

MSDU   MAC service data unit. The data unit between the LLC and PHY layers; internal to the device.

MT   Mobile terminal; synonym for MS, mobile station.

MTSO   Mobile telephone switching office. Located between a cell site and a conventional wireline switching office, the MTSO links cellular phone calls to the rest of the public landline telephone system. An MTSO also handles the routing of traffic within a system. Because of its hardened, secure facilities, with redundant power supplies, it is typically the site of choice for CDPD's MD-IS controller.

Multipath   The signal variation caused when radio signals take multiple paths from transmitter to receiver.

Multipath fading   A type of fading caused by signals taking different paths from the transmitter to the receiver and, consequently, interfering with each other.

Multiplexer   A network component that combines multiple signals into one composite signal in a form suitable for transmission over a long-haul connection, such as leased 56-Kbps or T1 circuits.

Multistation access unit (MAU)   A multiport wiring hub for token-ring networks.

Musical Instrument Digital Interface (MIDI)   A standard protocol for the interchange of musical information between musical instruments and computers.

MUX   Multiplexing sublayer. A sublayer of the L2CAP layer.

NABER   National Association of Business and Educational Radio.

NACK or NAK   Negative acknowledgment. This can be a deliberate signal that the message was received in error or can be inferred by a time-out.

Name discovery   The mechanism to request and receive a device name.

NAP   Nonsignificant address portion. A 16-bit section of the BD_ADDR. *See also* LAP and UAP.

Narrowband system   A wireless system that uses dedicated frequencies assigned by the FCC licenses. The advantage of narrowband systems is that if interference occurs, the FCC will intervene and issue an order for the interfering source to cease operations. This is especially important when operating wireless MANs in areas having a great deal of other operating radio-based systems.

NAV   Network allocation vector. A counter maintained on each side that indicates the amount of time that remains before the medium will become available. The station will not initiate transmissions if the NAV is not 0, regardless of whether or not the media is busy.

NCC   Network control center for Mobitex systems.

NCL   Native control language.

NCP   Network communications processor. Built originally by Motorola, it has been upgraded and is now maintained by ARDIS.

Network Basic Input/Output System (NetBIOS)   A standard interface between networks and PCs that allows applications on different computers to communicate within a LAN. NetBIOS was created by IBM for its early PC network, was adopted by Microsoft, and has since become a de facto industry standard. It is not routable across a WAN.

Network file system (NFS)   A distributed file system enabling a set of dissimilar computers to access each other's files in a transparent manner.

Network interface card (NIC)   *1.* A network adapter inserted to a computer to enable the computer to be connected to a network. An NIC is responsible for converting data from the form stored in the computer to the form transmitted or received. network layer. It also provides the routing of packets from source to destination. *2.* A circuit board installed in each network station to allow communications with other stations

Network management   A variety of practices undertaken to protect the network from disruption and provide proactive control of the configuration of the network.

Network management station   Executes management applications that monitor and control network elements.

Network monitoring   A form of operational support enabling network management to view the inner workings of the network. Most network monitoring equipment is nonobtrusive and can be used to determine the network's utilization and to locate faults.

Network reengineering   A structured process that can help an organization proactively control the evolution of its network. Network reengineering consists of continually identifying factors influencing network changes, analyzing network modification feasibility, and performing network modifications as necessary.

Network service access point (NSAP)   A point in the network where OSI network services are available to a transport entity.

NFS   *See* Network file system.

NIC   *See* Network interface card.

NIF   Network Interconnection Facility for Metricom's Ricochet system.

NIST   National Institute of Standards & Technology

Node   Any network-addressable device on the network, such as a router or network interface card. Any network station.

Nonconnectable device   A device that does not respond to paging is said to be in nonconnectable mode. The opposite of a nonconnectable device is a connectable device.

Nondiscoverable device   A device that cannot respond to an inquiry is said to be in nondiscoverable mode. The device will not enter the inquiry response state in this mode.

NSA   National Security Agency.

NSAP   *See* Network service access point.

NULL packet   Bluetooth: A 126-bit packet consisting of the CAC and packet header only. It is used to return link information to the source. The NULL packet does not have to be acknowledged.

OBEX   Object EXchange protocol.

ODBC   *See* Open Database Connectivity.

ODI   *See* Open Data-Link Interface.

OEM   *See* Original equipment manufacturer.

OFDM   Orthogonal frequency division multiplexing. A set of frequency-hopping codes that never use the same frequency at the same time. Used in IEEE 802.11a for high-speed data transfer.

One-time pad   Encipherment operation performed using each component k_i of the key, K, only once to encipher a single character of the plaintext. Therefore, the key has the same length as the message. The popular interpretation of one-time pad is that the key is used only once and never used again. Ideally, the components of the key are truly random and have no periodicity or predictability, making the ciphertext unbreakable. The one-time pad is usually implemented as a stream cipher using the XOR function. The elements, $k_1, k_2, ..., k_n$, of the key stream are independent and uniformly distributed random variables. This requirement of a single, independently chosen value of k_i to encipher each character of the plaintext is stringent and may not be practical for most commercial IT applications.

Open Database Connectivity (ODBC)   A standard database interface enabling interoperability between application software and multivendor ODBC-compliant databases.

Open Data-Link Interface (ODI)   Novell's specification for network interface card device drivers, allowing simultaneous operation of multiple protocol stacks.

Open Shortest Path First (OSPF)   Routing protocol for TCP/IP routers that bases routing decisions on the least number of hops from source to destination.

Open system authentication   The IEEE 802.11 default authentication method, which is a very simple, two-step process: First the station wanting to authenticate with another station sends an authentication management frame containing the sending station's identify. The receiving station then sends back a frame alerting whether it recognizes the identity of the authenticating station. The station wanting to authenticate with another station sends an authentication frame with the WEP bit = 0, indicating it will use open system authentication. The receiving station responds with an authentication frame indicating success or failure.

Open System Interconnection (OSI)   An ISO standard specifying an open system capable of enabling the communications between diverse systems. OSI has seven layers of distinction: physical, data link, network, transport, session, presentation, and application. These layers provide the functions necessary to allow standardized communications between two application processes.

Original equipment manufacturer (OEM)   A manufacturer of products for integration in other products or systems.

OS   Commonly used abbreviation for operating system.

OSI   *See* Open System Interconnection.

OSPF   *See* Open Shortest Path First.

Package   In this context, a reusable set of either functional or assurance components (e.g., an EAL), combined to satisfy a set of identified security objectives.

Packet   A basic message unit for communication across a network. A packet usually includes routing information, data, and (sometimes) error-detection information.

Packet format   A packet consists of three entities: the access code, the packet header, and the payload. There are a number of different packet types.

Packet header   Contains link-control information and consists of six fields: AM_ADDR, the active member address; TYPE, the type code; FLOW, flow control; ARQN, acknowledge indication; SEQN, the sequence number; and HEC, the header error check. The total size of the header is 54 bits.

Packet radio   Uses packet switching to move data from one location to another across radio links.

Packet-switched   A network that routes data packets based on an address contained in the data packet is said to be a packet-switched network. Multiple data packets can share the same network resources. A communications network that uses shared facilities to route data packets from and to different users. Unlike a circuit-switched network, a packet-switched network does not set up dedicated circuits for each session.

Packet type   Thirteen different packet types are defined for the baseband layer of the Bluetooth system. All higher layers use these packets to compose higher-level PDUs. The packets defined for both SCO and ACL links are ID, NULL, POLL, FHS, and DM1. DH1, AUX1, DM3, DH3, DM5, and DH5 are defined for ACL links only. HV1, HV2, HV3, and DV are defined for SCO links only

PACT   Personal Air Communications Technology. An AT&T wireless proposal for two-way paging over narrowband PCS. The proposal failed in 1996 at great cost to prospective users.

PAD   Acronym for packet assembly/disassembly.

Page (hopping) response sequence   The page-response sequence covers 32 (16 for the 23-MHz system) unique response frequencies that all are in one-to-one correspondence to the current page-hopping sequence. The master and slave use different rules to obtain the same sequence.

Page (hopping) sequence   A sequence of 32 (16 for the 23-MHz system) frequencies. Each frequency is calculated using the BD_ADDR of the unit being paged (which was obtained earlier, such as in an inquiry operation). The phase in the sequence is derived from an estimate of clock of the unit being paged. Although, theoretically, it should be able to calculate the predicated hop frequency of the unit being paged, and page it straight away, inevitably clock drift will occur, so 32 frequencies are used to handle this, using the calculated main center frequency and 31 other frequencies. These frequencies have an of offset of 16. A new center frequency is calculated every 1.28 seconds. To handle all 32 frequencies, the page-hopping sequence switches between two paging trains of 16 frequencies each.

Page state   A mode that a device enters when searching for other devices. The device sends out a page packet (ID packet), using the page-hopping sequence, to notify other devices that it wants to know about the other devices and/or their services.

Paging procedure   With the paging procedure, an actual connection can be established. The paging procedure typically follows the inquiry procedure. Only the Bluetooth device address is required to set up a connection. Knowledge about the clock (clock estimate) will accelerate the setup procedure. A unit that establishes a connection will carry out a page procedure and will automatically be the master of the connection.

Pairable mode   A device that accepts pairing is said to be in pairable mode. The opposite of pairing mode is nonpairable mode.

Pairing   The creation and exchange of a link key between two devices. The devices use the link key for future authentication when exchanging information.

PAL   Personal access link. Term used for early PCSI implementation of the "smart phone."

Park mode   In park mode, a device is still synchronized to the piconet but does not participate in the traffic. Parked devices have given up their MAC (AM_ADDR) address and occasionally listen to the traffic of the master to resynchronize and check on broadcast messages. Park mode has the lowest duty cycle (power efficiency) of all three power-saving modes (sniff, hold, and park).

Payload format   Each packet payload can have one of two possible fields: the data field (ACL) or the voice field (SCO). The different packets, depending on whether they are ACL or SCO packets, can only have one of these fields. The one exception is the DV packets, which have both. The voice field has a fixed-length field, with no payload header. The data field consists of three segments: a payload header, a payload body, and a CRC code (with the exception of the AUX1 packet).

PBCC   Packet binary convolutional coding. An optional modulation technique for DSSS to allow higher throughput rates.

PC   Point coordinator.

PCF   *See* Point coordination function.

PCM   *See* Pulse code modulation.

PCMCIA (Personal Computer Memory Card International Association.)   The industry group that defines standards for PC cards (and the name applied to the cards themselves). These roughly credit card-sized adapters for memory and modem cards, to name a few, come in three thicknesses: 3.3, 5, and 10.5 mm.

PCS   *See* Personal communications services.

PCSI   Pacific Communication Sciences. An early participant in CDPD design, it offered a variety of multiprotocol modems. The company failed in May 1997.

PDA   Personal digital assistant. A handheld device using either the Palm or Windows CE operating system. Common characterization of devices such as the Korn PalmPilot, Everex Freestyle, or HP620LX.

PDC   Personal digital cellular.

PDN   Public data network.

PDU   Protocol data unit; for example, a message.

PED   Personal electronic device.

Peer-to-peer network   1. A network in which a group of devices can communicate. A peer-to-peer LAN does not depend upon a dedicated server, but allows any node to be installed as a nondedicated server and share its files and peripherals across the network. Peer-to-peer LANs are normally less expensive because they do not require a dedicated computer to store applications and data. They do not perform well, however, for larger networks. 2. A network design in which each computer shares and uses devices on an equal basis.

PER   Packet error rate.

Performance modeling   The use of simulation software to predict network behavior, allowing developers to perform capacity planning. Simulation makes it possible to model the network and impose varying levels of utilization to observe the effects.

Performance monitoring   Tracks performance of a network during normal operations. Performance monitoring includes real-time monitoring, during which metrics are collected and compared against thresholds that can set off alarms; recent-past monitoring, for which metrics are collected and analyzed for trends that may lead to performance problems; and historical data analysis, for metrics are collected and stored for later analysis.

Personal Communications Services (PCS)   *1.* Microcellular wireless services providing voice, paging, and short-message data communications. In selected areas, PCS it is a clear, viable alternative to conventional cellular offerings. *2.* One-number services that associate a number with an individual. The microcellular design permits low-power operation, allowing smaller, lighter telephones with a longer time between battery charges. *3.* A spectrum allocation located at 1.9 GHz, a new wireless communications technology offering wireless access to the World Wide Web, wireless email, wireless voice mail, and cellular telephone service. *4.* Narrowband PCS is a term used to describe Skytel's data-only, two-way paging systems.

PGP   Pretty good privacy.

PHY   *See* Physical layer.

Physical layer (PHY)   The layer of the OSI model that provides the transmission of bits through a communication channel by defining electrical, mechanical, and procedural specifications, and establishes protocols for voltage and data transmission timing and rules for "handshaking."

Physical layer convergence procedure sublayer (PLCP)   Prepares MAC protocol data units (MPDUs) as instructed by the MAC layer for transmission, and delivers incoming frames to the MAC layer.

Physical link   A synchronized Bluetooth baseband-compliant RF hopping sequence. It is a baseband level association between two devices established using paging. A physical link comprises a sequence of transmission slots on a physical channel alternating between master and slave transmission slots.

Physical medium dependent sublayer   A sublayer of the physical layer that receives and transmits the bits on the medium. Provides the actual transmission and reception of physical layer entities between two stations via the wireless medium. Three types are defined for 802.11b: infrared, DSSS and FHSS.

Piconet   A collection of devices connected via Bluetooth technology in an ad hoc fashion. A piconet starts with two connected devices, such as a portable PC and cellular phone, and may grow to eight connected devices. All Bluetooth devices are peer units and have identical implementations. However, when establishing a piconet, one unit will act as a master and the other(s) as slave(s) for the duration of the piconet connection. All devices have the same physical channel defined by the master device parameters (clock and BD_ADDR).

PICS   Protocol implementation conformance statement.

PIFS   Priority inter-frame space. The 30-μs interval before transmission of a new frame sequence at the start of a contention-free period.

PIN   Acronym for personal identification number. The Bluetooth PIN is used to authenticate two devices that have not previously exchanged a link key. By exchanging a PIN, the devices create a trusted relationship. The PIN is used in the pairing procedure to generate the initial link that is used for further identification.

PIN(BB)   The PIN used on the baseband level. The PIN(BB) is used by the baseband mechanism for calculating the initialization key during the pairing procedure.

PIN(UI)   The character representation of the PIN that is entered on the UI level.

PKI   Public key infrastructure.

Plain old telephone system (POTS)   The original common analog telephone system, which is still in wide use today.

Plaintext   Text in human-readable form.

PLCP   *See* Physical layer convergence procedure.

PLMP   Private land mobile radio.

PM_ADDR   In Bluetooth, parked member address, an 8-bit member (master-local) address that separates the parked slaves. The PM_ADDR is only valid as long as the slave is parked.

PMD   *See* Physical medium dependent sublayer.

Point coordination function (PCF)   An IEEE 802.11 mode that enables contention-free frame transfer based on a priority mechanism. Enables time-bounded services that support the transmission of voice and video.

Point-to-Point Protocol   Provides router-to-router and host-to-network connections over both synchronous and asynchronous circuits. PPP is the successor to SLIP.

POLL packet   In Bluetooth, similar to the NULL packet, except it requires a confirmation from the destination. Upon reception of a POLL packet the slave must respond with a packet.

Portability   Defines network connectivity that can be easily established, used, then dismantled.

Portal   A logical point where MPDUs from a non-IEEE 802.11 LAN enter the distribution system of an extended service set wireless network. The logical point where frames pass between the WLAN and LAN.

POTS   *See* Plain old telephone system.

PPDU   PLCP data unit.

PPP   *See* Point-to-Point Protocol.

PRBS   Pseudorandom bit sequence.

Presentation layer   Layer of the OSI model that negotiates data transfer syntax for the application layer and performs translations between different data types, if necessary.

Privacy   In this context, the service used to allow the content of messages to be read only by the intended recipient. A bit in the frame indicates when this is enabled.

PRNG   Pseudo-random number generator.

Processing gain   Equal to the data rate of the spread direct sequence signal divided by the data rate of the actual data.

Product   IT software, firmware and/or hardware, providing functions designed for use or incorporation within a multiplicity of systems.

Profile   A description of the operation of a device or application.

Project charter   Formal recognition of a project; identifies the business need that the project is addressing, and gives a general description of the resulting product.

Project management   The overseers needed to make sure actions are planned and executed in a structured manner.

Protection profile (PP)   An implementation-independent set of security functional and assurance requirements for a category of IT products that meet specific consumer needs.

Protocol   Rules for communicating, particularly for the format and transmission of data.

Prototyping   A method of determining or verifying requirements and design specifications. The prototype normally consists of network hardware and software that support a proposed solution. The approach to prototyping is typically a trial-and-error experimental process.

PS   Power save mode.

PSDU   PLCP service data unit.

Pseudo-noise   An actual signal having a long pattern that resembles noise.

PSF   PLCP signaling field.

PSK   Phase shift keying.

PS-Poll power save poll   Frame from a mobile unit to the AP to request cached frames.

PSTN   Public-switched telephone network. The general phone network.

Pulse code modulation (PCM)   A common method for converting analog voice signals into a digital bit stream. The position of a pulse is varied to represent different binary symbols. The changes in pulse positions maintain the information content of the signal.

QAM   Quadrature amplitude modulation.

QoS   Quality of service.

QPSK   Quadrature phase shift keying. A modulation technique that changes the phase of the signal to represent different 4-bit binary words.

RA   Receiver address. Address of the MAC to which the frame is sent over the wireless medium. Individual or group address.

Radio frequency (RF)   *1.* The international unit for measuring frequency, in terms of Hertz (Hz), which is equivalent to the older unit of cycles per second: 1 Megahertz (MHz) is 1 million Hertz; 1 Gigahertz (GHz) is 1 billion Hertz. The standard U.S. electrical power frequency is 60 Hz; the AM broadcast radio frequency band is 0.55 to 1.6 MHz; the FM broadcast radio frequency band is 88 to 108 MHz; and microwave ovens typically operate at 2.45 GHz. *2.* A generic term for radio-based technology.

Radio layer   In the Bluetooth system, the lowest defined layer. It details the requirements needed for a Bluetooth device transceiver to operate in the Bluetooth radio band. Two different ranges have been defined for the radio layer: a 23-MHz range and a 79-MHz range; both are in the 2.4-GHz ISM band. The 23-MHz range is only used in certain countries (such as Spain and France) that have national limitations on the number of frequencies available. Different hop systems are used for both.

RADIUS   Remote Authentication Dial-in User Service.

RAM   Random access memory. The short name applied to RAM Mobile's public, two-way data radio service. RAM became operational in 1990 and, in steps, became wholly owned by BellSouth Mobility in 1998.

RAP   RIM's radio access protocol.

RBOC   Regional Bell operating company.

RC4   RSA cipher algorithm 4.

RD-LAP   Radio data-link access procedure. The 19,200-bps Motorola protocol first deployed commercially by ARDIS in October 1992.

Reassociation frame   An 802.11 frame that allows a station to change its association to different access points as it moves through the extended service set.

Reassociation service   Enables an IEEE 802.11 station to change its association with different access points as the station moves throughout the facility.

Red Book   A document of the United States National Security Agency (NSA) that defines criteria for secure networks.

ReFLEX   A Motorola protocol used for narrowband PCS. While there are many variants, a one-of-a-kind implementation, ReFLEX50, is used by Skytel. An unbalanced protocol, ReFLEX uses high-speed FLEX outbound, employing simulcast to greatly improve building penetration. There are multiple, 9600-bps inbound receivers for each outbound transmitter. ReFLEX trades off long latency in order to greatly extend device battery life.

Relay node   Implements a routing protocol that maintains the optimum routes for the routing tables, forwarding packets closer to the destination.

Remote bridge   A bridge that connects networks separated by longer distances. Organizations use leased 56-Kbps circuits, T1 digital circuits, and radio waves to provide long-distance connections between remote bridges.

Repeater   *1.* A network component that provides internetworking functionality at the physical layer of a network's architecture. A repeater amplifies network signals, extending the distance they can travel. *2.* A device used to extend cabling distances by regenerating signals.

Requirements analysis   The process of defining what the network is supposed to do, providing a basis for the network design.

RF   *See* Radio frequency.

RFCOMM   Bluetooth serial cable emulation protocol, based on ETSI TS 07.10. The RFCOMM protocol provides emulation of RS232 serial ports over the L2CAP protocol.

RFC   Acronym for request for comment.

RFID   Radio frequency ID.

RFP   Acronym for request for proposal.

RIM   Research In Motion Limited, the designer, manufacturer, and marketer of BlackBerry wireless email and text devices. RIM is sometimes used to refer to any such device.

Ring topology   A topology where a set of nodes are joined in a closed loop.

RIP   *See* Routing Information Protocol.

RM   RadioMail.

Roaming   Movement of a wireless node between two microcells. Roaming usually occurs in infrastructure networks built around multiple access points. Going from one access point to another without having to reestablish the connection.

ROM   Read-only memory.

router   A component that provides internetworking at the network layer of a network's architecture by allowing individual networks to become part of a WAN. A router works by using logical and physical addresses to connect two or more separate networks. It determines the best path by which to send a packet of information.

Routing Information Protocol (RIP)   A common type of routing protocol. RIP bases its routing path on the distance (number of hops) to the destination. RIP maintains optimum routing paths by sending out routing update messages if the network topology changes. For example, if a router finds that a particular link is faulty, it will update its routing table, then send a copy of the modified table to each of its neighbors.

RS-232   A serial communications interface. Serial communication standards are defined by the Electronic Industries Association (EIA). The RS-232 standard specifies up to 20-Kbps, 50-foot, serial transmission between computers and peripheral devices.

RS-422   An EIA standard specifying electrical characteristics for balanced circuits (i.e., both transmit and return wires are at the same voltage above ground). RS-422 is used in conjunction with RS-449.

RS-423   An EIA standard specifying electrical characteristics for unbalanced circuits (i.e. the return wire is tied to ground). RS-423 is used in conjunction with RS-449.

RS-449   An EIA standard specifying a 37-pin connector for high-speed transmission.

RS-485   An EIA standard for multipoint communications lines.

RSA   RSA refers to Ronald L. Rivest, Adi Shamir, and Leonard Adleman, inventors of the RSA algorithm.

RSSI   Received signal strength indicator. An optional part of the radio layer, used to determine the link quality and thus whether to increase broadcast power.

RTS   Request to send frame, used by Mobile.

RTX timer   The response timeout expired timer used in the L2CAP layer to terminate the channel when the remote endpoint is unresponsive to signaling requests. It is started when a signaling request is sent to a remote device.

RX   Receiver.

S   *1.* In Bluetooth, used as an abbreviation for slave. *See* slave device. *2.* Used to indicate steady-state network throughput, the average number of successful transmissions per packet transmission time.

SA   Source address. Address of the MAC that originated the frame. Always an individual address.

SAP *See* Service access point.

SAR Segmentation and reassembly. Bluetooth: A sublayer of the L2CAP layer.

SBU Abbreviation for sensitive but unclassified; an information designation.

Scatternet In Bluetooth, multiple, independent, and nonsynchronized piconets.

SCID Source channel identifier. Used in the L2CAP layer to indicate the channel endpoint on the device sending the L2CAP message. It is a device local name only. *See also* DCID.

SCO Synchronous connection-oriented link. One of the two Bluetooth data-link types defined. A synchronous (circuit-switched) connection for reserved bandwidth communications (e.g., voice) between two devices created on the LMP level by reserving slots periodically on a physical channel. This type of link is used primarily to transport SCO packets (voice data). SCO packets do not include a CRC and are never retransmitted. SCO links can be established only after an ACL link has been established. *See also* ACL.

SDAP Service discovery application profile.

SDDB Service discovery database.

SDLC Synchronous data-link control.

SDP Service Discovery Protocol. A Bluetooth-defined protocol provided for or available through a Bluetooth device. Essentially offers a means for applications to discover which services are available and to determine the characteristics of those available services.

SDP client May retrieve information from a service record maintained by the SDP server by issuing an SDP request.

SDP server Maintains a list of service records that describe the characteristics of services associated with the server.

SDP session   The exchange of information between an SDP client and an SDP server, which is referred to as an SDP transaction.

SDP transaction   Bluetooth: The exchange of an SDP request from an SDP client to an SDP server, and the corresponding SDP response from an SDP server back to the SDP client.

Security functional requirements   Requirements, preferably from the Common Criteria, Part 2, that, when taken together specify the security behavior of an IT product or system.

Security mode 1   One of three Bluetooth device security modes. In security mode 1, the device will not initiate any security. A nonsecure mode.

Security mode 2   One of three Bluetooth device security modes. In security mode 2, the device does not initiate security procedures before channel establishment on L2CAP level. This mode allows different and flexible access policies for applications, especially those with different security requirements running in parallel. A service level-enforced security mode.

Security mode 3   One of three Bluetooth device security modes. In security mode 3, the device initiates security procedures before the link setup on an LMP level is completed. A link-level-enforced security mode.

Security objective   A statement of intent to counter specified threats and/ or satisfy specified organizational security policies and assumptions.

Security target (ST)   A set of security functional and assurance requirements and specifications to be used as the basis for evaluation of an identified product or system.

SEQN   Sequential numbering scheme, used to order the data packet stream.

Serial interface   An interface to provide serial communications service. A service that one device provides for others; for example, printers, PIM synchronization servers, modems (or modem emulators).

Serial Line Internet Protocol (SLIP)   An Internet protocol used to run IP over serial lines and dial-up connections.

Server-oriented network   A network architecture whose network software is split into two pieces, one for the client and one for the server. The server component provides services for the client software; the client part interacts with the user. The client and server components run on different computers, and the server is usually more powerful than the client. The main advantages of a server-oriented network is less network traffic. Networks that support a large number of users usually achieve better performance using server-oriented networks.

Service (SDP layer)   Any entity that can provide information, perform an action, or control a resource on behalf of another entity. A service may be implemented as software, hardware, or a combination of hardware and software.

Service access point (SAP)   *1.* A point at which the services of an OSI layer are made available to the next higher layer. *2.* An internal port between layers that allow messages to pass from layer to layer. Each port has a unique identifier, usually called the SAP, to ensure the message is handled by the correct code in the adjacent layer.

Service advisor   The portion of the user interface that handles Bluetooth services.

Service attribute   Describes a single characteristic of a service.

Service class   An instance of a service class. The service class definition provides the definitions of all attributes contained in service records that represent the instances of that class.

Service discovery   *See* SDP.

Service layer   The group of protocols that provides services to the application layer and the driver layer in a Bluetooth device.

Service primitive   A communications element for sending information between network architectural layers.

Service record   Contains all of the information about a service that is maintained by an SDP server.

Service record database   Contains service discovery-related information.

Service record handle   A 32-bit number that uniquely identifies each service record within an SDP server.

Service set identifier (SSID)   An identifier attached to packets sent over the wireless LAN that functions as a "password" for joining a particular radio network (basic service set, BSS). All radios and access points within the same BSS must use the same SSID, or their packets will be ignored.

Session layer   One of the seven OSI model layers. Establishes, manages, and terminates sessions between applications.

SFD   Start of frame delimiter.

SFR   Single-frequency reuse.

Shared key authentication   A type of authentication that assumes each station has received a secret shared key through a secure channel, independent from an 802.11 network. Stations authenticate through shared knowledge of the secret key. Use of shared key authentication requires implementation of the 802.11 Wireless Equivalent Privacy (WEP) algorithm. A type of authentication that allows a mobile station to encrypt data using a common key. Four frames are exchanged in the authentication process.

SIFS   Short interframe space. The 10-μs interval between DATA and ACK frames, before RTS, in response to a poll or frames in a burst.

SIG   Acronym for special interest group.

Simple Mail Transfer Protocol (SMTP)   The Internet electronic mail protocol.

Simple Network Management Protocol (SNMP)   The network management protocol of choice for TCP/IP based Internets. Widely implemented with 10BASET Ethernet. A network management protocol that defines the transfer of information between management information bases (MIBs). Most high-end network monitoring stations require the implementation of SNMP on each of the components the organization wishes to monitor.

Slave device   In Bluetooth, a device in a piconet that is not the master. There can be many slaves per piconet.

SLIP   *See* Serial Line Internet Protocol.

Slot time   The 20-µs constant value object in the MIB used to calculate the time between frames.

SMDS   *See* Switched Multimegabit Digital Service.

SMF   Novell's Standard Message Format.

SMRS   Special mobile radio. Originally an analog voice dispatch system, SMR frequencies are now being used to support digital voice and data. SMR was originally local but has become nationwide via carriers such as Nextel.

SMS   Short (or small) message service.

SMTP   *See* Simple Mail Transfer Protocol.

SNA   *See* Systems Network Architecture.

SNADS   IBM's SNA Distribution Services.

SNET   Southern New England Telephone.

Sniff mode   In Bluetooth, devices synchronized to a piconet can enter power-saving modes in which device activity is lowered. In the sniff mode, a slave device listens to the piconet at reduced rate, thus reducing its duty cycle. The sniff interval is programmable and depends on the application. It has the highest duty cycle (i.e., is the least power-efficient) of the power-saving modes (hold and park are the other two).

SNMP   *See* Simple Network Monitoring Protocol.

SNR   Signal-to-noise ratio.

SONET   *See* Synchronous Optical NETwork.

Source   In Bluetooth, the device initiating an action to another Bluetooth device. The device receiving the action is called the destination. The source is typically part of an established link, though not always (such as in inquiry/page procedures).

Spectrum analyzer   An instrument that identifies the amplitude of signals at various frequencies.

Spread spectrum *1.* A modulation technique that spreads a signal's power over a wide band of frequencies. Using spread spectrum, the signal becomes much less susceptible to electrical noise and interferes less with other radio-based systems. IEEE 802.11 uses two such techniques: direct sequence spread spectrum (DSSS) and frequency-hopping spread spectrum (FHSS). *2.* A radio transmission technology that spreads the user information over a much wider bandwidth than otherwise required in order to gain benefits such as improved interference tolerance and unlicensed operation.

SQL *See* Structured Query Language.

SR Scan repetition. A mode used in the baseband layer to determine how long the device will continue to scan for a page response

SSI *1.* Signal strength indicator. Sometimes called RSSI for received signal strength indicator. *2.* Service Systems International.

SSID *See* Service set identifier.

SSL Secure Sockets Layer.

ST connector An optical fiber connector that uses a bayonet plug and socket.

STA Short for "station." In IEEE 802.11, any device that contains the IEEE 802.11 MAC and physical layers.

Star topology A topology wherein each node is connected to a common central switch or hub.

Station In IEEE 802.11 networks, any device that contains an IEEE 802.11-compliant medium access control and physical layers.

Station Basic Rate (SBR) A data transfer rate belonging to the extended basic service set (ESS) that is used by stations for specific transmissions. SBR changes dynamically to reflect the media conditions.

Structured Query Language (SQL) An international standard for defining and accessing relational databases.

Switched Multimegabit Digital Service (SMDS) A packet switching connectionless data service for WANs.

SYNC   Short for synchronization.

Synchronous Optical NETwork (SONET)   A fiber optic transmission system for high-speed digital traffic. SONET is part of the B-ISDN standard.

Synchronous transmission   Type of communications data synchronization whereby frames are sent within defined time periods. It uses a clock to control the timing of bits being sent. Compare asynchronous transmission.

System   A specific IT installation, with a particular purpose and operational environment.

System testing   Type of testing that verifies the installation of the entire network. Testers normally complete system testing in a simulated production environment, simulating actual users in order to ensure the network meets all stated requirements.

Systems Network Architecture (SNA)   IBM's proprietary network architecture.

T1   A standard specifying a time division multiplexing scheme for point-to-point transmission of digital signals at 1.544 Mbps.

TA   Transmitter address. Address of the MAC that transmitted the frame onto the wireless medium. Always an individual address.

Target of evaluation (TOE)   Another name for an IT product or system described in a PP or Station. The TOE is the entity that is subject to security evaluation.

TBTT   Target beacon transmission time.

TCM   Trellis-coded modulation. Additional (redundant) signal points added to a transmission, with only specific patterns of allowable sequences. If an impairment occurs, the closest pattern is selected to correct errors without retransmission. TCM is backed up by a CRC in case the correction decision is incorrect.

TCP   *See* Transmission Control Protocol.

TCP/IP   *See* Transmission Control Protocol/Internet Protocol.

TCS-AT   A set of AT-commands by which a mobile phone and modem can be controlled in the multiple usage models. In Bluetooth, AT-commands are based on ITU-T recommendations v.250 and ETS 300 916(GSM 07.07). In addition, the commands used for fax services are specified by the implementation. TCS-AT will also be used for dial-up networking and headset profiles.

TCS-BIN   Telephony Control Protocol Specification Binary. Bluetooth's Telephony Control protocol. Specification using bit-oriented protocol. TCS-BIN is used for wireless telephony profiles and call control.

TCSEC   Trusted computer security evaluation criteria.

TDD   Time division duplex.

TDMA   Time division multiple access. An approach to access control that subdivides the channel into multiple time slots. A particular form of TDMA was developed by L. M. Ericsson and implemented by AT&T Wireless as its voice technologies for digital cellular telephone service. *See also* CDMA and FDMA.

TDR   *See* Time-domain reflectometer.

Technical Service Bulletin 67 (TSB 67)   Published by the Link Performance Task Group, a subcommittee of the Telecommunications Industry Association's TR41 Standards Committee, describes how to test Category 5 twisted pair cable.

Technology comparison matrix   A documentation method that compares similar technologies based on attributes such as functionality, performance, cost, and maturity.

Telecommuting   The concept of electronically extending a corporate office to include an employee's home or other off-site work environment.

Telnet   A virtual terminal protocol used in the Internet, enabling users to log in to a remote host. A terminal emulation defined as part of the TCP/IP protocol suite.

Terminal node controller (TNC)   Interfaces computers to ham radio equipment. TNCs act much like a telephone modem, converting the computer's digital signal into one that a ham radio can modulate and send over the airwaves using a packet-switching technique.

Test case   An executable test with a specific set of input values and a corresponding expected result.

TGAP   Timer used in the general access profile (GAP).

TIA   Telecommunications Industry Association.

TIM   Traffic indication map. Field in beacon frames that indicates there are frames cached on the access point for stations in power save mode.

Time Division Multiple Access   *See* TDMA.

Time slot   A single time slot in the Bluetooth system lasts 625 μs. A time slot can be thought of as the time it takes to send one packet from one Bluetooth device to another.

Time unit   A measurement of time equal to 1024 μs.

Time-domain reflectometer (TDR)   Mechanism used to test the effectiveness of network cabling.

TLA   Top-level architecture.

TLS   Transport layer security.

TNC   *See* Terminal node controller.

Token bus   A network that uses a logical token-passing access method. Permission to transmit is usually based on the node address rather than the position in the network, as in a token-passing ring. A token bus network uses a common cable set with all signals broadcast across the entire LAN.

Token ring   A local area network (LAN) standard developed by IBM that uses tokens to control access to the communication medium. A medium access method that provides multiple access to a ring-type network through the use of a token. FDDI and IEEE 802.5 are token ring standards.

Top-down design   Design process in which high-level specifications that directly satisfy network requirements are defined first, followed by the remaining elements in an order that satisfies the specifications already determined.

Topography   In this context, a description of the network's physical surface spots. Topography specifies the type and location of nodes with respect to one another.

Topology   A description of the network's geographical layout of nodes and links.

TP0   OSI Transport Protocol Class 0 (Simple Class), useful only with very reliable networks.

TP4   OSI Transport Protocol Class 4 (Error Detection and Recovery Class), useful with any type of network. The functionality of TP4 is similar to that of TCP.

Transceiver   A device for transmitting and receiving packets between the computer and the medium.

Transmission Control Protocol (TCP)   Protocol in wide use for establishing and maintaining communications between applications on different computers. TCP provides full-duplex, acknowledged, and flow-controlled service to upper-layer protocols and applications.

Transmission Control Protocol/ Internet Protocol (TCP/IP)   The de facto, industry-standard protocol for interconnecting disparate networks. Standard protocols that define both the reliable full-duplex transport level and the connectionless, "best effort" unit of information passed across an Internet. Developed for wireline systems, it is used with little change for CDPD applications.

Transport layer   OSI model layer that provides mechanisms for the establishment, maintenance, and orderly termination of virtual circuits, while shielding the higher layers from the network implementation details.

TRIB   Transfer rate of information bits. The number of information bits accepted and the total time needed to send all bits (sync, header, CRC) to get those information bits accepted.

TSB 67   *See* Technical Service Bulletin 67.

TSF   Time synchronization factor.

TTP   Tiny Transport Protocol between OBEX and UDP.

TU   Time units.

Twisted pair wire   Medium that uses metallic-type conductors twisted together to provide a path for current flow. The wire is twisted in pairs to minimize the electromagnetic interference between one pair and another.

TX   Abbreviation for transmit.

UA Channel   User asynchronous data channel. One of the five logical channels defined for the Bluetooth system. The UA channel carries L2CAP transparent asynchronous user data. It is normally carried in the ACL link.

UAP   Upper address portion. A 8-bit section of the BD_ADDR. *See also* LAP and NAP.

UART   Universal asynchronous receiver transmitter. A device that converts parallel data into serial data for transmission, or converts serial data into parallel data for receiving data.

UBER   Undetected bit (sometimes block) error rate. The percent of errors that escape error correction or detection and pass into the system.

UC   Abbreviation for user control.

UDP   *See* User Datagram Protocol.

UDP/IP   User Datagram Protocol/Internet Protocol.

UI channel   User isochronous data channel. One of the five logical channels defined for the Bluetooth system. The UI channel carries L2CAP transparent isochronous user data. It is normally carried in the ACL link. It is supported by timing start packets at higher levels.

UMTS   Universal Mobile Telecommunications System.

Unacknowledged connectionless service   A datagram-style service that does not involve any error-control or flow-control mechanisms.

Unit testing   Type of testing that verifies the accuracy of each network component, such as servers, cables, hubs, and bridges. The goal of unit testing is to make certain the component works properly by running tests that fully exercise the internal workings of the component.

USAISEC   U.S. Army Information Systems Engineering Command. U.S. Army Information Systems Engineering Command.

US channel   User synchronous data channel. One of the five logical channels defined for the Bluetooth system. The UI channel carries transparent synchronous user data. It is carried in the SCO link only.

User Datagram Protocol   (UDP) A protocol that uses the underlying Internet Protocol (IP) to transport a message. This is an unreliable, connectionless delivery scheme. It does not use acknowledgments to ensure that messages arrive and does not provide feedback to control the rate of information flow. UDP messages can be lost, duplicated, or arrive out of order. In addition to the data, each UDP message contains both a destination and source number; thus the user can construct a more reliable application.

User profile requirements   Identify the attributes of each person who will be using the system, providing human factors that designers can use to select or develop applications.

UUID   Universal unique identifier. Used in the SDP layer.

V.21   An ITU standard for asynchronous 0-300 bps full-duplex modems.

V.21FAX   An ITU standard for facsimile operations at 300 bps.

V.34   An ITU standard for 28,800 bps modems.

VAN   Value-added network. Wireline transmission facility such as America Online, CompuServe, Geisco, Telenet, and Tymnet, which are employed to connect private computing facilities to data radio switching centers.

VIM   Lotus' Vendor-independent messaging system.

VLSI   Very large-scale integrated.

VTAM   Virtual telecommunications access method.

WAM   Wide area mobile.

WAN   *See* Wide area network.

WAP   Wireless Application Protocol. A standard commonly used for the development of applications for wireless Internet devices. WAP enables graphical data to be received, displayed, and manipulated on micro-browser screens and for user input to be relayed to a server. WAP is not part of the IEEE 802.11 standards.

WBS   *See* Work breakdown structure.

W-CDMA   Wideband CDMA.

WECA   Wireless Ethernet Compatibility Alliance.

WEP   *See* Wired Equivalent Privacy.

Wide area network (WAN)   A network that interconnects users over a wide area, usually encompassing different metropolitan areas.

Wi-Fi   Wireless fidelity. 1. Wireless Ethernet Compatibility Alliance (WECA) brand identity for the IEEE 802.11b standard. 2. WECA certification that ensures products compatibility.

WIM   Wireless identification module.

Wired Equivalent Privacy (WEP)   An optional IEEE 802.11 function that offers frame transmission privacy similar to that of a wired network. WEP generates secret shared encryption keys that both source and destination stations can use to alter frame bits to avoid disclosure to eavesdroppers.

Wireless   Describes any computing device that can access a network without a wired connection.

Wireless metropolitan area network (wireless MAN)   Provides communications links between buildings, avoiding the costly installation of cabling or leasing fees and the downtime associated with system failures.

Wireless network interface   Couples the digital signal from the end-user appliance to the wireless medium, which is air.

Wireless node   A user computer with a wireless network interface card (adapter).

Wiremap test   Used to ensures a link has proper connectivity by testing for continuity and other installation mistakes, such as the connection of wires to the wrong connector pin.

WLAN   Wireless local area network.

Work breakdown structure (WBS)   Diagram of how a team will accomplish the project at hand by listing all tasks the team will need to perform and the products they must deliver.

Work function (factor)   The difficulty in recovering the plaintext from the ciphertext as measured by cost and/or time. The security of the system is directly proportional to the value of the work function. The work function need only be large enough to suffice for the intended application. If the message to be protected loses its value after a short period of time, the work function need only be large enough to ensure that the decryption would be highly infeasible in that period of time.

WPAN   In Bluetooth, wireless personal area network.

WTLS   Wireless Transport Layer Security.

wVPN   Wireless virtual private network.

X.12   An ITU standard for EDI.

X.21   An ITU standard for a circuit-switching network.

X.25   An ITU standard for an interface between a terminal and a packet-switching network. X.25 was the first public packet-switching technology, developed by the CCITT and offered as a service during the 1970s and still available today. X.25 offers connection-oriented (virtual circuit) service; it operates at 64 Kbps, which is too slow for some high-speed applications.

X.75   An ITU standard for packet switching between public networks.

X.121   An ITU standard for international address numbering.

X.400   An ITU standard for OSI messaging.

X.500   An ITU standard for OSI directory services.

Xcvr transceiver   A combination radio transmitter and receiver.

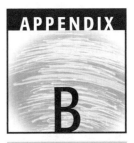

APPENDIX

B

A WLAN Exploitation Guide

Deployment of IEEE 802.11b wireless local area networks is increasing around the globe due to their cost compared to wired infrastructures, availability, versatility, and recent performance gains in the areas of transmission speed. Coupled with its ease of implementation, IEEE 802.11b wireless local area networks provide a viable solution for convenient information access. Unfortunately, wireless LANs remain a new technology not fully understood by the organizations implementing them.

IEEE 802.11b wireless local area networks are extremely vulnerable to intrusion and exploitation due to their broadcast infrastructure. Adding a wireless network to an organization's internal LAN may open a potential backdoor into the existing wired network.

This appendix will provide the initial key steps involved in exploiting an IEEE 802.11b WLAN for the purpose of gaining access into the backbone wired network. It explores the use of AiroPeek, an IEEE 802.11b COTS network monitoring and packet analysis software, and its capabilities in exploiting the 802.11b standard through its Media Access Control (MAC) Layer.

A discussion on the Wired Equivalent Privacy (WEP) protocol and procedures on installing and configuring an open source decryption tool are also included.

While organizations and governments have invested a considerable amount of time and effort in securing their network's connection to the Internet, the addition of a wireless extension anywhere within the existing internal network will undoubtedly create a potential backdoor into the target wired network (see Figure B.1). Due in part to the fact that wireless LANs are used primarily for convenient access to the internal wired network (intranet), wireless access points are usually placed behind the network's demilitarized zone (DMZ). By gaining access into the wireless access point, an attacker can essentially "'plug into" the wired network as an internal user, bypassing the target network's firewall, intrusion detection system (IDS), or any other standard security mechanisms designed to prevent intrusion through the most common port of entry—the Internet. Figure B.1 demonstrates a potential backdoor into a WLAN.

WLAN Configurations

The IEEE 802.11 WLAN architecture is built around a basic service set (BSS). A BSS is a set of stations, mobile or fixed, that communicate with one another. By definition, a station can be any of two types: a stationary Access Point or a wireless node (fixed or mobile). The simplest WLAN configuration is an independent basic service system (IBSS) also known as "Ad hoc" mode. When all of the stations in the BSS are mobile stations and there is no connection to a wired network, the Ad hoc mode is being implemented. The IBSS is the entire WLAN, and only those stations communicating with each other in the IBSS are part of this local area network. Figure B.2 shows how the basic service set is configured in an independent basic service system.

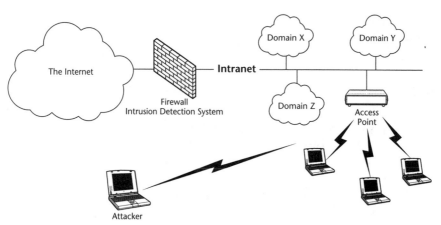

Figure B.1   WLAN potential backdoor.

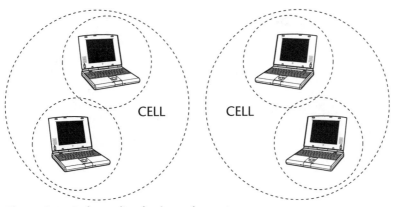

Figure B.2   Independent basic service system.

When a basic service set includes an access point (AP), the BSS is no longer independent and is called an infrastructure BSS. An access point (AP) is a dual-mode device that provides wireless relay services and connection to a wired network. It can be used for both indoor and outdoor connectivity.

In an infrastructure BSS, all mobile stations communicate with the access point. The AP provides both local relay functions for the BSS and connection to the wired LAN. Therefore, if a mobile station in the BSS must communicate with another mobile station, the communication must first be sent to the AP and then from the AP to the desired destination, as shown in Figure B.3.

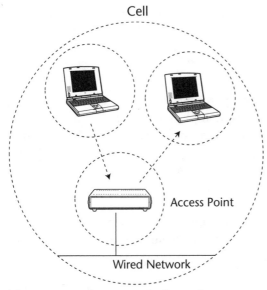

Figure B.3   Infrastructure basic service set.

The IEEE 802.11 Physical (PHY) Layer

According to the FCC, unlicensed wireless networks can operate in three areas of the radio spectrum, referred to as the Industrial, Scientific, and Medical (ISM) bands.

The frequencies for these regions are:

- 902 – 928 MHz

- 2.4 – 2.4835 GHz

- 5.725 – 5.825 GHz

IEEE 802.11b operates in the 2.4 – 2.4835 GHz frequency spectrum.

Since there are a host of other unlicensed devices that operate in these same regions of the E-M spectrum, techniques are needed to avoid interference. One such technique, developed by the military to help secure its transmission, involves spreading transmissions across a range of frequencies, rather than transmitting on one frequency all the time. This is commonly referred to as spread spectrum modulation.

Direct Sequence Spread Spectrum

Spread spectrum modulation techniques are used to widen the RF bandwidth of a signal so the transmitted bandwidth is much wider than would be necessary for information transmission alone. This type of communication makes the signal resistant to noise and interference.

Direct sequence spread spectrum combines a data signal at the sending station with a high-bit sequence commonly referred to as a chipping code. This is the only spread spectrum technique implemented in IEEE 802.11b.

Regulatory Requirements

WLAN IEEE 802.11-compliant radios operating in the 2.4-GHz Industrial, Scientific, and Medical (ISM) bands must comply with the local geographical regulatory domains before operating in this spectrum. These technical requirements are specified to comply with the regulatory requirements for WLANs to minimize the amount of interference a radio can generate or receive from another in the same proximity.

The IEEE 802.11 standard identifies the minimum technical requirements for interoperability and compliance based upon established regulations for Europe, Japan, and North America. The lists and tables below specify the current regulatory and technical requirements for various geographical areas.

IEEE 802.11 Media Access Control Frame Formats

The primary objective of this section is to provide a brief overview of the IEEE 802.11b MAC Layer and to "zero in" on the primary information we need to retrieve in order to gain access into the WLAN.

General Frame Format

The general IEEE 802.11 frame structure is depicted in Figure B.4. This frame structure is found in all frames, regardless of frame types.

It should be strongly noted the MAC header is never encrypted. Only the data content in the Frame body can be encrypted to prevent eavesdropping.

IEEE 802.11 Management Frame Type

The main purpose of this frame is to allow mobile stations to join the WLAN. This is the frame we want to enumerate with AiroPeek. We want to retrieve the "SECRET WLAN Infrastructure Name" or Service Set Identification (SSID). This is the key into joining our target IEEE 802.11b WLAN and the connected wired backbone network. The following management frame subtypes are our primary targets:

- Beacons
- Probe request and Probe response
- Association request
- Reassociation request

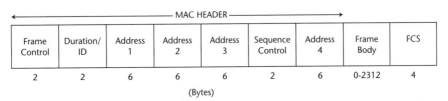

Figure B.4   IEEE 802.11 general frame format.

Beacon Frame

Access Points will periodically transmit a beacon frame, about 10 frames a second, to provide synchronization among the mobile stations and to announce its capabilities. All station clocks are synchronized by these beacons while operating in infrastructure mode. These wireless broadcasts are used by mobile stations to find a particular Access Point or other stations that match its parameters. The following information is included in every beacon frame:

- Timestamp
- Beacon Interval (usually every 100 milliseconds)
- Capability Information
- SSID
- Supported Rates (1, 2, 5.5, and/or 11 Mbps)
- Other parameters

Probe Request and Probe Response Frames

Mobile stations will send a Probe Request Frame to quickly locate an IEEE 802.11 WLAN. To find a particular Access Point, a mobile station will broadcast a Probe Request frame to all channels with the SSID of the AP it wishes to find. The station can also send a Probe Request with the broadcast address in the SSID field. It will then check all the Probe Responses for the SSID that matches the SSID it wishes to join. The body of the Probe Request Frame contains two subfields:

- SSID
- Supported Rates (1, 2, 5.5, 11 Mbps)

By definition, in an infrastructure BSS, the Access Point will always, *always*, respond to a Probe Request Frame!

The Probe Response Frame is identical to the Beacon Frame.

Association Request

The Association Request Frames is sent by a mobile station to request an association with an Access Point. The Association Request Frame contains the following information:

- Capability Information
- Listen Interval (how often a mobile station wakes to listen to Beacons)
- SSID
- Supported Rates

Reassociation Request

The Reassociation Request Frames contain the following information:

- Capability Information
- Listen Interval
- Current Access Point Address
- SSID
- Supported Rates

Systematic Exploitation of an 802.11b WLAN

802.11b Exploitation Software: AiroPeek

The information contained in the IEEE 802.11b MAC headers will always provide an attacker with the critical information needed for a successful attack against an 802.11b WLAN as these header frames are never encrypted. By utilizing an 802.11b protocol analyzing software, an attacker will be able to retrieve the information required to authenticate and associate with the target Access Point and gain access into the backbone wired network.

The release of the AiroPeek software suite configured an IEEE 802.11b-compliant PCMCIA card into *promiscuous* mode. In this condition, the PCMCIA card can monitor and capture all IEEE 802.11b broadcast and multicast traffic within its sensitivity range. Such tools are known as "sniffers" and they allow an attacker to *passively* harvest a wealth of information on a target in order to execute a focused and surgical attack. It should be noted that only the Cisco 342 card was tested. Specific details on supported PCMCIA cards can be found through AiroPeek's website (www.wildpackets.com).

Nevertheless, due to the inherent vulnerabilities in the IEEE 802.11b standard, in particular the transmitting of the Media Access Control (MAC) headers in the clear, an IEEE 802.11b WLAN can now be easily exploited with this particular software. AiroPeek will capture the entire IEEE 802.11b MAC header and display, in great detail, the information contained in each field and subfield.

The remainder of this section will focus on the capabilities of this sniffer and introduce a systematic approach in exploiting an IEEE 802.11b wireless local area network to gain access into the backbone wired network. It is important to note that the exploitation methodology described in this appendix is dependent upon the successful eavesdropping on IEEE 802.11b signals.

AiroPeek: Getting Started

AiroPeek captures all conversation on a network segment and provides a wealth of features for dissecting this traffic. To see live traffic on your network, just follow these steps-by-step instructions:

1. Launch the program choosing AiroPeek from the Start menu.

2. Select an interface for the software to use in capturing network traffic.

3. Choose New from the File menu. This will open the Capture Buffer Options dialog , where you can set the size of the capture buffer for the new Capture window and determine how it will be used during capture. A capture window can be set to use the capture buffer in one of three ways. It can stop capture when the buffer becomes full, or it can continue capturing, either by periodically saving the buffer's contents to disk or by dumping the contents and refilling the buffer.

4. Once you have made your selections and changes, click OK. A Capture window will open.

5. Click Start Capture. You will now begin to see packets from your network processed and displayed in the Capture window just created. You can customize the display of information in the Packets view of any Capture window. The default Packets view layout shows the following information for each packet:

- Source and Destination Address
- BSSID
- Data Rate
- Channel
- Signal Strength
- Packet Size
- Timestamp showing the moment of capture
- Protocol of the packet

The Customizable Packet List is shown in Figure B.5. The column content, color, and format in which packet information is displayed in Capture windows and Packet File windows can be changed and rearranged for customized viewing. For example, you can view names and logical and physical addresses side by side, colorized web server traffic, change timestamp representations, and more.

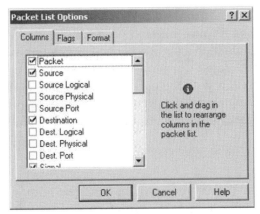

Figure B.5   Customizable packet list.

To customize the columns that appear in packet lists, follow these steps:

1. With a packet list active, right-click and choose View Options.

2. Check the columns you would like displayed in the Packets view.

3. Uncheck any columns you do not wish to see displayed.

4. Click and drag in the list to arrange the order of columns.

5. Click OK.

Systematic Exploitation

The methodology to exploit an IEEE 802.11b WLAN to gain access into the backbone wired network can be broken down into three phases: Reconnaissance, Analysis, and Access.

Step 1: Reconnaissance

Reconnaissance is necessary to ensure that all pieces of information related to a specific target are analyzed and collected in order to create a complete profile of an organization. By utilizing AiroPeek, the collection and monitoring of IEEE 802.11b signals is now easily accomplished. This phase involves five steps: time of day, optimum collection profile, passive analysis of IEEE 802.11b packets, identification and selection of active channels, and collection of IEEE 802.11b packets.

Time of Day

The optimum time to conduct a reconnaissance mission on a specific target will vary depending on the target organization's work schedule. For example, heavy network traffic is usually encountered during an organization's shift change. By convention, morning hours provide the optimum collection time since workers are busily logging on to their workstations. The day of the week, holidays, and breaks are other factors that should be considered while profiling a target network.

Optimum Collection Profile

By placing the PCMCIA card within the beam width of the transmitting WLAN antenna and having a direct line of sight to the target, an attacker will undoubtedly have a higher probability of collecting and analyzing IEEE 802.11b signals.

Passive Analysis of IEEE 802.11b Signals

Due to the inherent vulnerability in the IEEE 802.11b standard of transmitting the Medium Access Control (MAC) headers in the clear, an attacker will always have the opportunity to enumerate this information. By utilizing AiroPeek, an attacker can take advantage of this vulnerability. This software provides the unique capability of passively analyzing and recording all IEEE 802.11b MAC headers in real time and displaying selected results in an easily understood graphical format. A particular feature of AiroPeek is its capability of displaying the entire IEEE 802.11b channel spectrum.

This display provides a quick snapshot of channel activities and their associated packet information. Specifically, this feature of AiroPeek provides the attacker with the vendor-specific Access Point, or BSSID, for each channel as well as its associated signal strengths relative to the attacker. Vendor-specific information will undoubtedly help the attacker focus on a particular method of attack. Proprietary configurations can now be exploited. The amount of data traffic for each channel can also be enumerated from this statistical display.

To create a quick sample of traffic across the IEEE 802.11b spectrum, follow these steps:

1. Open a new Capture window.

2. Choose Options from the Tools menu to open the Options dialog, and click the 802.11 Tab to open the 802.11 view.

3. Check the Scan option. By default, AiroPeek will scan channels 1 through 11 (five seconds for each channel). You can change these settings by hitting the Edit Scanning Options button.

4. Click OK.

5. Click View, Start Capture.

AiroPeek will report the channels on which the NIC is actually listening in the Channel column, and the signal strength for each packet in the Signal column. You can immediately see what IEEE 802.11b traffic is present across the spectrum

Since we're interested in joining our target WLAN in order to connect to the backbone wired network, we need to enumerate IEEE 802.11b Access Points. The easiest method to effectively select *only access points* is as follows:

1. Go to the Protocols view and find and choose a Beacon frame.

2. Right-click to open the Context menu; or use the Edit menu and choose Select Related Packets. In the Selection Results dialog, choose By Protocol and Hide Unselected. The Packets view now shows all the properly formed beacon packets present on all channels during the sample period. Because beacon packets are broadcast, the MAC addresses shown in the Nodes view and the Conversations view will be those of the access points in the sample. You now know the BSSID of each access point whose signals could be detected on any channel at the location from which you took the sample.

3. To determine the *channel* on which each access point is broadcasting, you will need to look at the *decodes* of the beacon packets. Double-click on a beacon packet to open it in a Packet Decode window. Scroll down to the body of the packet and find the *Element ID:3* called *Direct Sequence parameter set*. The channel the access point is operating on will be identified here.

Identification and Selection of Active Channels

The objective of this step is to identify and individually select each active channel of interest. Due to the limitations of AiroPeek, an accurate analysis of a particular channel cannot be achieved unless all other channels are filtered out. However, the attacker should be aware of channel overlap. Since only three channels are entirely separated, co-channel interference will undoubtedly occur. To select an individual channel of interest, do the following:

1. Choose Options from the Tools menu. This will open the Options dialog box.

2. Click on the 802.11 tab and select Channel.

3. Select desired channel, as shown in Figure B.6.

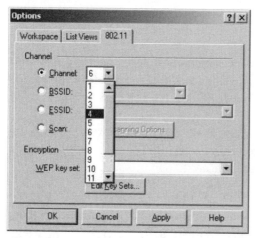

Figure B.6   Selection of desired channel.

Step 2: Analysis

The objective of this phase is to analyze the IEEE 802.11b packets captured by AiroPeek. Specifically, an attacker will be looking for the following information:

- Proprietary WLAN security mechanisms
- SSID
- IP information. (Subnet Mask or DHCP)
- WEP (if enabled)

The Decode window of the software is used to enumerate this information.

WLAN Security Mechanisms

Some proprietary access points (e.g., Lucent's AP-1000) employ an optional closed wireless system mode; see Figure B.7. In this setting, the SSID is not advertised in the access point's beacon frame. Thus, wireless nodes must be configured with a specifically matched infrastructure name before they're allowed to authenticate and associate with the AP. However, there are four other frames that contains the Service Set Identification (SSID).

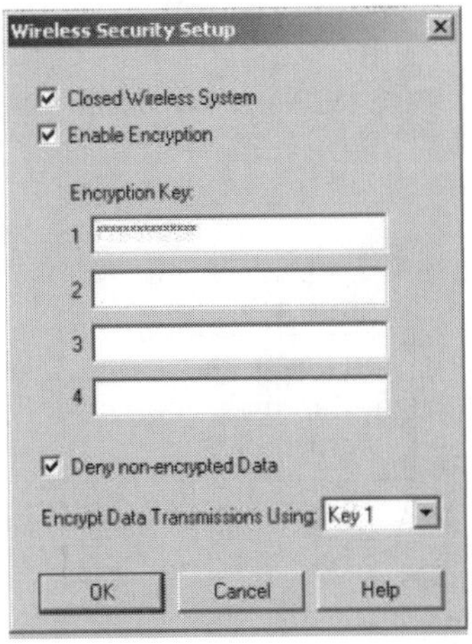

Figure B.7   Lucent's AP-1000 proprietary security mechanism.

The following IEEE 802.11b management frame types will always contain the SSID subfield:

- Beacon
- Probe request and Probe response
- Association request
- Reassociation request

Retrieving the SSID, or infrastructure name, is critical when an access point is operating in a closed wireless network mode (as in the case of the AP-1000). As indicated earlier, when this mode is invoked, the advertisement of the SSID is no longer present in the AP's beacon frame. However, due to another inherent vulnerability in the IEEE 802.11b standard, the other aforementioned management frame types will still display this information, even if any type of encryption is enabled.

An easy method to enumerate the target's SSID is for the attacker to intercept and capture an authorized wireless node's probe request to join the target IEEE 802.11b WLAN; see Figure B.8.

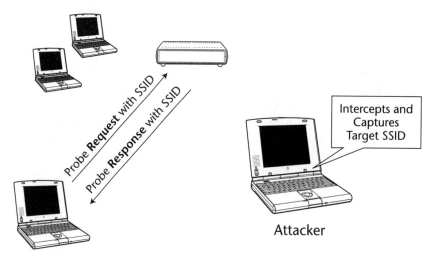

Figure B.8 Intercepting and capturing the SSID.

Nevertheless, capturing an IEEE 802.11b access point's beacon frame is the simplest method in enumerating your target WLAN's SSID. The following steps will enable you to select a beacon frame and enumerate the SSID from AiroPeek's Decode window:

1. Select the desired channel.

   ■ Choose Options from the Tools menu. This will open the Options dialog box.

   ■ Click on the 802.11 tab and select the desired Channel.

2. Start a Capture Window.

3. Click the Start Capture button.

4. Filter out the Beacon frame

   ■ Go to Protocols view tab (on bottom) and find and choose a Beacon frame.

   ■ Right-click to open the context menu; or use the Edit menu and choose Select Related Packets. In the Selection Results dialog, choose By Protocol and Hide Unselected. The Packets view now shows all the properly formed beacon packets.

5. Select a Beacon packet.

6. Place cursor in Decode window (below packet view) and left-click.

7. Hit F4. This will expand the Decode window for the selected beacon packet.

8. Scroll down until you see "802.11 Management - Beacon."

   ▪ Look for Element ID:0 SSID.

   ▪ SSID information will be displayed here.

IP Information

The enumeration of the target WLAN's Internet Protocol addressing scheme, as well as its associated subnet mask and default gateways, can be achieved through various options in AiroPeek. However, higher-level protocols, OSI layers 3 and above, require the use of WEP, the adopted IEEE 802.11 encryption scheme, to be either disabled on the target access point or decrypted by the attacker. IP information will not be displayed if an unknown WEP key string is being utilized by the target IEEE 802.11b WLAN. For a known encryption key string (or WEP disabled on the access point), AiroPeek will display the IP addressing scheme. For the sniffer to decipher the encrypted packets, you must first enter the 5 ASCII characters (40-bit) or 13 ASCII characters (104-bit) into the appropriate configuration setting of the software.

AiroPeek allows you to specify the WEP shared key for its network. Using the secret shared key set, AiroPeek can decode the network data contained in the target's 802.11b WLAN packets in the same way that every other station on the target's network does. To enable AiroPeek to decode higher-level protocols (i.e., IP layer) on your target network where WEP is in use:

1. Choose Options from the Tools menu to open the Options dialog.

2. Choose the 802.11 tab to bring up the 802.11 view.

3. In the Encryption section of the 802.11 view, use the pop-up menu labeled "WEP key set" to choose the key set to use for this session of AiroPeek from the list of available key sets. To use a key set, highlight its name in this list and click the Apply button to apply the new key set without closing the 802.11 view; or click OK to enable the new key set and close the Options dialog.

4. To create a *new* WEP key set:

   ▪ Click the Edit Key Sets button to open the WEP Key Sets window.

   ▪ Click the Insert button in the WEP Key Sets window to open the WEP Key Set dialog;, see Figure B.9.

   ▪ Enter the Name for this key set. This name will appear in the WEP Key Set window and in the pop-up menu in the Encryption section of the 802.11 view of the Options dialog, where you can enable each key set by name.

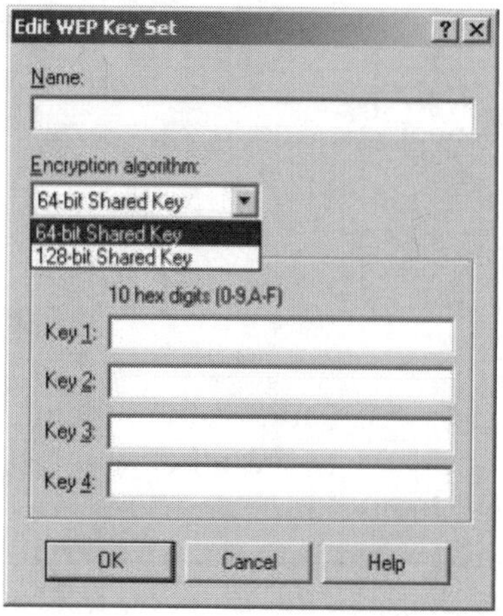

Figure B.9   WEP Key Set window.

- Choose an encryption algorithm from the pop-up menu. You can choose 64-bit Shared Key or 128-bit Shared Key.
- Enter the keys in hexadecimal notation in the numbered text entry boxes in the section labeled Key Set. If you chose 64-bit shared key encryption, you will need to enter 10 hexadecimal numbers. For 128-bit shared key encryption, the keys are 26 hexadecimal numbers long.

Once the secret WEP key has been entered and selected, AiroPeek will now be able to decode higher-layer protocols (IP layer and above).

NOTE You still need to calculate the subnet mask to join the WLAN. However, if your target is running a DHCP server, then getting an IP address will be trivial.

Step 3: Access

As mentioned previously, the following information is needed for an attacker to authenticate and associate with the target IEEE 802.11b access point in order to gain access into the backbone wired network:

- Service Set Identification (SSID)
- WEP encryption key string (if enabled)
- IP Address/Subnet Mask

The retrieval of the target's SSID and IP information were explained previously. The attacker has two options to authenticate and associate with the target IEEE 802.11b access point: manually configure the 802.11b PCMCIA driver or utilize the vendor-specific utility software associated with the target AP. The manual configuration of the 802.11b PCMCIA driver is identical to configuring your conventional wired NIC card to join a wired network. The configuration of the Cisco 342 PCMCIA utility software is explained below:

1. Start the Aironet Client Utility software.

2. Select Edit Properties from the Commands menu. You should be in the System Parameters tab.

3. Enter the target's SSID. Confirm that Infrastructure has been selected under Network Type.

4. If WEP is enabled on the target access point, select the RF Network tab and check the Enable WEP (Wired Equivalent Privacy) box.

5. Accept the default setting for the rest of the options.

6. Start the Client Encryption Manager software; see Figure B.10.

7. Enter default password of "Cisco" (case-sensitive).

8. Select Enter WEP key under the Commands menu. Enter he WEP key in hexadecimal numbers. Check the appropriate key size (40- or 128-bit).

9. Click OK. You are now in the target's WLAN.

Once authenticated and associated, the attacker has essentially plugged into the WLAN's access point and can enjoy the full privileges of an authorized user.

Furthermore, since the target IEEE 802.11b WLAN is configured either as a Basic Service Set (BSS), the attacker now has a direct connection to the backbone wired network. Should the access point be placed behind the firewall or network intrusion detection system, the attacker now has the same privileges and trust level as an internal user on that particular local area network. For all practical purposes, a computer network attack via an IEEE 802.11b access point will appear as an internal job.

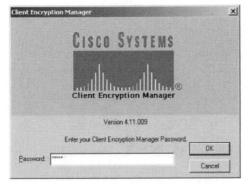

Figure B.10   Aironet Client Encryption Manager software.

It should be noted that tracing the source of the attack would be substantially difficult, especially if the attack were conducted from literally miles away. With the use of high-gain antennas and low-noise amplifiers, an attacker would be virtually impossible to trace. The only substantial evidence logged for this unauthorized entry through the target network's IEEE 802.11b access point would be the MAC address of the attacker's 802.11b PCMCIA card.

802.11 REGULATORY REQUIREMENTS

General Europe

Approval Standards: European Telecommunications Standards Institute

Documents: ETS 300-328, ETS 300-339

Approval Authority: National Type Approval Authorities

France

Approval Standards: La Reglementation en France pour les Equipements fonctionnant

dans la bande de fréquences 2.4 GHz "RLAN-Radio Local Area Network"

Documents: SP/DGPT/ATAS/23, ETS 300-328, ETS 300-339

Approval Authority: Direction Generale des Postes et Telecommunications

Japan

Approval Standards: Research and Development Center for Radio Communications

(RCR)

Documents: RCR STD-33A

Approval Authority: Ministry of Telecommunications (MKK)

North America

Approval Standards, Canada: Industry Canada (IC) *Documents*: GL36

Approval Authority, Canada: Industry Canada (Canada)

Approval Standards, United States: Federal Communications Commission (FCC)

Documents: CFR47, Part 15, Sections 15.205, 15.209, 15.247.

Approval Authority, United States:FCC

Spain

Approval Standards: Supplemento Del Numero 164 Del Boletin Oficial Del Estado

(Published July 10, 1991, Revised June 25, 1993)

Documents: ETS 300-328, ETS 300-339

Approval Authority: Cuadro Nacional De Atribucion De Frecuesias

Table B.1 shows 802.11b transmit power levels for the three major geographic regions.

Table B.1 Transmit Power Levels for Different Regions

MAX OUTPUT POWER	GEOGRAPHIC LOCATION	COMPLIANCE DOCUMENT	
1000 mW	USA	FCC 15.247	
100 mW	(EIRP)	EUROPE	ETS 300-328
10 mW/MHz	JAPAN	MPT	Ordinance 79

Table B.2 breaks out the different DSSS frequencies by geographic region. Figure B.11 is a diagram showing the shape of the transmitted channel.

Table B.2 Direct Sequence Spread Spectrum (DSSS) Frequencies for Different Regions

CHANNEL NUMBER	FREQUENCY GHZ	NORTH AMERICA	EUROPE	SPAIN	FRANCE	JAPAN-MKK
1	2.412	X	X			
2	2.417	X	X			
3	2.422	X	X			
4	2.427	X	X			
5	2.432	X	X			
6	2.437	X	X			
7	2.442	X	X			
8	2.447	X	X			
9	2.452	X	X			
10	2.457	X	X	X	X	
11	2.462	X	X	X	X	
12	2.467		X		X	
13	2.472		X		X	
14	2.483					X

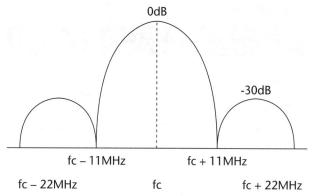

Figure B.11   Transmit channel shape.

Figure B.12. shows the minimum spacing allowable between channels in North American DSSS networks.

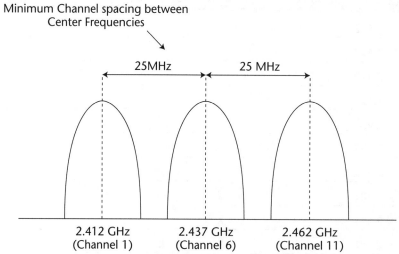

Figure B.12   Minimum channel spacing for North American DSSS networks.

Wired Equivalent Privacy (WEP)

To protect from eavesdropping, IEEE 802.11 incorporates a 40-bit or 104-bit encryption mechanism called Wired Equivalent Privacy. Only Data Frames and Management Frames of subtype Authentication can be encrypted. It should be noted that only the frame body of data frames is encrypted. The complete MAC header of the data frame and the entire frame of other frame types are transmitted unencrypted. According to the IEEE 802.11 standard:

> *The privacy service of IEEE 802.11 is designed to provide an equivalent level of protection for data traversing the WLAN as that provided by a wired network that exists in an office building with physical access to the network plant. This service protects the data only as it traverses the wireless medium. It is not designed to provide complete protection of data between applications running over a mixed network environment that happens to include an IEEE 802.11 WLAN.*

This privacy mechanism adopted by IEEE 802.11 is inherently vulnerable to network exploitation.

The dot11PrivacyInvoked attribute controls the use of WEP in each station. If this attribute is set to false, all frames are sent without encryption. If it is true, all frames will be sent with encryption enabled.

RC4 is the encryption algorithm used in WEP. It is a symmetric stream cipher that supports variable key lengths up to 256 bytes. Since the cipher is symmetric, both encryption and decryption are accomplished using the same key. Therefore, only those stations sharing the same key can correctly decrypt data frames. IEEE 802.11 has chosen to use the 40-bit key.

The WEP algorithm can be broken down into five steps.

At the sending station:

1. WEP first runs the unencrypted data through an integrity algorithm that generates a 4-octet check value that will be sent with the data and verified at the receiving station. This integrity check value (ICV), as noted previously, is used to check the integrity of the received frame.

2. The secret encryption key is then concatenated with a 24-bit initialization vector (IV) and processed through a pseudo-random number generator (PNRG) to create a key sequence. The length of the key sequence is equal to the plaintext and ICV.

> **NOTE** PNRG is the critical component of this process, since it transforms a short secret key into an arbitrarily long key sequence. The secret key can remain constant while the IV can change periodically. Each new IV results in a new key sequence. The IV is transmitted in the clear since it provides no information about the secret key.

3. WEP then uses a bitwise XOR on the plaintext and ICV with the key sequence to create the ciphertext.

At the receiving station:

4. WEP deciphers the ciphertext using its shared key and the received initialization vector.

5. Station then calculates its own ICV and ensures it matches the one sent with the frame.

The sequence of events at the sending station is depicted in Figure B.13.

> **NOTE** The terms 40-bit and 64-bit encryption keys are synonymous, since a 24-bit initialization vector is concatenated to the 40-bit key. With the same reasoning, a 128-bit encryption scheme uses only a 104-bit key.

WEP Key Details

Two mechanisms are provided by the IEEE 802.11 standard to select a key for encrypting or decrypting a frame:

- Default Keys
- Key Mapping

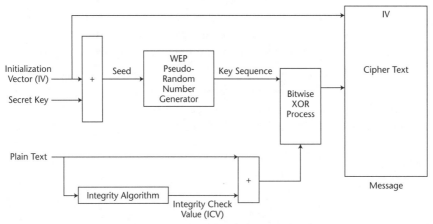

Figure B.13   Wired Equivalent Privacy (WEP) sequence of events.

Up to four default keys can be shared by all stations in a BSS or an ESS. An algorithm, which is not defined in the IEEE 802.11 standard, decides which key will be used to encrypt the frame body. Figure B.14 displays the WEP frame body. The default key used to encrypt the frame is indicated in the KeyID segment of the WEP frame header.

The reception of encrypted frames is also controlled by the dot11PrivacyInvoked attribute located in each Access Point. This attribute, which was discussed previously, controls the reception of frames corresponding to its Boolean value. When set to False, all frames, encrypted or unencrypted, are received. When set to True, only encrypted frames are received. Unencrypted frames will be discarded.

Open Source WEP Decryption Scripts

In July 2001, two open source WEP decryption software applications were released on the Internet. According to their creators, their scripts will decrypt IEEE 802.11b WEP-encrypted packets no matter what the key size, either 40-bit or 104-bit. These open source tools, AirSnort and Wep_Tools, can be found through the following websites:

http://airsnort.sourceforge.net

www.lava.net/~newsham/wlan

Only AirSnort will be discussed. It is the author's opinion that Newsham's WEP-Cracking Tool will compile and execute with the same results.

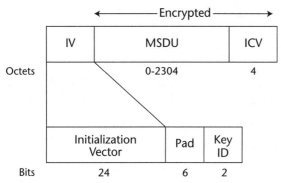

Figure B.14   WEP frame body.

Required Gear

Below is a listing of the hardware and software required to run AirSnort. I've listed some WLAN cards that are compliant.

1. IEEE 802.11b WLAN Card with PRISM2 chipset
   - D-Link DWL-650
   - Linksys WPC-11
   - SMC 2632W
   - Addtron AWP-100
   - BROMAX Freeport
   - Compaq WL 100
   - GEMTEK WL-211
   - Samsung SWL2000-N
   - Z-COM XI300
2. OS-Linux (Redhat 7.1 with 2.4.2-2 Kernel)
3. Kernel pcmcia
4. Linux-wlan-ng-0.1.8-pre13 package
5. Wlan-monitor-patch (patches wlan-ng-0.1.8)
   - Pcmcia-cs-3.1.29

Required Packages

- Full install of Redhat 7.1 (all packages)
- Download pcmcia-cs driver package (http://pcmcia-cs.sourceforge.net)
- Download linux-wlan-ng-0.1.8-pre13 (www.linux-wlan.com)
- Download wlan-monitor.patch (http://airsnort.sourceforge.net)
- Download AirSnort (http://airsnort.sourceforge.net)

Installation Procedures

The following is a detailed listing of the procedures to install the required packages to successfully run AirSnort. They must be executed exactly as given.

1. Untar pcmcia-cs driver package in /usr/src/linux-2.4.2.
2. Run "make config" from within the expanded pcmcia-cs directory.
   - Change from the default: Specify correct kernel source directory.

3. Run "make all" from within the directory.

4. *Do not run* "make install" for pcmcia-cs.

5. Untar linux-wlan-ng-0.1.8-pre13 into any directory

6. Run "make config" from within the expanded linux-wlan-ng directory.

   - Change the following from their defaults:
     - Specify correct kernel source directory: usr/src/linux-2.4.2/ (for Redhat 7.1 only)
     - Specify correct pcmcia-cs source directory: /usr/src/linux-2.4.2/pcmcia-cs-3.1.29/ (for Redhat 7.1)
     - Ensure that the PCMCIA card services are the only modules built (vice PCI/PLX services).

7. Run "make all" from within the directory.

8. Run "make install" from within the directory.

9. Make the following changes to the file wlan-ng.opts:

   - Change the field parameter DesiredSSID="linksys"
   - Ensure PrivacyInvoked = "false"
   - Ensure AuthType = "opensystem"

10. Run netconfig, changing the interface name from "irlan0" to "wlan0."

11. Edit /etc/pcmcia/config file, adding a line at the end: source ./wlan-ng.conf.

12. Edit /etc/sysconfig/network-scripts/ifcfg-wlan0:

    - DEVICE="wlan0"
    - USERCTL="yes"
    - ONBOOT ="yes"
    - BOOTPROT="dhcp"
    - NETWORK="192.168.1.0"
    - NETMASK="255.255.255.0"
    - BROADCAST="192.168.1.255"
    - GATEWAY="192.168.1.1"
    - IPADDR=""

13. Apply wlan-monitor.patch

    - patch -p0 < wlan-monitor.patch

14. After patch is applied run:
    - "make config" for linux-wlan-ng-0.1.8-pre13
    - "make all" for linux-wlan-ng-0.1.8-pre13
    - "make install" for linux-wlan-ng-0.1.8-pre13

15. Reboot machine

16. After reboot, bringing up interface wlan0 may fail; this is normal because pcmcia drivers are loaded after interface initialization.

17. Restart the pcmcia and network services:
    - /etc/rc.d/init.d/pcmcia restart
    - /etc/rc.d/init.d/network restart

18. Examine the card status to ensure proper operation:
    - ifconfig -a
    - iwconfig
    - cardctl status
    - cardctl ident

19. Untar AirSnort into any directory.

20. Run "make" in the expanded AirSnort directory.

21. Within the scripts subdirectory, run shell script:
    ./dopromisc.sh

22. Within the airsnort/src subdirectory, run:
    /capture -c <outputfilename>

23. After enough interesting packets have been captured (some 3 hours worth of sample), run:
    ./crack <outputfilename>

Table B.3 lists the specifications of the ORiNOCA AP-1000 access point, and Table B.4 lists the specs for the Cisco 340 PC card.

Test Equipment Specifications

Table B.3   ORiNOCO AP 1000 Access Point Specifications

Features	Dual PC Card slot architecture
	Wireless-to-Wireless Bridging
	10/100 Mb Ethernet Support
	IEEE 802.11b (Wi-Fi)-compliant
	Spanning Tree Algorithm
	IEEE 802.1D Transparent Bridging
	Selective protocol filtering
	Access Control Table and radio-based authentication
	DHCP and BOOTP
	Multichannel support
	Roaming Support
	RC4-based encryption support
Management	ORiNOCO AP Manager software
	SNMP MIB II, 802.3, 802.1D, and 802.11 MIB-compliant
	Windows-based user interface
	TRAPS: power-up, authentication, link-up/down
	Site Survey Tools
	Remote Point-to-Point diagnostics

(continues)

Table B.3   ORiNOCO AP 1000 Access Point Specifications *(Continued)*

LEDs	4 LEDs:
	-Power
	-Ethernet LAN Activity
	-ORiNOCO Activity on Slot A
	-ORiNOCO Activity on Slot B
Interface	Ethernet 802.1
	-100Base-T (RF 45 Connector)
	ORiNOCO
	Two slots for ORiNOCO PC Cards
	RS-232
	Unit Configuration (Supported with future software release)
Dimensions	50 mm × 185 mm × 261 mm (2.0 in. × 7.3 in. × 10.2 in.)
Weight	1.75 kg (3.86 lb.)
Power Supply	Integrated Module
	Autosensing 100/240 VAC 50/60 Hz
	0.2 A
Operating Temperature	0 to +40 C
	(20% to 80% relative humidity)

Table B.4   CISCO Aironet 340 PC Card Specifications

Network Architecture Types	Supports peer-to peer networking and communication to wired networks via access points
Range at 1 Mbps (typical)	1500 ft. (460 m) open environment; 300ft. (90m) office
Range at 11 Mbps (typical)	400 ft. (120m) open environment; 100 ft. (30m) office

Table B.4 *(Continued)*

Encryption	AIR-PCM340: No WEP option
	AIR-PCM341: 40- bit WEP option
	AIR-PCM342: 128-bit WEP option
Antenna	Integrated internal antenna with diversity support
Device Drivers Available	NDIS2, NDIS3, NDIS4, NDIS5, ODI, and packet
System Interface	PC Card type II slot PC Card Type II slot
LED Indicators	Link status and link activity Link status and link activity
Receive Sensitivity	90 dBm @ 1 Mbps
	88 dBm @ 2 Mbps
	87 dBm @ 5.5 Mbps
	83 dBm @ 11 Mbps
Max Output Power	30 mW (U.S., Canada, ETSI)
	4.5 mW/MHz (EIRP, Japan)
Power Consumption	Transmit: 350 mA
	Receive: 250 mA
	Sleep: under 10 mA
Certifications	FCC Class B, FCC Part 15.247,
	Canada ICES Class B, CE, UL, CSA
Operating Temperature	32° to 158° F (0° to 70° C)
	95% max. humidity (non condensing)
Humidity	10 to 90%
Dimensions	2.13 x 4.37 x 0.1 in. (5.4 x 11.1 x .5cm)
Weight	1.6 oz. (45 g)

Figure B.15 shows the Cisco Aironet 340 PC card.

Figure B.15   Cisco Aironet 340 PC Card.

The Demo Version of AiroPeek

The 30-day evaluation version of AiroPeek is included on the accompanying website, or can be downloaded from the company's website at www.wildpackets.com.

The demonstration version of AiroPeek differs from the full-featured version in the following ways:

- Each capture window is limited to 30 seconds, and no more than 250 packets.
- Only five Capture windows can be opened per launch.
- Only the first 250 packets of a saved file will be loaded into Packet File windows.
- Global statistics are captured for only five minutes.
- Printing and Saving are disabled.
- Only AiroPeek native file format (*.apc) files can be loaded.
- Allows an unlimited number of launches before the expiration date.

Minimum System Requirements (all versions):

- Pentium 166 MHz or faster processor with 64-MB RAM
- Windows 95 (release B), Windows 98, Windows ME, Windows NT 4.0 (SP3 or later), or Windows 2000
- Cisco Aironet 340 adapter card (including utility software)

Written by Mel K. Yokoyama, Jr.
Mr. Yokoyama, Jr. is a wireless security consultant currently on government assignment.

Using the Fluhrer, Mantin, and Shamir Attack to Break WEP

Written by Adam Stubblefield[1], John Ioannidis, and Aviel D. Rubin August 6, 2001[2]. Reproduced with permission from the Internet Society. The Internet Society is a nonprofit, nongovernmental, international, professional membership organization. Its more than 150 organization and 6,000 individual members in over 170 nations worldwide represent a veritable who's who of the Internet community. More information can be found at: www.isoc.org.

Abstract

We implemented an attack against WEP, the link-layer security protocol for 802.11 networks. The attack was described in a recent paper by Fluhrer, Mantin, and Shamir. With our implementation, and permission of the network administrator, we were able to recover the 128 bit secret key used in a production network, with a passive attack. The WEP standard uses RC4 IVs improperly, and the attack exploits this design failure. This paper describes the attack,

[1] Research done while a summer intern at AT&T Labs.

[2] Stubblefield, A., J. Ioannidis, & A. Rubin, "Using the Fluhrer, Mantin, and Shamir Attack to Break WEP," AT&T Labs Technical Report TD-4ZCPZZ, August 6, 2001.

how we implemented it, and some optimizations to make the attack more efficient. We conclude that 802.11 WEP is totally insecure, and we provide some recommendations.

1 Introduction

Wireless networking has taken off, due in large part to the availability of the 802.11 standard. While another standard, Bluetooth, is also gaining in popularity, the longer range and higher speeds achieved by 802.11 make it the protocol of choice for wireless LANs. Office buildings, conferences, and even many residences now offer 802.11 connectivity. The PC cards that are most often used in these networks provide a security protocol called Wired Equivalent Privacy (WEP).

WEP is easy to administer. The device using the 802.11 card is configured with a key, that in practice usually consists of a password or a key derived from a password. The same key is deployed on all devices, including the access points. The idea is to protect the wireless communication from devices that do not know the key.

Borisov, Goldberg and Wagner demonstrated some security flaws in WEP[3]. They explained that WEP fails to specify how IVs for RC4 are specified. Several PC cards reset IVs to zero every time they are initialized, and then increment them by one for every use. This results in high likelihood that keystreams will be reused, leading to simple cryptanalytic attacks against the cipher, and decryption of message traffic. The authors verified this experimentally and describe other weaknesses as well. For example, the space from which IVs are chosen is too small, virtually guaranteeing reuse, and leading to the same cryptanalytic attacks just described. The paper also shows that message authentication in WEP is broken.

Fluhrer, Mantin, and Shamir describe a passive ciphertext-only attack against RC4 as used in WEP[4]. The attack exploits the method in which the standard describes using IVs for the RC4 stream cipher. In their paper, the authors state, "Note that we have not attempted to attack an actual WEP connection, and hence do not claim that WEP is actually vulnerable to this attack". Based on the description in their paper, we successfully implemented the attack, proving that WEP is in fact completely vulnerable. The purpose of this paper is to describe our implementation, along with some enhancements to improve the performance of the attack.

[3]BORISOV, N., GOLDBERG, I., AND WAGNER, D. Intercepting mobile communications: The insecurity of 802.11. MOBICOM 2001 (2001).

[4]FLUHRER, S., MANTIN, I., AND SHAMIR, A. Weaknesses in the key scheduling algorithm of RC4. Eighth Annual Workshop on Selected Areas in Cryptography (August 2001).

2 Overview of the WEP Attack

In this section we present an overview of the WEP protocol and review briefly how the attack of Fluhrer, Mantin, and Shamir can be applied to WEP. For a detailed description of WEP we refer the reader to the official 802.11 standard[5].

Encryption in WEP uses a secret key, k, shared between an access point and a mobile node. To compute a WEP frame, the plaintext frame data, M, is first concatenated with its (non-cryptographic) checksum c(M), to produce M · c(M) (where · denotes concatenation). Then, a per packet initialization vector (IV) is prepended to the secret key, k, to create the packet key, IV · k. The RC4 stream cipher is then initialized using this packet key, and the output bytes of the cipher are exclusive-ored (denoted ⊕) with the checksummed plaintext to generate the ciphertext:

```
C = (M · c(M)) ⊕ RC4(IV · k)
```

The actual WEP data is the per-packet IV prepended to this ciphertext, C.

2.1 The Known IV Attack of Fluhrer, Mantin, and Shamir

For completeness, we include a short description of the attack of Fluhrer, Mantin, and Shamir[6] here. We refer the reader to the original paper for the motivation and details.

To begin, we describe the structure of the RC4 stream cipher (a full description can be found in[7]). RC4 consists of two parts, a key scheduling algorithm and an output generator. In WEP, the key scheduling algorithm uses either a 64-bit packet key (40-bit secret key plus 24-bit IV) or a 128-bit key (104-bit secret key plus 24- bit IV) to set up the RC4 state array, S, which is a permutation of { 0, . . . , 255 } . The output generator uses the state array S to create a pseudorandom sequence.

The attack utilizes only the first word of output from the pseudorandom sequence, so we focus our attention there. The equation for this first byte of output is given by S[S[1] +S[S[1]]]. Thus, after the key setup stage, this first byte depends on only three values of the state array (S[1], S[S[1]], S[S[1] +S[S[1]]]). The attack is based on our ability to derive information about the key by

[5]L. M. S. C. OF THE IEEE COMPUTER SOCIETY. Wireless LAN medium access control (MAC) and physical layer (PHY) specifications. IEEE Standard 802.11, 1999 Edition (1999).

[6]FLUHRER, S., MANTIN, I., AND SHAMIR, A. Weaknesses in the key scheduling algorithm of RC4. Eighth Annual Workshop on Selected Areas in Cryptography (August 2001).

[7]SCHNEIER, B. Applied Cryptography - Protocols, Algorithms, and Source Code in C. John Wiley & Sons, Inc., 1994.

observing this value. We defer the discussion of how to recover the value of this first byte from a WEP ciphertext stream until Section 3.

To mount the attack, we search for IVs that place the key setup algorithm into a state which leaks information about the key. Using the terminology of Fluhrer *et al.*, we refer to these key-leaking cases as *resolved*. It is simple to test whether a particular packet provides an IV and output byte that result in a resolved condition, though we refer the reader to the Fluhrer *et. al.* paper for the conditions under which they occur[8]. Each resolved packet leaks information about only one key byte, and we must correctly guess each key byte before any packet gives us information about a later key byte.

We say we must "guess" each key byte as the attack is statistical in nature; each resolved packet gives us a 5% chance of guessing a correct key byte and a 95% chance of guessing incorrectly. However, by looking at a large number of these resolved cases, we can expect to see a bias toward the true key bytes.

3 Implementation

In implementing this attack, we had three goals. First and foremost, we wanted to verify that the attack could work in the real world. Second, we were interested in how cheaply and easily the attack could be launched. Lastly, we wanted to see what improvements could be made to both the general RC4 attack and the WEP attack in particular. In this section we report on our success at the first two goals, while reserving discussion about attack optimizations to Section 4.

3.1 Simulating the Attack

Before trying to break WEP, we created a simulation of the RC4 attack to both verify our understanding of the weakness and to gather information about how many resolved packets we could expect would be required when mounting the actual attack. The coding of the simulated attack took under two hours, including a few optimizations. The simulation showed that the attack was always able to recover the full key when given 256 probable resolved cases[9]. We also observed that although 60 resolved cases (the number recommended in the Fluhrer *et. al.* paper) were usually enough to determine a key byte, there were instances in which more were required. Because at this point we had not thoroughly investigated how accurately we would be able to determine the first output byte of the RC4 pseudorandom sequence, we also simulated the

---

[8]It is important to use the criteria given in section 7 (of Fluhrer) rather than the criteria given in appendix A.

The IVs listed in appendix A are only a subset of the IVs which can resolve. We return to this in section 4 of this paper.

[9]Cases corresponding to IVs of the form (B+3, 255, N) as in the Fluhrer et. al. paper.

effect that sometimes guessing wrong would have on the attack. We were pleased to see that as long as the number of incorrect guess was kept small, the correct key byte would still be returned, though sometimes more resolved cases were needed.

3.2 Capturing the Packets

Surprisingly, capturing WEP encrypted packets off of our wireless network proved to be the most time consuming part of the attack. There are a number of commercial software programs that are able to both capture and decode 802.11 packets, such as NAI's "Sniffer" and Wildpacket's "AiroPeek," though both products cost thousands of dollars. Because we wanted to show that the attack could be done by an adversary with limited resources, we purchased a $100 Linksys wireless card, based on the Intersil Prism II chipset. We made this choice because the Prism II allows much of its computation to be completed in software and because there was a Linux driver available that could grab raw WEP-encrypted packets. Though we did not know it at the time, this chipset has been used by others to mount dictionary and brute force attacks against WEP[10].

We used both the linux-wlan-ng prism2 driver[11] and a modified version of Tim Newsham's patch to re-enable raw packet monitoring[12], to get the card working in Linux. We were then able to use a modified version of the packet sniffer Ethereal[13] to capture raw WEP encrypted packets and to decode the data necessary for our attack tool.

There is one problem with using this card as opposed to a more sophisticated solution. The prism2 chipset does request a transmission timeslot even when in monitor mode. Many inexpensive base stations do not report this, though a software hack can allow Linux computers running as access points to register an SNMP trap each time that a node joins or leaves the network[14]. This information does not directly indicate likely attackers, but could be combined with other information in an IDS to locate users who register with a base station but not with whatever network level access controls exist. Also, we know of no practical reason why this "registration" with the network is necessary; there may even exist consumer 802.11 chipsets which support listening without registering (perhaps even the prism2 chipset in some other undocumented mode).

---

[10]See Blackhat '01 presentation at http://www.lava.net/~newsham/wlan/WEP_password_cracker.ppt.

[11]Available from http://www.linux-wlan.com/.

[12]Available from http://www.lava.net/~newsham/wlan/.

[13]Available from http://www.ethereal.com/.

[14]HAMRICK, M. Personal communications, 2001.

Even with the hardware and software problems, from the time that we first decided to look at this problem, it took less than a week for the card to be ordered and shipped, the test bed to be set up, the problems to be debugged, and a full key to be recovered.

3.3 *Mounting the Attack*

The last piece in actually mounting the attack was determining the true value of the first plaintext byte of each packet, so that we could infer the first byte of the pseudorandom sequence from the first ciphertext byte. We originally looked at tcpdump output of decrypted traffic (using a correctly keyed card[15]), and were planning on using packet length to differentiate between ARP and IP traffic (both of which have well known first bytes in their headers) as these were by far the two most common types of traffic on our network. After implementing this, however, we discovered that the attack didn't seem to work. We then tried hand decrypting packets to determine whether tcpdump was working correctly and discovered that an additional 802.2 encapsulation header is added for both ARP and IP traffic[16, 17]. This discovery actually made the attack even easier, as all IP and ARP packets would now have the same first plaintext byte (0xAA, the SNAP designation)[18, 19]. If the network in question also carries legacy IPX traffic, the first plaintext byte will not be 0xAA for these packets. However, as we showed in our simulation, as long as the IP and ARP packets greatly outnumber the IPX packets, the attack is still possible. If the network carries mostly IPX traffic, the attack should be modified to use either 0xFF or 0xE0 instead of 0xAA.

```
RecoverWEPKey()
        Key[0...KeySize] = 0
        for KeyByte = 0...KeySize
                Counts[0...255] = 0
                foreach packet?  P
                        if P.IV ∈ { (KeyByte +3, 0xFF, N) | N∈ 0x00...0xFF)
                                Counts[SimulateResolved(P,Key)]+=1
                Key[KeyByte] = IndexOfMaximumElement(Counts)
                return Key
```

Figure C.1   The basic attack on WEP.

[15]Note that a correctly keyed card is not needed; we simply used one to design the attack.

[16]We eventually traced this back to RFC 1042.

[17]POSTEL, J., AND REYNOLDS, J. K. Standard for the transmission of IP datagrams over IEEE 802 networks. Request for Comments 1042, Internet Engineering Task Force, Feb. 1988.

[18]Some vendors, such as Cisco use a proprietary OID. Fortunately, it also beings with 0xAA.

[19]CAFARELLI, D. Personal communications, 2001.

Although our actual attack used the improvements discussed in the next section, we present an outline of how a naive attack could work here. It is interesting to note that even this baseline version of the attack would still be successful in a short period of time (a day or two at most) and with an even smaller amount of computation when compared to the improved implementation, assuming that the wireless network in question had a reasonable amount of traffic.

To begin, we collected a large number of packets from our wireless network. To speed the process up for some of our experiments late at night when network volume was low, we artificially increased the load on the wireless network by ping flooding a wireless node. (We could have waited until more traffic was created; this is not an active attack.) Because we are able to predict the value of the first byte of any plaintext, the fact that we changed the makeup of the network traffic did not affect these experiments. In looking at the IVs of these collected packets, we discovered that the wireless cards use a simple counter to compute the IV, wherein the first byte is incremented first[20, 21].

Figure C. 1 shows the basic attack used to recover a WEP key[22]. In section A.1 of Fluhrer et. al., the authors postulate that 4,000,000 packets would be sufficient with this baseline attack; we found the number to be between 5,000,000 and 6,000,000 for our key. This number is still not unreasonable, as we were able to collect that many packets in a few hours on a partially loaded network.

4 Improving the Attack

In this section we discuss several modifications that can be made to improve the performance of the key recovery attack on WEP. While not necessary for the compromise to be effective, they can decrease both time and space requirements for an attacker.

4.1 Choosing IVs

In the baseline attack (the one described in Appendix A of Fluhrer *et. al.*), only IVs of a particular form are considered (those corresponding to (*KeyByte* +3, 0x*FF*, N) where *KeyByte* is the current KeyByte we are guessing and N is unrestricted). However, we found that there are other IVs that can result in a

---

[20]Other cards have been reported to choose IVs at random, to count in big endian order, or to switch between two IVs. This last class are cards are not vulnerable to the attack in this paper, although they break badly under the attacks of Borisov et al.

[21]BORISOV, N., GOLDBERG, I., AND WAGNER, D. Intercepting mobile communications: The insecurity of 802.11. MOBICOM 2001 (2001).

[22]Depending on the actual key used, this attack can take between 4,000,000 and 6,000,000 packets to recover a 128-bit key. The SimulateResolved function computes the value described in section 7.1 of Fluhrer et al.

resolved state, and that testing all IVs instead of only the subset suggested by the Fluhrer *et. al.* paper can be done in parallel with receiving packets. This conclusion was verified by Adi Shamir[23], who also noted that these packets appear more often for higher key bytes.

4.2 Guessing Early Key Bytes

As the Fluhrer, Mantin, and Shamir attack works by building on previously discovered key bytes, recovering early key bytes is critical. There are two approaches that we tried both separately and together. The first utilized the way that the IVs were generated, namely that we would receive packets that resolved for lots of different key bytes before necessarily receiving enough resolving packets to predict the early key bytes[24]. We would therefore use the resolving cases that we had received to narrow down the possibilities for the early key bytes. We were then able to test candidate keys by determining if the WEP checksum on a decrypted packet turned out correctly.

The second approach exploited the poor key management available in WEP implementations. Since WEP keys have to be entered manually, we assumed that instead of giving clients a long string of hex digits, a user memorable passphrase would be used. After examining the test wireless cards at our disposal, we determined that the user-memorable passphrase is simply used raw as the key (i.e. the ASCII is used; no hashing is done). Although hashing does not protect against a dictionary attack, it would have helped in this circumstance, as we were able to determine directly whether each key byte was likely to be part of a user memorable passphrase by checking whether the byte value corresponded to an ASCII letter, number, or punctuation symbol.

This pair of optimizations turned out to provide an astounding decrease in the number of packets required. In parallel with receiving packets (on another machine, though this is not really necessary), we were continually attempting to guess the key by choosing the most likely candidates based on the resolved cases we had already gathered. In the event of "ties" for the next most likely byte, we gave priority first to (in order): lowercase letters, uppercase letters, numbers, symbols, other byte values.

4.3 Special Resolved Cases

As Shamir pointed out to us, there are cases when a resolved case can provide an even better indication as to a particular key byte. If there is a duplication among the three values at positions $S[1]$, $S[S[1]]$, and $S[S[1]+S[S[1]]]$ (i.e. these

---

[23]SHAMIR, A. Personal communications, 2001.

[24]See Figure 6 of Fluhrer et. al.; resolved cases are much more likely to occur for later key bytes.

```
RecoverWEPKeyImproved(CurrentKeyGuess, KeyByte)
        Counts[0...255] = 0
        foreach packet? P
                if Resolved?(P.IV)
                        Counts[SimulateResolved(P,CurrentKeyGuess)]+
                =Weight(P,CurrentKeyGuess)
        foreach SelectMaximumIndexesWithBias(Counts) ? ByteGuess
                CurrentKeyGuess[KeyByte] = ByteGuess
                if Equal? (KeyByte, KeyLength)
                        if CheckChecksums(CurrentKeyGuess)
                                return CurrentKeyGuess
        else
                        Key = RecoverWEPKeyImproved(CurrentKeyGuess, KeyByte + 1)
                        if notEqual? (Key,Failure)
                                return Key
        return Failure
```

Figure C.2   The Improved attack on WEP.

are only two distinct values), then the probability that these positions in the S permutation remain unchanged jumps from $e^{-3} \sim 5\%$ to $e^{-2} \sim 13\%$. We can thus treat the evidence from these cases as about three times more convincing as a standard resolved case.

4.4 Combining the Optimizations

Figure C.2 shows the key recovery algorithm after all of the improvements described above[25]. The improvements drop the number of packets required from around 5,000,000 to around 1,000,000.

5 Discussion

There are many variables that can affect the performance of the key recovery attack on WEP. In this section we summarize the effect of some of these variables and look at how the WEP design could be slightly altered to prevent this particular attack.

---

[25]Depending on the actual key used, this attack can take between 1,000,000 and 2,000,000 packets to recover a 128-bit key. The SimulateResolved function computes the value described in section 7.1 of Fluhrer et al., the CheckChecksums checks to see if a key causes the checksums in the WEP packets to come out correctly, and the Resolved? predicate checks to see if a given packet results in a resolved condition. The SelectMaximalIndicesWithBias function corresponds to the optimization in section 4.2. The Weight function returns 3 if the resolved case corresponds to a special resolved case as described in section 4.3, and 1 otherwise.

5.1 IV Selection

Since the WEP standard does not specify how IVs should be chosen, there are a variety of IV generation in use in current 802.11 cards. The majority of cards seem to use one of three methods: counters, random selection, or value-flipping (i.e. switching between two IV values). This attack is possible with either of the first two types of IV selection. Value-flipping prevents this attack at the expense of reusing the pseudorandom stream every other packet. This is not a reasonable tradeoff.

Counter modes are the most accommodating of this attack. In these cards, the IV is incremented with each packet sent (starting either at 0 or at some random value when the card is powered on). With counter mode cards, an attacker is practically guaranteed a nice distribution of resolving packets among the key bytes. Random selection of each IV is not much better, as there are enough expected resolved cases that although the distribution might not be quite as good as the counter modes, it won't be much worse.

In short, there does not seem to be a way of choosing IVs to mitigate the effects of this attack without explicitly testing each IV and key pair to see if it resolves before sending it. This would require extra processing power and would decrease the already small space of IVs.

5.2 Key Selection

The lack of key management in WEP certainly contributes to the ease of the key recovery attack. Most networks use a single shared key between the base station and all mobile nodes. Besides the suite of "disgruntled ex-employee who knows the key" style attacks, there is also the problem of distributing this key to the users. Many sites use a human memorable password to easy this key distribution. There is however no standard way of mapping these passwords to a WEP key. The current solution is mapping the ASCII value directly to a key byte. We would recommend switching to either using a secure (nonmemorable) WEP key or having the key setup software hash the password to the key using a cryptographic hash function. Note that neither of these solutions prevent the attack, only make it slightly more difficult.

There do exist proprietary solutions that allow each mobile node to use a distinct WEP key, most notably Cisco's LEAP protocol. LEAP sets up a per-user, per-session WEP key when a user first authenticates to the network. This complicates the attack, but does not prevent it so long as a user's "session" lasts sufficiently long. We would recommend securely rekeying each user after every approximately 10,000 packets.

5.3 RC4

RC4 is an efficient stream cipher that can be used securely. The implementation of RC4 in SSL is not affected by the Fluhrer *et. al.* attack. The reasons are that SSL pre-processes the encryption key and IV by hashing with both MD5 and SHA-1[26]. Thus different sessions have unrelated keys. In addition, in SSL, RC4 state from previous packets is used in future packets, so that the algorithm does not rekey after each packet.

A further recommendation (RSA Security Inc.'s standard recommendation) is for applications to discard the first 256 bytes of RC4 output. This may be a bit expensive for very small packets, but if session state is maintained across packets, that cost is amortized.

In summary, RC4 can be used as part of a security solution. However, care must be taken when implementing it so that key material is not leaked. One of the risks of algorithms that have such caveats is that protocol designers without a strong grounding in cryptography and security may not be aware of the correct way to implement them, and this is exactly what happened in the case of WEP.

6 Conclusions and Recommendations

We implemented the attack described by Fluhrer *et. al.* in several hours. It then took a few days to figure out which tools to use and what equipment to buy to successfully read keys off of 802.11 wireless networks. Our attack used off of the shelf hardware and software, and the only piece we provided was the implementation of the RC4 attack, along with some optimizations. We believe that we have demonstrated the ultimate break of WEP, which is the recovery of the secret key by observation of traffic.

Since our technical report appeared, others have duplicated our results. Although we did not release our code, there are now two publicly available tools for breaking WEP keys. As always, once security attacks become known, exploits are available to *script kiddies*, who do not need to understand the technical details to break systems. The two tools that we know of are AirSnort and WEPCrack.

Given this attack, we believe that 802.11 networks should be viewed as insecure. We recommend the following for people using such wireless networks.

---

[26]DIERKS, T., AND ALLEN, C. The TLS Protocol, Version 1.0. Internet Engineering Task Force, Jan. 1999. RFC-2246, ftp://ftp.isi.edu/ in-notes/rfc2246.txt.

- Assume that the link layer offers no security.

- Use higher-level security mechanisms such as IPSec[27] and SSH[28] for security, instead of relying on WEP.

- Treat all systems that are connected via 802.11 as external. Place all access points outside the firewall.

- Assume that anyone within physical range can communicate on the network as a valid user. Keep in mind that an adversary may utilize a sophisticated antenna with much longer range than found on a typical 802.11 PC card.

The experience with WEP shows that it is difficult to get security right. Flaws at every level, including protocol design, implementation, and deployment, can render a system completely vulnerable. Once a flawed system is popular enough to become a target, it is usually a short time before the system is defeated in the field.

Acknowledgments

We thank Bill Aiello, Steve Bellovin, Scott Fluhrer, Bob Miller, Ron Rivest, Adi Shamir, Dave Wagner, and Dan Wallach for helpful comments and discussions. We informed Stuart Kerry, the 802.11 Working Group Chair, that we successfully implemented the Fluhrer, et al. attack. Stuart replied that the 802.11 Working Group is in the process of revising the security, among other aspects, of the standard and appreciates this line of work as valuable input for developing robust technical specifications.

[27] KENT, S., AND ATKINSON, R. Security architecture for the Internet protocol. Request for Comments 2401, Internet Engineering Task Force, November 1998.

[28] YLONEN, T. SSH - secure login connections over the Internet. USENIX Security Conference VI (1996), 37-42.

NASA White Paper on the Wireless Firewall Gateway

Written by Nicole K. Boscia and Derek G. Shaw,
and used by permission from NASA Advanced Supercomputing Division.

1 Introduction

With the deployment of wireless network access in the workplace, the requirement for a more enhanced security design emerges. Wireless technology offers a more accessible means of connectivity but does not address the security concerns involved with offering this less restrained service. In order to facilitate management of this network, maintain a secure network model, and keep a high level of usability, a multi-functional device to do these tasks must be placed in the wireless environment.

2 Design Objectives

The WFG (Wireless Firewall Gateway) is designed to take on several different roles in order for the process to be near transparent to the user. Since the wireless network is considered to be an untrusted environment, access is restricted in order to limit the amount of damage that can be inflicted on internal systems and the Internet if an intruder invokes an attack. This impedes the convenience of the wireless service to users who wish to access external sites on the Internet. Since unknown users are difficult to identify and hold accountable for damages, a method of user authentication is needed to ensure that the user takes responsibility for their actions and can be tracked for security concerns.

A trusted user can then gain access to services and the commodity Internet from which unauthenticated users are blocked. Keeping simplicity in mind, the WFG acts as a router between a wireless and external network with the ability to dynamically change firewall filters as users authenticate themselves for authorized access. It is also a server responsible for handing out IP addresses to users, running a website in which users can authenticate, and maintaining a recorded account of who is on the network and when.

Users of the wireless network are only required to have a web browser, if they wish to authenticate, and dynamic host configuration (DHCP) software, which comes standard on most operating systems. Minimal configuration is required by the user, allowing support for a variety of computer platforms with no additional software. The idea is to keep the wireless network as user-friendly as possible while maintaining security for everyone.

3 Internals

Given the multiple functionalities and enhanced security required for this device, a PC running OpenBSD Unix was chosen with three interfaces on different networks: wireless, external (gateway), and internal (management). The following sections elaborate upon the services that constitute the device's various roles:

Dynamic Host Configuration Protocol (DHCP) Server

DHCP is used to lease out individual IP addresses to anyone who configures their system to request one. Other vital information such as subnet mask, default gateway, and name server are also given to the client at this time. The WFG uses a beta DHCPv3 open-source server from the Internet Software Consortium with the additional ability to dynamically remove hosts from the firewall access list when DHCP releases a lease for any reason (client request, time-out, lease expiration, and so on).

Configuration files for the server are located in /etc and follow the ISC standard (RFC) format. However, the server executable is customized and does not follow these standards. If the server needed to be upgraded, then the source code would need to be re-customized as well.

The DHCP server is configured to only listen on the subnet interface of the wireless network. This prevents anyone from the wired network to obtain a wireless IP address from this server. As an added security measure, packet filters prevent any DHCP requests coming in on any other interfaces.

IP Filtering

Stateful filtering is accomplished using OpenBSD's IPF software. IP routing is enabled in the kernel state allowing for the packet filtering to occur between the wireless and external network interfaces. Static filters are configured on boot up in the /etc/ipf.rules file and are designed to minimize remote access to the WFG. Only essential protocols such as NTP, DNS, DHCP, and ICMP are allowed to reach the system. This builds a secure foundation for the restricted environment. For the users who do not require an authenticated session, access is granted to selected servers for email, VPN, and web. Where applicable, packet filtering is done at a transport layer (UDP or TCP) to allow for stateful inspection of the traffic. This adds a higher level of security by not having to explicitly permit dynamic or private port sessions into the wireless network.

The same script that authenticates a user over the web also enables their access to the unrestricted environment. When a user connects to the web server, their IP address is recorded and upon successful login, gets pushed to the top of the firewall filter list, permitting all TCP and UDP connections out of the wireless network for that IP address.

In order to prevent succeeding users from being allowed trusted access when the IP address is recycled, the in-memory database software removes the firewall filter permit rule whenever the user's next lease binding state is set to free, expired, abandoned, released, or reset. The DHCP server will not issue the same IP address until it frees the lease of the last client. This helps avoids the security issue of someone hijacking an IP address that's been authenticated and using it after the valid user is no longer using the wireless service

Web Authentication

The need for web-based authentication is necessary so that any user running any platform can gain access to the wireless network. Apache (open-source) web server is designed to securely handle this task. The server implements Secure Sockets Layer (SSL) for client/server public-and-private key RSA encryption. Connecting to the web server via HTTP automatically redirects the client browser to use HTTPS. This ensures that the username and password entered by a user will not be sent in clear text. To further increase security, the SSL certificate is signed by VeriSign, a trusted Certificate Authority (CA), which assures that an attacker is not imitating the web server to retrieve a user's password information.

A website is set up where a user can go to type in their username and password information. This site displays the standard government system access warning and shows the IP address of the user's system (using PHP). Once a user has typed their username and password at the website where prompted, a Perl/CGI script then communicates with a RADIUS server with RSA's MD5 digest encryption to determine if the information submitted is correct. If the account information matches what is in the RADIUS database, then commands to allow their IP address, obtained through the Apache environment variables, are added to the IPF access rules. If the user is not found in the RADIUS database, or if the password entered is incorrect, a web page stating

"Invalid Username and Password" is displayed to the user. If everything is successful, the user is notified of their privileged access.

Security

Every step is taken to ensure that a desirable security level is maintained both on the WFG system and the wireless network while not hindering functionality and usability. Only hosts connecting from the wireless network can access the web server. For system management purposes, Secure Shell (OpenSSH) connections are permitted from a single, secured host. All other methods of direct connection are either blocked by the firewall filters or denied access through the use of application-based TCP wrappers.

User's authentication information is encrypted throughout the process: SSL encryption with a certificate signed by a trusted CA between the client's web browser and the server, and MD5 digest encryption between the web server and the RADIUS system for account verification.

Logs are kept for all systems that gain access to both the restricted and authorized network. The DHCP server keeps a record of what MAC address (NIC address) requests an IP address and when it is released, then passes that information to syslog. Syslog then identifies all logging information from DHCP and writes it to /var/log/dhcpd. Additionally, any user who attempts to authenticate via the web interface has their typed username and source IP address logged with the current time along with whether or not they were successful. When a lease on an IP address expires and is removed from the firewall filters, it is noted with the authentication information in /var/log/wireless. These logs are maintained by the website script and DHCP server software, not syslog. Combined, it is possible to identify who is on the network at a given time(either by their userid or by their burned-in physical address, for auditing purposes.

Developer: Nichole K. Boscia, Network Engineer, Computer Sciences Corp., NASA Advanced Supercomputing Division, M/S 258-6, Moffett Field, CA 94035, nboscia@nas.nasa.gov

Designer: Derek G. Shaw, Senior Security Analyst, AMTI, NASA Advanced Supercomputing Division, M/S 258-6, Moffett Field, CA 94035, shawd@nas.nasa.gov

orig. 08.20.01 -nkb-rev 08.30.01 -nkb

Referenced Documents and URLs

802.11b Wired Equivalent Privacy (WEP) Security, www.wirelessethernet.org/pdf/Wi- FiWEPSecurity.pdf, Wired Compatibility Ethernet Alliance, February 19, 2001.

"Advisory Name: PalmOS Password Lockout Bypass," March 1, 2001, @Stake, Inc., www.atstake.com/research/advisories/2001/a030101-1.txt.

"Affidavit in Support of Criminal Complaint, Arrest Warrant and Search Warrants," www.fas.org/irp/ops/ci/hanssen_affidavit.html (March 26, 2001). Albright, Peggy. "With Popularity Comes Security Concerns," *Wireless Week,* April 16, 2001, www.wirelessweek.com/index.asp?layout=print_page&articleID=CA72302 (September 16, 2001).

Anand, Nikhil. "An Overview of Bluetooth Security," February 21, 2001, www.sans.org/infosecFAQ/wireless/bluetooth.htm (April 2001).

Andersson, Christoffer. *GPRS and 3G Wireless Applications.* New York: John Wiley & Sons Inc. 2001.

Anderson, Ross. *Security Engineering.* New York: John Wiley & Sons Inc. 2001.

Andress, Mandy. "Wireless LAN Security," www.blackhat.com/presentations/bh-usa-01/MandyAndress/bh-usa-01-Mandy-Andress.ppt, Black Hat Briefings, August 2001.

ANSI/IEEE "Std 802.11 1999 Edition," September 20, 2001, pp. 59-69; a957.g.akamai.net/7/957/3680/v0001/standards.ieee.org/reading/ieee/std/lanman/802.11-1999.pdf.

Arar, Yardena. "PDA-Based Cell Phones Deliver All-in-One Convenience," November 28, 2000, www.pcworld.com/news/article/0,aid,35241,00.asp (March 26, 2001).

Arbaugh, William A., N. Skankar, Narendar, Y. C. J. Wan, "Your 802.11 Wireless Network Has No Clothes," March 30, 2001, www.cs.umd.edu/~waa/wireless.pdf.

Armstrong, Illena. "Plugging the Holes in Bluetooth," *SC Magazine*, February 2001, www.scmagazine.com/scmagazine/2001_02/cover/cover.html (July 17, 2001).

Army Regulation 380-53, Security Information Systems Security Monitoring, April 29, 1998.

Associated Press. "Users of Wireless Beware: Electronic Eavesdropping Is Easier Than Ever." MSNBC, August 24, 2001, www.msnbc.com/local/rtroa/m83951.asp (September 16, 2001).

Austin, Tom. *PKI*. New York: John Wiley & Sons Inc. 2001.

Baran, Suzanne. "Networking Begins at Home." *InternetWorld*. June 15, 2001, www.internetworld.com/magazine.php?inc=061501/06.15.01feature6.html (July 17, 2001).

Bedell, Paul. *Wireless Crash Course*. New York: McGraw-Hill Telecom. 2001.

Bernatchez, E. "What Is Bluetooth—often spelled Blue Tooth—About?" cellphones.about.com/gadgets/cellphones/library/glossary/bldef_blue_tooth.htm (March 26, 2001),

biz.yahoo.com/prnews/000828/ca_mcafee_.html. Berners-Lee, T., R. Fielding, and L. Masinter "Uniform Resource Identifier (URI): Generic Syntax," August 1998, www.ietf.org/rfc/rfc2396.txt.

"Binary XML Content Format Specification," WAP Forum, , November 4, 1999, www.wapforum.org/.

Bisdikian, C., & B. Miller. *Bluetooth Revealed*. Upper Saddle River, NJ: Prentice-Hall PTR, 2001.

Bluetooth SIG. "Bluetooth Security FAQ," www.bluetooth.com/bluetoothguide/faq/5.asp (January 5, 2001).

Bluetooth v1.1 Specifications and Bluetooth v1.1 Profiles, www.bluetooth.com/developer/specification/Bluetooth_11_Specifications_Book.pdf; and www.bluetooth.com/developer/specification/Bluetooth_11_Profiles_Book.pdf.

"Bluetooth Wireless Technology Bridging the Gap between Computing and Communication," www.intel.com/mobile/bluetooth/index.htm (February 18, 2001).

Borisov, N., I. Goldberg, & D. Wagner. "Intercepting Mobile Communications: The Insecurity of 802.11," August 2001, www.isaac.cs.berkeley.edu/isaac/wep-draft.pdf.

—. "Security of the WEP Algorithm: Internet Security, Applications, Authentication, and Cryptography (ISAAC)," Computer Science Division, UC Berkeley, February 2001, www.isaac.cs.berkeley.edu/isaac/wep-faq.html.

Boulton, Clint. "IBM Ripples Security Waves with 802.11 Wireless Auditing Tool." InternetNews.Com. July 12, 2001, www.internetnews.com/infra/article/0,,10693_800221,00.html.

Bowman, Lisa M. Wireless Networks Leave Holes for Hackers. news.cnet.com/news/0-1004-201-4722179-0.html?tag=owv, CNET News.com, February 5, 2001.

Bray, T., et al. "Extensible Markup Language (XML), W3C Proposed Recommendation, December 8, 1997, PR-xml-971208," December 8, 1997, www.w3.org/TR/PR-xml.Version 04 November 1999. Buchanan, Ronald M. "The Internet in the Palm of Your Hand," *SANS Information Security Reading Room*, August 27, 2001.

Buckingham, Simon. "3GSM: The Future of Communications," *GSM World*, June 20, 2001, www.gsmworld.com/technology/3g_intro.html#3.

Bugtraq Archive, www.securityfocus.com/archive/1/26008.

"By the Numbers." Information Security, January 2001: 24Capslock. "Securing the Wireless Internet: Seven Critical Success Factors," www.itsecurity.com/papers/capslock1.htm (March 26, 2001).

Camacho, Jose Luis. "SNMP Security Enhancement," March 28, 2001, www.sans.org/infosecFAQ/netdevices/SNMP_sec.htm.

Carlson, A.B. *Communication Systems*, 3rd ed., New York: McGraw-Hill, 1986, pp. 230, 401, 514-536, 554.

Certicom Corporation. www.certicom.com/products/movian/movianvpn.html (October 6, 2001).

Cheney, Ann. "HomeRF Working Group Unveils Faster Standard for Multimedia Wireless Networks," May 2, 2001, www.homerf.org/data/press/homerf/homerf20_ratification_50201.pdf.

Chinitz, Leigh. "HomeRF Technical Overview," May 9, 2001, www.homerf.org/data/events/past/pubseminar_0501/tech_overview.pdf.

—. "Cisco Aironet Security Solution Provides Dynamic WEP to Address Researchers' Concerns," 2001, www.cisco.com.

Cisco Product Bulletin No. 1327. "Cisco Comments on Recent WLAN Security Paper from University of Maryland."

Cisco Product Bulletin. "Cisco Aironet Security Solution Provides Dynamic WEP to Cisco Systems, Inc. "Cisco Aironet 350 Series Wireless LAN Security," September 20, 2001, www.cisco.com/warp/public/cc/pd/witc/ao350ap/prodlit/a350w_ov.htm.

—. "Catalyst 6000 Family Software Configuration Guide (5.4)," www.cisco.com/univercd/cc/td/doc/product/lan/cat6000/sw_5_4/config/e_trunk.htm.

—. "Cisco Aironet 350 Series," www.cisco.com/warp/public/cc/pd/witc/ao350ap.

—. "Cisco Internet Mobile Office Hot Spots," www.cisco.com/pcgi-bin/cimo/Home.

Cohn, Michael. "Personal Networks," *InternetWorld*. June 15, 2001, www.internetworld.com/magazine.php?inc=061501/06.15.01feature1_p1.html.

Connell, Peter. "Binion Jurors Take the Stand," *Las Vegas Journal Review*, August 12, 2000.

Cope, James. "Palms Pose New Demands on IT Managers," *Computerworld*, March 20, 2001, www.computerworld.com/cwi/story/0,1199,NAV47_STO41923,00.html (March 26, 2001).

Cowell, Ruth. "War Dialing and War Driving: An Overview," www.sans.org/infosecFAQ/wireless/war.htm, June 11, 2001.

Cox, J. "High-Speed Wireless LANs Are Coming," *Network World*, April 9, 2001.

Crabb-Guel, Michele. "Model Security Policies: Determining Level of Control," SANS Institute Resources, www.sans.org/newlook/resources/policies/bssi3/sld012.htm.

"Dedicated VPN Hardware Market Hits $835 Million, Firewall Market Hits $1.1 Billion in 2000," February 21, 2001, www.itsecurity.com/tecsnews/feb2001/feb452.htm.

Dell Computer Corporation. "802.11 Wireless Security in Business Networks," February 2001, http://www.dell.com/us/en/biz/topics/vectors_2001-wireless_security.htm.

Department of Defense. DoD 5200.40 Instruction, DoD Information Technology Security Certification and Accreditation Process (DITSCAP), December 30, 1999.

— DoD Directive 5200.28, Security Requirements for Automated Information Systems (AIS), 21 March 1988.

— DoD Directive 5200.28-STD, Trusted Computer Security Evaluation Criteria (TCSEC), December 1985.

DeRose, James F. *The Wireless Data Handbook*. New York: John Wiley & Sons Inc. 1999.

Dr. Who. "WaveLAN," www.l0pht.com/~oblivion/radionet/reference/ wavelan/sin_wavelan.html.

Durkin, Brian. "Wireless Local Area Networking." Fall 1999, polaris. umuc.edu/~bdurkin/wireless_lan.htm.

Elachi, Joanna. "Researchers Find Hole in 802.11 Security," February 6, 2001, www.commweb.com/article/COM20010206S0001.

Ellingson, Jorgen. "Layers One & Two of 802.11 WLAN Security," August 3, 2001. www.sans.org/infosecFAQ/wireless/WLAN_sec/htm.

Ellison, Craig. "Exploiting and Protecting 802.11b Wireless Networks," *ExtremeTech*, September 4, 2001. www.extremetech.com/article/ 0,3396,s%253D1034%2526a%253D13880,00.asp.

Evans, William F. "RADIUS: A Protocol for Centralized Authentication," October 27, 2000, www.sans.org/infosecFAQ/authentic/radius2.htm.

Fairleigh Dickinson University. "Wireless Local Area Network IEE 802.11," alpha.fdu.edu/~anandt/security.html.

Federal Information Processing Standard (FIPS) Publication 140-1, Security Requirements for Cryptographic Modules, January 11, 1994.

Fisher, Dennis. "Symantec Offers Virus Protection for Palm," ZDNet E-Week, March 5, 2001, www.zdnet.com/zdnn/stories/news/ 0,4586,2692857,00.html.

—. "Flaws Found in Key Wireless Protocol," ZDNet, August 7, 2001, www.zdnet.com/eweek/stories/general/0%2C11011%2C2802134%2C00. html.

Fisher, D., & Nobel, C. "Wireless LANS Dealt New Blow," eWeek, August 10, 2001, www.zdnet.com/eweek/stories/general/0,11011,2803615,00.html.

—. "Wireless LAN Holes," eWeek, February 11, 2001, www.zdnet.com/eweek/stories/general/0,11011,2684337,00.html.

Flanagan, David. *JavaScript: The Definitive Guide*, O'Reilly & Associates, Inc. 1997,Version 04 November 1999.

Fluhrer, S., I. Mantin, & A. Shamir. "Weakness in the Key Scheduling Algorithm of RC4," September 20, 2001, www.eyetap.org/~rguerra/ toronto2001/rc4_ksaproc.pdf.

"The Forensic Challenge," The Honeynet Project, project.honeynet.org/ challenge/ March 26, 2001.

Fout, Tom. "Wireless LAN Technologies and Windows XP," July 2001, www.microsoft.com/technet/treeview/default.asp?url=/technet/prodtechnol/winxppro/evaluate/wrlsxp.asp.

Fox, Jim. "A Computer Virus Primer." WinPlanet, www.winplanet.com/winplanet/reports/1256/1/ March 26, 2001.

Garcia, Andrew. "WEP Remains Vulnerable." eWeek, March 26, 2001, www.zdnet.com/eweek/stories/general/0,11011,2700806,00.html.

Gardner, Dale. "Wireless Insecurities," *Information Security Magazine*, January 2002. www.infosecuritymag.com/articles/january02/cover.shtml#wireless.

Geier, Jim. "Spread Spectrum: Frequency Hopping vs. Direct Sequence, Wireless-Nets, Ltd.," May 1999, www.wireless-nets.com/whitepaper_spread.htm.

—. *Wireless LANs*, 2nd ed., Indianapolis, IN: SAMS, 2001.

Ghosh, Anup K. *Security & Privacy for E-Business*. New York: John Wiley & Sons Inc. 2001.

Gibilisco, Stan. *Handbook of Radio and Wireless Technology*. New York: McGraw-Hill, 1998.

Gillian, S. "Vulnerabilities within the Wireless Application Protocol," August 31, 2000, www.sans.org/infosecFAQ/WAP.htm.

Gomes, Lee. "Many Wireless Networks Open to Attack," April 27, 2001, www.zdnet.com/filters/printerfriendly/0,6061,2713009-2,00.html.

Graham-Rowe, Duncan. "Palmtop Plunder." *New Scientist*. 5 December 1998, www.newscientist.com/ns/981205/newsstory6.html.

Green, Jeff. "Keeping Your Palm Closed Tightly." BusinessWeek On-Line, March 8, 2001, www.businessweek.com/bwdaily/dnflash/mar2001/nf2001038_563.htm.

Griffin, Sean. "Security and the 802.11b Wireless LAN," *SANS Information Security Reading Room,* September 16, 2001.

Grogans, C., Bethea, J., and Hamdan, I. "RC4 Encryption Algorithm," North Carolina Agricultural and Technical State University, March 5, 2000, www.ncat.edu/~grogans/main.htm.

Gutzman, Alexis D. "The Who, What, and Why of WAP." Ecommerce-guide.com, May 26, 2000, ecommerce.internet.com/news/insights/ectech/article/0,,10378_381271,00.html.

Haagh, Jan. Wireless Network Security Bulletin. ftp://ftp.orinocowireless.com/pub/docs/IEEE/BULLETIN/ SALES/ORiNOCO%20security%20paper%20v1_2.pdf, April 5, 2001.

Harrison, Craig. "The Wireless Confusion," *SANS Information Security Reading Room,* November 13, 2000.

Harrison, Linda. "Judge Slams PalmPilot and Web Use in Las Vegas Murder Case," *The Register.* September 18, 2000, www.theregister.co.uk/content/1/13347.html.

Hayes, D. "Hacker U: Company Offers Security Service, Training Against Computer Invaders." Infowar.com, June 21, 1999, www.infowar.com/hacker/99/hack_062199b_j.shtml.

Hessing, Chris. "WAAC (Wireless Authenticated Access Control)," www.research.utah.edu/networking/anl/current_projects/wireless/WAACwhitepaper.html.

Hillson, Isaac. "Study: HomeRF Losing To 802.11x," *CommWeb.com,* 01/07/02 http://www.commweb.com/article/COM20020107S0005.

Hjelm, Johan. *Designing Wireless Information Systems.* New York: John Wiley & Sons Inc. 2000.

Hodges, Ken. "Is Your Wireless Network Secure?," *SANS Information Security Reading Room,* September 10, 2001.

Holes in Wireless Nets, http://www.eweek.com/article/0,3658,s=1864&a=10887,00.asp, eWeek, February 26, 2001.

Holm , Christopher J. "The Present and Coming Security Threat Security of Internet Appliances," *SANS Information Security Reading Room,* January 10, 2001.

HomeRF Working Group. "A Comparison of Security in HomeRF versus IEEE 802.11b, 2001," www.homerf.org/data/tech/security_comparison.pdf.Housley, Russ & T. Polk. *Planning for PKI.* New York: John Wiley & Sons Inc. 2001.

Hovar, Virgil L. "Personal Area Networks - How Personal are They?," *SANS Information Security Reading Room,* July 19, 2001.

Hurley, Chad. "Isolating and Securing Wireless LANs," *SANS Information Security Reading Room,* October 23, 2001.

"Hypertext Transfer Protocol—HTTP/1.1," R. Fielding, et al., January 1997, www.ietf.org/rfc/rfc2068.txt.

IBM Corporation. "Wireless Security Auditor (WSA), www.research.ibm.com/gsal/wsa (September 26, 2001) "Information Technology—Universal Multiple-Octet Coded Character Set (UCS) (Part 1: Architecture and Basic Multilingual Plane," ISO/IEC 10646-1:1993.

"Information Processing—Text and Office Systems—Standard Generalised Markup Language (SGML)," ISO 8879:1986.

Intel Corporation. "IEEE 802.11b High Rate Wireless Local Area Networks," June 2000, www.intel.com/network/documents/pdf/wireless_lan.pdf.

Intelligraphics. "Introduction to IEEE 802.11," www.intelligraphics.com/articles/80211_article.html.

Jackson, D., & R. Diercks. "Wireless Data/Internet Market Gains Momentum," Cahners In-Stat Group, August 2000.

Jackson, Joab. " Secure Wireless Networking at Last? Companies Solve Security Woes With VPN Techniques," *Washington Technology*, November 05, 2001. http://www.washingtontechnology.com/cgi-bin/udt/im.display.printable?client.id=wtonline-test&story.id=17394.

Jakobsson, M., & S. Wetzel. "Security Weaknesses in Bluetooth," www.bell-labs.com/user/markusj/bluetooth.pdf.

Jeffs, Tamzin. "Wireless Application Protocol 2.0 Security," *SANS Information Security Reading Room,* November 29, 2001.

Johnson, Scott. "War-Dialing: A Necessary Auditing Tool," September 20, 2000, www/sans.org/infosecFAQ/audit/war_dialing.htm.

Kaufman, Elizabeth & A. Newman. *Implementing IPsec.* New York: John Wiley & Sons Inc. 1999.

Kellner, Mark A. "Technology: Handheld Devices Are Viruses' Next Target," *The Nando Times*, March 15, 2001.

Kelly, S. J. "Chair of IEEE 802.11 Responds to WEP Security Flaws," February 15, 2001, slashdot.org/articles/01/02/15/1745204.shtml.

Knight, Will. "3G: Will 3G Devices Be Secure?" ZDNet, August 23, 2000, news.zdnet.co.uk/story/0,,s2080988,00.html.

Kobielus, James. "Network Strategy Overview, Wireless Application Protocol," v1, The Burton Group, April 7, 2000.

Kosiur, Dave. *Building and Managing Virtual Private Networks.* New York: John Wiley & Sons Inc. 1998.

Kozup, Chris. "Secure your WLAN now," *ZDNet Enterprise*, December 28, 2001. http://www.zdnet.com/filters/printerfriendly/0,6061,2835133-92,00.html.

Kraemer, Bruce. "IEEE 802.15 Publicity Committee," Rev. 0.4 (Modified: April 25, 2001), ieee802.org/15/pub/PC.html.

Laing, Alicia. "The Security Mechanism for IEEE 802.11 Wireless Networks," *SANS Information Security Reading Room,* November 24, 2001.

LAN MAN Standards Committee of the IEEE Computer Society, "Wireless LAN Medium Access Control (MAC) and Physical layer (PHY) Specifications," ANSI/IEEE Standard 802.11, 1999 edition.

Lansford, Jim. "HomeRF: Bringing Wireless Connectivity Home," May 2001.

Lau, Darrin." A Whole New World for the 21st Century," *SANS Information Security Reading Room,* March 28, 2001.

Lawton, George. "Lock Up Your Wireless," LAN.techupdate.zdnet.com/techupdate/stories/main/0,14179,2806945-1,00.html,ZDNet, August 23, 2001.

Lee, Chris. "Virus Attacks Pick Up Pace," ZDNet E-Week, March 19, 2001, www.zdnet.com/eweek/stories/main/0,10228,2698615,00.html.

Lemos, Robert. "Handhelds: Here Comes the Bugs?" ZDNet E-News. March 19. 2001. www.zdnet.com/zdnn/stories/news/0,4586,5079712,00.html.

—. "Passwords Don't Protect Palm data, Security Firm Warns," ZDNet E-News, March 2, 2001, news.cnet.com/news/0-1006-201-5005917-0.html?tag=cd_pr.

Lin, Yi-Bing & I. Chlamtac. *Wireless and Mobile Network Architectures.* New York: John Wiley & Sons Inc. 2001.

Lough, D. L., T. K. Blankenship, K.J. Krizman. "A Short Tutorial on Wireless LANs and IEEE 802.11," 1997 www.computer.org/students/looking/summer97/ieee802.htm.

Lynch, Ian. "Crackers Can Zap Data off PalmPilots." Vnunet.com. January 19, 2001, www.vnunet.com/News/1116644.

Mahan, Robert E. "Security in Wireless Networks," *SANS Information Security Reading Room,* November 14, 2001.

Malloy, Rich. "What You Can't See Can Hurt You," *Mobile Computing & Communications Magazine,* August 2001, p. 48.

Manion, Patrick. "Cipher Attack Delivers Heavy Blow to WLAN Security," EETimes.Com. August 6, 2001. www.eetimes.com/story/OEG20010806S0006.

Mann, Steve & S. Sbihli. *The Wireless Application Protocol.* New York: John Wiley & Sons Inc. 2000.

Maxwell, Kim. *Residential Broadband.* New York: John Wiley & Sons Inc. 2001.

McCoullough, Declan. "Old Spy, New Tricks," February 22, 2001, www.wired.com/news/wireless/0,1382,41950,00.html.

McFedries, Paul. "The Word Spy," February 17, 1997, www.logophilia.com/WordSpy/war-dialing.html.

McGill, Gregory A."Elements of Wireless Security," *SANS Information Security Reading Room,* October 1, 2001.

McMurry, Mike. "Wireless Security," www.sans.org/infosecFAQ/wireless/wireless_sec.htm, January 22, 2001.

Mehta, Princy C. "Wired Equivalent Privacy Vulnerability " *SANS Information Security Reading Room,* April 4, 2001.

Mekkala, Ritu. "Bluetooth Protocol Architecture," Version 1.0, August 29, 1999, www.bluetooth.com/developer/whitepaper/whitepaper.asp.

Meredith, Gail. "Securing the Wireless LAN," Packet, *Cisco Systems Users Magazine,* Volume 13, No 3, www.cisco.com/warp/public/784/packet/jul01/p74-cover.html.

Microsoft Corporation. "Microsoft Windows CE 3.0 Datasheet," September 1, 2000, microsoft.com/windows/embedded/ce/guide/datasheets/ce30datasheet.asp.

—. "System Requirements, Installing SQL Server CE," September 1, 2000, microsoft.com/sql/productinfo/cesysreq.htm.

—. "Enabling IEEE 802.11 Networks with Windows 'Whistler.'" November 30, 2000, www.microsoft.com/hwdev/wireless/IEEE802Net.htm.

"Microsoft Outlook Goes Mobile." *PDA News.* February 14, 2001, www.pdanews.com.au/index.php?dir=10018&show=10879&layout=10010.

Middleton, James. "Exclusive: hackers make chop suey of wireless security," *Vnunet.com,* 28-03-2002. http://www.vnunet.com/News/1130542.

Mitchell, Gordon L. "Wireless LANs: The Big New Security Risk," May 5, 2000, www.sans.org/infosecFAQ/LAN.htm.

Mobile Computing Online. "Comparison Report: Wireless LANs for All: Aironet 350," www.mobilecomputing.com/showarchives.cgi?149:4 September 26, 2001.

Molta, Dave. "Cisco Aironet 350 Series Tightens Wireless Security," February 5, 2001, www.networkcomputing.com/1203/1203sp1.html.

Mullen, Tim. "In the Air Tonight," SecurityFocus.Com, August 26, 2001, www.securityfocus.com/frames/?content=/templates/column.html%3Fid%3D19%26_ref%3D1081477708%26_ref%3D1564390234.

Muller, Nathan J. *Bluetooth Demystified.* New York: McGraw-Hill Telecom. 2001.Muller, Thomas. "Bluetooth Security Architecture," Version 1.0, July 15, 1999. www.bluetooth.com/developer/whitepaper/whitepaper.asp.

National Security Agency CCIB-98-026, Common Criteria for Information Technology Security Evaluation, Version 2.0, May 1998, Information Assurance Advisory No. 1AA-001-01.

Neel, Dan. " Microsoft to Wait on Bluetooth Backing in Windows XP," Network World Fusion, April 5, 2001, www.nwfusion.com/news/2001/0405msblue.html.

Nelson, Matthew G. "Untethered Doesn't Mean Unsecure," February 5, 2001, www.informationweek.com/shared/printArticle?article=infoweek/823/cisco.htm&pub=iwk.

Newsham, Tim. "Cracking WEP Keys," www.blackhat.com/presentations/bh-usa-01/TimNewsham/bh-usa-01-Tim-Newsham.ppt, Black Hat Briefings, August 2001.

OmniSky Corporation. "OmniSky Security White Paper," Revision 1.0. April 17, 2000, www.omnisky.com/support/security.jhtml.

Ow, Eng Tiong. "IEEE 802.11b Wireless LAN: Security Risks," *SANS Information Security Reading Room,* September 20, 2001.

Owens, Dave. "War Dialing Your Company: A How-To," December 10, 2000, www/sans.org/infosecFAQ/audit/war_dialing2.htm.

"Palm PDA User Security Notice." NASA Headquarters Information & Technology Division, www.hq.nasa.gov/office/codec/codeci/help/hardware/palm.htm March 26, 2001.

Palm, Inc. "Handbook for the Palm V Organizer," File: www/palm.com/support/handbooks/palm5.pdf January 4, 2001.

—. "Palm OS: A Flexible Architecture for Innovative Solutions," www.palmos.com/platform/architecture.html January 5, 2001.

Paro, Dwayne D. "Wireless Application Protocol (WAP)," *SANS Information Security Reading Room,* September 4, 2001.

Pascoe, Robert A. "Service Discovery Spans Platforms," Network World Fusion, May 29, 2000, www.nwfusion.com/archive/2000/93009_05-29-2000.html.

Personal Telco Project. "War Driving." May 17, 2001. www.personaltelco.net/index.cgi/WarDriving.

Pescatore, John. "Commentary: An Object Lesson in Managing Security Risks of New Technologies," www.techrepublic.com/article.jhtml?src=search&id=r00120010207ggp10.htm, TechRepublic, Inc. February 7, 2001.

Posluns, Jeffrey. "Wireless Communications Technologies: An Analysis of Security Issues," *SANS Information Security Reading Room,* April 26, 2001.

Post, E. Rehmi, M. Reynolds, M. Gray, J. Paradiso, & N. Gershenfeld. "Intra-body Buses for Data and Power," Physics and Media, MIT Media Lab.

Poulsen, Kevin. "War Driving by the Bay." SecurityFocus.Com, April 12, 2001, www.securityfocus.com/frames/?content=/templates/article.html%3Fid%3D192.

Powell, D., S. Schuster, & E. Amoroso. "Local Area Detection of Incoming War Dial Activity," www.att.com/isc/docs/war_dial_detection.pdf June10, 2001.

Proust, Albert. "Personal Area Network: A Bluetooth Primer," O'Reilly Network, November 3, 2000, www.oreillynet.com/pub/a/wireless/2000/11/03/bluetooth.html.

Publications and Communications, Inc. "Cisco and Microsoft Collaborate on Wireless Networking Security," May 2001, Cisco World, www.ciscoworldmagazine.com/monthly/2001/05/microsoft.shtml.

Raggett, D., et al. "HTML 4.0 Specification, W3C Recommendation, December 18, 1997, REC-HTML40-971218," September 17, 1997, www.w3.org/TR/REC-html40.

Redder, Greg. "Implementation of a Secure Wireless Network on a University Campus," *SANS Information Security Reading Room,* October 29, 2001.

Retallack, Roger. "Securing Linux Installations," June 15, 2001, www.sans.org/infosecFAQ/linux/sec_install.htm.

Ross, B.J. "Containing the Wireless LAN Security Risk." November 4, 2000, www.sans.org/infosecFAQ/wireless/wireless_LAN.htm.

Ross, Patrick. "FCC to Aid Wireless Carriers' Growth," November 9, 2000, www.news.cnet.com/news/0-1004-200-3605698.html/.

Ruber, Peter. "Building a Home-Office Network," *InternetWorld,* June 15, 2001, www.internetworld.com/magazine.php?inc=061501/06.15.01 feature5.html.

Saarinen, Juha. "Cracked by PC World." New Zealand PC World. September 3, 2001, www.pcworld.co.nz/pcworld/pcw.nsf/UNID/D613EE06F6D98222CC256AB5000913CE?OpenDocument.

Sandberg, Jared. Hackers Poised to Land at Wireless AirPort, www.zdnet.com/enterprise/stories/main/0,10228,2681947,00.html, ZDNet, February 5, 2001.

Sandstorm Enterprises, Inc. "PhoneSweep Identification: Peter Shipley Scans," www.sandstorm.net/phonesweep/ident.shtml June 9, 2001.

—. "PhoneSweep - Boston." www.sandstorm.net/phonesweep/ps-numbr.shtml June 10, 2001.

—. "Introducing PhoneSweepTM," www.sandstorm.net/phonesweep June 9, 2001.

Schenk, Rob. "Cisco Aironet 350 Series." February 15, 2001, www.zdnet.com/products/stories/reviews/0,4161,2682131,00.html.

Schenk, Rob, et al. "Wireless LAN Deployment and Security Basics," *ExtremeTech,* August 29, 2001, www.extremetech.com/article/0,3396,s%253D1034%2526a%253D13521,00.asp.

Schneier, Bruce. *Secrets & Lies: Digital Security in a Networked World.* New York: John Wiley & Sons Inc, 2000. Schroeder, Max. " Wireless Security," *Communications Convergence,* 11/05/01. http://www.cconvergence.com/article/printableArticle?doc_id=CTM20011031S0013.

"Securing Linux Step-by-Step, Version 1.0," the SANS Institute.

Seifired, Kurt. "802.11 Wireless Security," February 07, 2001, www. securityportal.com/closet/closet20010207.html.

Shah, Rawn. "Analysis: The Next Great Net Connection," August 23, 2000, www.cnn.com/2000/Tech/computing/08/23/next.great.connection/ index.html/.

Sharma, Chetan. *Wireless Internet Enterprise Applications*. New York: John Wiley & Sons Inc. 2001.

"Sharp Announces Linux PDA." *PDA News*, February 21, 2001, www. pdanews.com.au/index.php?dir=10018&show=10955&layout=10010.

Shim, Richard. "How to Fill Wi-Fi's Security Holes," www.zdnet.com/ enterprise/stories/main/0,10228,2693864,00.html, ZDNet, March 8, 2001.

Shivers, O. "BodyTalk and the BodyNet: A Personal Information Infrastructure," Personal Information Architecture Note 1, MIT Laboratory for Computer Science, Cambridge, MA December 1, 1993.

Sieberg, Daniel. "Off-the-Shelf Hack Breaks Wireless," encryption.www. cnn.com/2001/TECH/ptech/08/10/wireless.hack/index.html, CNN, August 11, 2001.

Somogyi, Stephen. "802.11 and Swiss Cheese," ZDNet, April 2001, www.zdnet.com/zdnn/stories/comment/0,5859,2707262,00.html.

Sprague, Robert. "Cisco's Aironet 350 - An Enterprise-Level Wireless Security Solution", *SANS Information Security Reading Room*, September 28, 2001.Song, Dug. "dsniff," www.monkey.org/~dugsong/dsniff/.

Stalling, W. *Networking Standards*. Reading, MA: Addison-Wesley, 1993, pp. 23-26.

Stallings, William. *Cryptography and Network Security: Principles and Practice*, 2nd edition. Upper Saddle River, NJ: Prentice Hall, 1999, pp. 264-269.

Standard ECMA-262: "ECMAScript Language Specification," ECMA, June 1997.

Stubblefield, A., J. Ioannidis, & A. Rubin. "Using the Fluhrer, Mantin, and Shamir Attack to Break WEP," AT&T Labs Technical Report TD-4ZCPZZ, August 6, 2001.

Sutherland, Ed. "Despite the Hype, Bluetooth has Security Issues That Cannot Be Ignored," *Mcommerce Times*, November 28, 2000, www. mcommercetimes.com/Technology/41.

—. "Would You Like a WLAN Card with Your Frappuccino, Sir?," *Mcommerce Times*, August 02, 2001. http://www.mcommercetimes.com/ Solutions/155.

Szacik, Bob. "HomeRF: Wireless with Security, for the Rest of Us?," *SANS Information Security Reading Room*, May 18, 2001.

3Com Corporation. "What Is 802.11 & 802.11B?" April 2001, www.pulsewan.com/data101/802_11_b_basics.htm.

"The Unicode Standard: Version 2.0," The Unicode Consortium, Addison-Wesley Developers Press, 1996, www.unicode.org/.

United States Government Accounting Office, Defense Spectrum Management. "More Analysis Needed to Support Spectrum Use Decisions for the 1755 – 1850 MHz Band, August 2001, www.gao.gov.

Uskela, Sami. "Security in Wireless Local Area Networks," Helsinki University of Technology, December 1997, www.tml.hut.fi/Opinnot/ Tik-110.501/1997/wireless_lan.html.

Uwakwe, Evan. "Wireless Computing - A Technological Breakthrough Laden with Risk?," *SANS Information Security Reading Room,* August 16, 2001.

vCalendar: The Electronic Calendaring and Scheduling Format; version 1.0; the Internet Mail Consortium (IMC), September 18, 1996, www.imc.org/pdi/vcal-10.doc.

vCard: The Electronic Business Card; version 2.1; the Internet Mail Consortium (IMC), September 18, 1996, www.imc.org/pdi/vcard-21.doc.

Viotti, Vicki. "Didgets: Turning Your PalmPilot into a Camera." *The Honolulu Advertiser.* May 5, 2000, the.honoluluadvertiser.com/2000/May/05/ business13.html.

Wagner, Jim. "Apple Boost AirPort Security, Features," Silicon Valley Internet News, November 13, 2001. http://siliconvalley.internet.com/news/ article/0,,3531_922651,00.html.

Walker, J. R. "Unsafe at Any Key Size: An Analysis of the WEP Encapsulation," IEEE 802.11-00/362, October 27, 2000.

Wang, S. "Threats and Countermeasures in Wireless Networking," December 20, 2000, www.sans.org/infosecFAQ/wireless/threats.htm.

Weatherspoon, Sultan. "Overview of IEEE 802.11b Security." developer.intel.com/technology/itj/q22000/pdf/art_5.pdf.

Weiser, M. "The Computer for the 21st Century," *Scientific American* 265, No. 3, September 1991, pp. 94-104.

Wilcox, Joe. "As Bluetooth Nibbles, Competition Lurks," September 15, 2000, www.canada.cnet.com/news/0-1006-200-2784702.html/.

Wild Packets, Inc., www.wildpackets.com/products/airopeek.

Wilson, Nancy. "VPN at Colorado State University," September 12, 2001, www.colostate.edu/acns/vpn.

—. "Wireless Networking at Colorado State University," September 17, 2001, www.colostate.edu/acns/wireless.

"Wireless Application Environment Specification," WAP Forum, November 4, 1999, www.wapforum.org/.

"Wireless Application Protocol Architecture Specification," Wireless Application WAP Forum, April 30, 1998, www.wapforum.org/.

"Wireless LAN Security, 802.11b and Corporate Networks," Internet Security Systems, 2001, documents.iss.net/whitepapers/wireless_LAN_security .pdf September 16, 2001.

"Wireless Markup Language Specification," WAP Forum, November 4, 1999, www.wapforum.org/.

"Wireless Session Protocol," WAP Forum, November 5, 1999, www. wapforum.org/.

"Wireless Telephony Application," WAP Forum, November 8, 1999, www.wapforum.org/.

"Wireless Telephony Application Interface Specification," WAP Forum, November 8, 1999, www.wapforum.org/.

"Wireless Transaction Protocol," WAP Forum, June 11, 1999, www. wapforum.org/.

"Wireless Transport Layer Security," WAP Forum, November 5, 1999, www.wapforum.org/.

WLANA: The Learning Zone for Wireless Networking, www.wlana.org/ learn/security.htm April 2001.

"WMLScript Language Specification," WAP Forum, November 4, 1999, www.wapforum.org/.

"WMLScript Standard Libraries Specification," WAP Forum, November 4, 1999, www.wapforum.org/.

Wood, Charles Cresson. "Information Security Policies (Made Easy)," Version 7, Baseline Software, 1999.Zeichick, Alan. "3G Wireless Explained," Red Herring, September 1, 2000, www.redherring.com/ index.asp?layout=story&channel=70000007&doc_id=1010013701.

Zeller, Tom. "Security Still Up in the Air." Network Computing. February 5, 2001, www.networkcomputing.com/1203/1203ws1.html.

Zimmerman, T. G. "Personal Area Networks: Near-Field Intrabody Communication," *IBM Systems Journal*, Vol 35, Nos 3 & 4, 1996,www.research. ibm.com/journal/sj/mit/sectione/zimmerman.html.

Zimmerman, T.G., J.R. Smith, J.A. Paradiso, D. Allport, & N. Gershenfeld, "Applying Electric Field Sensing to Human-Computer Interfaces," CHI'95 Human Factors in Computing Systems, Denver, May 9-11, 1995, New York: ACM Press.

Zurko, Ellen. "Listwatch: Items from Security-Related Mailing Lists," www.ieee-security.org/Cipher/Newsbriefs/2001/022001.ListWatch.html, IEEE, February 16, 2001.

Zyren, J.,& Al, P. IEEE 802.11 Tutorial. www.wirelessethernet.org/whitepapers.asp.

Index